Women, Literacy and Development

Are literate women more likely to use contraceptives or to send their children to school? This is a question that has dominated much development research and has led to women's literacy being promoted by governments and aid agencies as the key to improving the lives of poor families.

However, high drop-out rates from literacy programmes suggest that the assumed link between women's literacy and development can be disputed. This book explores why women themselves want to learn to read and write and why, all too often, they decide that literacy classes are not for them.

Bringing together the experiences of researchers, policy makers and practitioners working in more than a dozen countries, this edited volume presents alternative viewpoints on gender, development and literacy through detailed first-hand accounts. Rather than seeing literacy as a set of technical skills to be handed over in classrooms, these writers give new meaning to key terms such as 'barriers', 'culture', 'empowerment' and 'motivation'.

Divided into three sections, this text examines new research approaches, a gendered perspective on literacy policy and programming and implementation of literacy projects in African, Asian and South American contexts. With new insights and groundbreaking research, this collection will interest academics and professionals working in the fields of development, education and gender studies.

Anna Robinson-Pant is a Lecturer at the Centre for Applied Research in Education at the University of East Anglia. As a development planner, teacher trainer and researcher with various international aid agencies, she has spent much of her working life in South Asia. Her publications include *Why Eat Green Cucumber at the Time of Dying?* (2001), an ethnographic study of women's literacy programmes in Nepal which won the UNESCO International Award for Literacy Research.

Routledge studies in literacy
Edited by David Barton
Lancaster University

1 **Women, Literacy and Development**
   Edited by Anna Robinson-Pant

Women, Literacy and Development

Alternative perspectives

Edited by Anna Robinson-Pant

Routledge
Taylor & Francis Group

LONDON AND NEW YORK

Published 2014 by Routledge
First published 2004
by Routledge
2 Park Square, Milton Park, Abingdon, Oxfordshire OX14 4RN

Simultaneously published in the USA and Canada
by Routledge
711 Third Avenue, New York, NY 10017
First issued in paperback 2014

Routledge is an imprint of the Taylor & Francis Group, an informa business
Transferred to Digital Printing 2009

Typeset in Baskerville by Wearset Ltd, Boldon, Tyne and Wear

British Library Cataloguing in Publication Data
A catalogue record for this book is available from the British Library

Library of Congress Cataloging in Publication Data
A catalog record for this book has been requested

ISBN 978-0-415-32239-3 (hbk)
ISBN 978-1-138-86657-7 (pbk)

Contents

Illustrations

Contributors

Gillian Attwood is a lecturer in the School of Education at the University of the Witwatersrand. She received her BA and Honours degree in African Studies from the University of Cape Town, and her Master's degree in Adult Education from the University of the Witwatersrand. She is working on her PhD degree through the same university. Her research interests include community education, gender and development issues. She has published in South African and international journals, and in 2000 was selected by the University of Georgia, Athens GA, to participate in the Cyril O. Houle Scholars in Adult and Continuing Education Program.

Julia Betts completed her doctorate, an ethnographic study of literacy and livelihoods in rural El Salvador, at the University of Oxford in 2000. She subsequently worked for the UK Department for International Development for three years, in India and Malawi, before deciding to relocate home to the United Kingdom. She works in local government in Northumberland.

Lalage Bown worked in adult education from a university base for forty-four years, thirty-one of which were spent in African universities (in four different countries). Research interests have included adult education and development; the use of the media in adult education (including television centres for women's literacy); gender and literacy; higher education. She had programme responsibilities in Africa from 1960 to 1980 and in Scotland from 1981 to 1992 and has always been interested in working with policy makers in government and international agencies.

Donna Bulman is a PhD student at the University of Nottingham. Her thesis topic relates to how women in Atlantic Canada learn about HIV and how they may learn about it more effectively in the future. Her research interests include women's learning, HIV, gender-related issues and literacy. She completed a Master's degree in Adult Education from Saint Francis Xavier University in Canada, where her focus was on literacy education for women with disabilities. She has presented papers at a variety of international conferences.

Jane Castle is an associate professor in adult education at the University of the Witwatersrand, in Johannesburg. Her teaching and research interests lie in adult literacy and development, HIV/AIDS in social context, experiential learning and qualitative research design.

Priti Chopra is completing a PhD at King's College London. Her research is based on an ethnographic study of communication practices for women in three north Indian villages. She completed a postgraduate degree in Language Studies and Adult Education from Lancaster University. She has been working as an adult education practitioner and researcher in the United Kingdom and India.

Marc Fiedrich studied in Hamburg (Political Science) and Brighton (MPhil/DPhil Development Studies). He is working with the European Commission in Abuja, Nigeria, focusing on Good Governance issues. He was previously involved with a long-term research project for ActionAid Uganda, analysing women's engagement with literacy programmes. He has experience as a trainer of trainers using the REFLECT approach and as an educator for children and adults with special needs.

Claudia Flores-Moreno is at an advanced stage of her PhD at the Institute of Education, University of London. Her research is concentrated on an ethnographic study of how activists become teachers, and on the micro-politics of popular schools in Mexico. She took her MA in Education, Gender and Development in 1998/99 and developed an interest in gendered literacies and numeracies.

Sujata Khandekar is a founder member and Director of a Mumbai-based NGO, CORO for Literacy. An electrical engineer turned development activist, she has been working in urban slums for capacity building of Dalit (scheduled caste) community women since 1989. She completed her MA in Education, Gender and International Development at the University of London, and is a fellow of MacArthur Foundation. She has authored a book in Marathi, *Aashevin Aasha* (Hope without Hope), a social documentation of urban slum life in Mumbai.

Juliet McCaffery has worked in the field of adult literacy for over twenty-five years. Since 1995 she has run Consultancy & Training Services, a small consultancy firm, specialising in gender, adult education and social development. She has worked in many countries in the Middle East, Africa and the Indian subcontinent, designing and advising on basic education programmes and training adult literacy facilitators. She joined the literacy campaign in the United Kingdom at its inception, working at the Friends Centre (NGO) in Brighton, in a team developing a variety of literacy programmes for adults. She worked in adult education in London before moving to the British Council to develop a gender policy for its global operations. She was Chair of the British Association for Literacy in Development. She is an elected councillor with responsibility for basic education and is also undertaking doctoral studies at the University of Sussex on the education of marginalised communities.

Juliet Millican is a freelance educational consultant and a lecturer involved in widening participation at the University of Brighton. She has worked as a project manager and adviser with a range of international development projects in the area of literacy, adult education and capacity building, in North, West and Southern Africa, India and Nepal. She has written a number of training materials for field workers and policy makers and is enrolled on a doctorate of Education at the University of Brighton.

Archana Patkar is a consultant with JunctionSocial, a small consulting firm based in Mumbai. After studying social policy and planning for a Master's programme at the London School of Economics, she engaged in consultancy work in many countries and especially in South Asia. Among her interests are poverty and equity, girls' education and the use of ICT for development.

Anna Robinson-Pant is based at the Centre for Applied Research in Education at the University of East Anglia, where she teaches research methods courses and co-ordinates the PhD programme. She is researching children's and teachers' communicative practices within school councils as part of an action research project in Norwich primary schools. She has spent much of her working life in Nepal, working as development planner, researcher and teacher trainer. Her particular interest has been in adult literacy and the assumed links with 'development' – she completed a DPhil on this topic at the University of Sussex, published as *Why Eat Green Cucumber at the Time of Dying?* (2001).

Alan Rogers is an independent consultant in adult learning in development. He holds visiting professorships at the Universities of East Anglia and Nottingham. He has engaged in fieldwork in many countries, especially India, and has written extensively on adult learning and literacy.

L.S. Saraswathi is an independent consultant in literacy and social development. Based in Chennai, India, she has worked in many countries.

Her main interest lies in anthropological studies of women, especially rural women.

Chizu Sato is a Japanese doctoral candidate at the Center for International Education, University of Massachusetts, Amherst, and has a graduate certificate in advanced feminist studies. Her research examines how women participants' subjectivities in adult literacy, micro-credit and legal advocacy training are formed through their participation in those activities in Nepal and what consequences these formations have on those subjects as well as ourselves.

Suzanne Smythe is an adult literacy researcher and educator who lives in Vancouver. She has worked in community-based literacy projects in South Africa and Vancouver and is project manager for a national community literacy initiative in Canada. She is completing her doctoral dissertation, a feminist history of advice to mothers about their children's literacy development.

Brian V. Street is Professor of Language in Education at King's College London and Visiting Professor of Education in the Graduate School of Education, University of Pennsylvania. He undertook anthropological fieldwork on literacy in Iran during the 1970s, and taught social and cultural anthropology for over twenty years at the University of Sussex, before taking up the Chair of Language in Education at King's College. He has written and lectured extensively on literacy practices from both a theoretical and an applied perspective, and has a long-standing commitment to linking ethnographic-style research on the cultural dimension of language and literacy with contemporary practice in education and in development. His books include *Literacy in Theory and Practice* (1985), the edited volume *Cross-cultural Approaches to Literacy* (1993), *Social Literacies* (1995) and *Literacy and Development: Ethnographic Perspectives* (2001). He is also involved in research projects on academic literacies (co-editor of *Student Writing in the University: Cultural and Epistemological Issues*, 2000) and on home/school literacy and numeracy practices (co-author of *Numeracy Practices at Home and at School*, forthcoming).

Shirin Zubair is Associate Professor in the Department of English at Baha-ud-Din Zakariya University, Multan, in Pakistan. Her PhD was on women's literacies and multiple identities in rural Pakistan. She used qualitative and ethnographic methods for her research, which resulted in several papers in journals and edited volumes. More recently she was based at University of Texas, Austin, as a Fulbright Research Fellow. She is researching issues relating to Pakistani women's identity, literacy and higher education; recent publications include articles in *Changing English* and *South Asia Research.*

Introduction

Anna Robinson-Pant

Are literate women healthier, wealthier and even wiser than illiterate women? This is a question that has dominated debates on school and adult education in countries of the South.[1] Women's and girls' education has been taken up by many governments and development agencies as the key to improving the lives of poor families. In particular, women's literacy classes are often run as the entry point to other development interventions, such as family planning and child nutrition programmes. High drop-out rates from such programmes suggest however that the assumed link between women's literacy and development can be disputed. Do women themselves feel that they need to read and write in order to learn about contraceptives or to find out about immunisation for their children? What are the real reasons why some women want to come night after night to study in literacy classes? Do they want to learn to decipher the labels on medicine bottles or to read religious texts or to write about their lives? This book, collecting together experiences from countries as diverse as El Salvador, India and Uganda, tries to answer some of these questions.

The belief that literacy will contribute to women's greater participation in development has resulted in a proliferation of women's literacy programmes run by both governments and NGOs. Researchers and evaluators have attempted to measure the impact of literacy on women's lives, using indicators as varied as 'empowerment', child mortality or fertility. Policy makers have focused on the barriers to women's participation in education, the high drop-out rates in literacy programmes and poor long-term retention of skills. Only recently have questions been raised about the purpose of educating women, challenging the efficiency arguments of the past. Is it only so that women can become better mothers and wives?

This edited volume brings together writing by researchers, policy makers and practitioners working within a new paradigm of gender, development and literacy. Though working in contrasting contexts and countries, these writers share a concern to promote literacy as a human right, for women (and men) as individuals, not only as parents or workers. Rather than seeing literacy as a set of technical skills to be handed over in classes, these writers explore how the processes of literacy, gender and development are interwined and interact. They expand the debate beyond 'literacy for women' to consider, for example, gender issues implicit in the choice of a certain language as a medium of instruction or analysing literacy programmes in relation to gendered everyday literacy practices. The contributions reflect the richness of research and practice currently to be found in innovative literacy programmes and give a new meaning to key issues identified in previous discussions on women's literacy, such as 'barriers', 'culture', 'empowerment' and 'motivation'.

Background to this book

In 1990, Lalage Bown conducted a survey of women's literacy programmes to analyse the 'impact of female literacy on human development and the participation of literate women in change' (Bown 1990). Her report, *Women, Literacy and Development*, was the first systematic attempt to bring together research on adult women's literacy (as distinguished from school girls' literacy) in order to inform government and NGO educational policy. Over the 1990s, the emphasis widened to a research and policy focus on Gender (rather than 'Women'), Literacy and Development, where 'literacy' does not just mean reading and writing in the classroom but also in everyday life, and where 'development' is seen less as a definable outcome than as a process with a specific discourse that determines what can be measured or counted.

Research on women's literacy has gained momentum and diversity, no longer focused on statistical correlations between literacy rates and indicators like child mortality or fertility rates (see Chapter 1). Theoretical developments in the field of literacy, notably the New Literacy Studies (Street 1993), Real Literacies Movement (Rogers 1999) and REFLECT (Archer 1998), have influenced the kind of research carried out and the methods of analysis. Whereas ten years ago Bown's study was one of the few qualitative research studies on women's literacy, there are now numerous ethnographic studies from around the world. This volume is intended to complement Street's *Literacy and Development: Ethnographic Perspectives* (2001) by bringing ethnographic accounts of literacy programmes more directly into the arena of development and gender policy. Several of the contributors (Chopra, Zubair, Street and myself) to Street's 2001 volume have taken up the challenge, posed by Rogers in the Afterword, to explore the relevance of their findings to planners and implementers of literacy programmes.

My own personal journey through 'development' also lies behind this book. From training women facilitators and developing materials for a girls' literacy programme in the far west of Nepal, I moved gradually into a planning and policy role with various international and local NGOs. After conducting ethnographic research on women's literacy for my PhD, I found myself adopting a more critical stance on my previous work as planner and teacher trainer. I questioned, for example, the assumption that women would want to learn literacy only in their mother tongue, as it became apparent that they equated learning English or the national language (Nepali) as a higher-status 'male' education (like that provided by the local schools). I became aware too of conflicting discourses: that language policy decisions were generally made on educational and economic grounds (which literacy would be more accessible to women and how materials could be provided cheaply), rather than taking into account issues of power and status.

Now that I am working as a lecturer in a United Kingdom university, I am all too aware of the barriers set up by us as academics concerned with theoretical constructs of literacy on the one hand, and by policy makers, on the other hand, who dismiss any evidence that is not quantifiable as 'anecdotal' and regard 'efficiency' as the only measure of success. I hope that this book – written by people who have crossed these assumed boundaries with their multiple identities as planners, implementers, trainers and researchers – will help to develop a shared language and understanding about how literacy and development interventions could respond to the needs of women and men in a diversity of settings. Although the book is focused on poorer countries, Bulman's case study from Canada serves to illustrate that many issues around gender and literacy policy objectives are similar in countries of the North too.

From research to policy and practice

Though this book is divided into three parts, there is much overlap between the issues that arise and approaches described in relation to research (Part I), policy (Part II) and practice (Part III). By establishing boundaries in the form of these three separate parts, my intention is to illuminate the ways in which the same issues are discussed in different contexts (e.g. research and policy) and to follow through how issues addressed in research studies have been addressed in educational programmes. The danger of dividing the book in this way is, of course, that the reader who is a researcher will read only the first part and the policy maker only the second!

Adopting new research approaches, as Part I illustrates, involves 'speaking back' (Chopra) to the dominant literacy discourse. Throughout the book, the stereotype of the 'illiterate woman' which has informed most policy on literacy development is countered through case studies of women who are confident, have developed other strategies to survive without literacy and, for those who do attend literacy classes, challenge the assumptions of planners and trainers. The writers in Part I not only analyse the ways in which the 'illiterate' woman has been constructed, but also look critically at their own representations and question how researchers can encourage the participants to shape their text and research agenda (see Sato's chapter). Because of the desire to reflect what is important to the non-literate women they describe, some of these writers do not focus on literacy per se. To a large extent, this section is defining what literacy and development have come to be about (from the perspective of the individual women involved) and this is reflected in later parts of the book where several accounts focus on the non-literacy aspects of projects (Khandekar, Fiedrich, Attwood *et al.*). These researchers also take a more holistic view of literacy practices in the communities they study (Betts, Chopra, Street). The ethnographic accounts here have direct implications for the policy issues raised in Part II: for example, would the personal literacy practices (such as journal writing) of women in the Seraiki community (Zubair) be promoted as 'functional' literacy (see Rogers *et al.*)?

Taking a reflexive approach as a researcher has become accepted practice within qualitative studies. However, planning and policy formulation still tend to be seen as a 'technical' role and it is perhaps less usual to reflect on how the individual's values and identity shape educational structures, policy objectives and literacy teaching methods. The writers in Part II explore how to adopt a more reflexive approach to training and planning in order to respond effectively to women and men's literacy needs. Looking at literacy interventions through a gender lens reveals the limitations of a functional literacy approach which focuses on only one kind of work-related literacy, and Rogers *et al.* suggest ways in which literacy support could be developed to recognise women's varied roles (both leisure and work). Part II suggests that the conventional learning structure of the literacy class is valued by women in particular, because of providing a new space where they can meet together and raise issues not normally addressed in public (Attwood *et al.*). There are however constraints in running women-only programmes, not least in terms of finding female facilitators and risking gender-stereotyped activities and materials (McCaffery; Rogers *et al.*).

This part brings out the difficulties of developing programmes for women as a group, too – their multiple identities imply multiple literacies, which are rarely acknowledged in the traditional literacy packages for women. As Part I showed too, women participating in programmes have differing desires and needs according to factors such as age, family responsibilities (McCaffery; Rogers *et al.*) and disability (Bulman). By recognising these differences among women as a group, and the desire of each individual woman to participate in an appropriate educational intervention, these writers all promote the objective of education as human right, above the economic efficiency rationale for educating women.

These critical points emerging about policy and programme objectives when seen from a gendered perspective are followed through in the last part of the book. Here we examine the implementation of more innovative approaches to literacy through detailed case studies. Looking at practice in relation to the programme's stated objectives can reveal the ways in which people transform the intended approaches. We see how the REFLECT circles set up in Uganda were valued by women more for the status of attending than as a space for discussion of new information about health practices (Fiedrich). In contrast, the literacy classes in Santosh Nagar (Khandekar) and Muthande (Millican) developed into new spaces for discussing problems, when the original aim had been to provide literacy support. In programmes designed to promote functional and 'real' literacies, women may value instead the symbolic importance of literacy learning and the feeling of being 'schooled' (Flores-Moreno, Millican).

What is interesting about these case studies is that – unlike the traditional women's literacy programmes discussed earlier in the book – these were intended to be more bottom-up approaches to literacy provision, responding to participants' needs and desires. Several of the chapters point to the complexity of introducing ideologies and literacy methods from 'outside' the local context (McCaffery, Millican, Fiedrich, Attwood *et al.*) and the implications for ownership of the programme. Although participatory approaches such as PNA[2] and PRA are intended to enable local communities to have more influence over programme objectives and methods, these case studies present a less optimistic picture (similar to Cooke and Kothari 2003). This also relates to attempts to initiate change in gender relations more directly (Attwood *et al.*) through apparently participatory yet 'contrived' (Fiedrich) discussion. These case studies raise questions about attempts to present models of 'desirable' or 'typical' gender relations or roles in any culture and how far development projects can influence these. Even the word 'gender' may not translate easily into another language, posing a challenge for gender trainers (see Attwood *et al.* and McCaffery). Where the participants have succeeded in transforming the literacy intervention described here, this seems to be in spite of, rather than in support of, the project objectives. In all these cases, the participants move the debate on to a wider vision of 'education', in preference to 'literacy'.

Where do we go from here?

Since we started working on this book, over three years ago, there have been several major changes in the area of adult education policy. In the Jomtien Education for All (EFA) discussions in 1990, adult education hardly featured, the emphasis being on increasing girls' school attendance and enrolment. However, there has been growing recognition of the need to include adult education within the EFA endeavour and to stress the justification for women's education on the grounds of human rights (see EFA Global Monitoring Report, UNESCO 2002). Since the year 2000, several of the major multilateral and bilateral aid agencies have written strategy papers on adult education, underlining the role that literacy support can play in relation to other sectoral activities (see DfID 2002; World Bank 2001).

Most recently, the World Bank has held a series of consultations to develop its draft strategy papers on adult basic education. In the latest policy documents, there has been a noticeable move away from considering literacy and education to be synonymous, and the term 'adult basic education' is adopted in preference to 'adult literacy'. As the World Bank concept paper (2003) suggests, this has implications not just for who participates in programmes (lifelong learning for all, rather than just the 'illiterate') but also for the kind of education provided. Literacy provision is to be based on 'effective demand' and the actual uses of literacy (as revealed through research in Part I of this book), as opposed to a policy maker's imagined vision of how literacy could be used – the usual starting point for mass literacy programmes. The World Bank paper also advocates different forms of organisation for literacy interventions, fitting into other sectoral activities at the point of need (such as specific literacy needs for health assistants) rather than literacy as an entry point.

This policy shift towards what has been termed a 'real literacies' approach is in part a recognition of the failure of literacy programmes in the past to build on people's everyday literacy practices (the gap between the 'functional' element and the literacy, as Rogers *et al.* point out). However, there has been little indication of the World Bank and other major players in the policy arena beginning to follow the other implications of adopting an 'ideological' approach to literacy. In Oxenham's review (2003), the search for a universal indicator to monitor progress is based on the assumption that literacy attainment across differing cultural and linguistic contexts can be easily measured and compared. This conflicts with the findings in this book, which demonstrate how literacy practices are embedded in their cultural and political context.

Throughout Oxenham's review, the economic rationale for promoting a certain approach dominates over a 'rights' perspective, meaning that instrumental uses of literacy are promoted rather than those around women's empowerment and personal literacy practices. The idea that policy decisions are made for reasons of 'efficiency' leads to the technical aspects being stressed above the ideological arguments. For example, language policy is viewed in isolation from issues around social and political power structures: 'the choice of language of instruction made little difference to effective demand for instruction or to the learning outcomes' (Oxenham 2003: 12). Similarly, the use of volunteers is justified because they are cheap, even though the report acknowledges that 'the argument for paying literacy honoraria in hard cash remains powerful in terms of justice and equity' (2003: 94). Even 'knowledge' is discussed in technical terms, suggesting that there is one kind of knowledge which is useful for literacy programmes – that 'NFE programs ... should commission a proper survey of what the unschooled public already knows of these urgent issues' (2003: 132) and then seek to fill the gap through their adult education programmes.

What is most striking about the recent World Bank papers is the failure to disaggregate the target groups of adult education, other than to mention that they will be focused on 'the poorest'. All the above points could be viewed from a gendered perspective – especially given that the majority of participants in the programmes reviewed were women – since policy statements may have differing implications for women and men. For example, the idea of moving literacy support out of the classroom and creating new learning structures other than the class may not be welcomed by women whose main motivation was to come and meet as a group to discuss their lives. Mother-tongue language policy may be seen as an attempt to exclude women from the language of formal education to which their husbands and brothers had access. Using women as volunteer (rather than paid) facilitators may not enhance their status as a role model within the community and could contribute to the common conception that women's literacy is a second-rate education. The relationship between non-formal and formal education becomes more problematic when adult education is seen as only a women's domain, and especially if the vocational element of functional literacy programmes is associated only with stereotyped women's work (such as kitchen gardening instead of commercial agriculture). Above all, if a 'rights' perspective on adult women's education were adopted (as suggested by several writers in this book – see Bulman), this might mean that different kinds of literacy are promoted, such as religious literacy and legal literacy, and that more attention would be given to recognising the differing literacy practices and desires of individual women according to age, ethnic group and location.

The World Bank discussion documents reviewed above suggest that adult education programmes should build on people's everyday literacy practices and link more integrally with other sectoral interventions. However, it is clear that the evidence drawn upon in those papers is largely based on statistical evaluation of literacy interventions or measuring impact in tangible ways (drawing on some qualitative research studies too for this aspect). The evidence presented in this book, in the form of participants' perspectives on literacy interventions, is more complex and not so easy to relate directly to policy objectives. I hope that by suggesting a way of 'reading' ethnographic research in a policy context, we will perhaps have signalled ways in which adult education policy could begin to address issues around gender inequality.

Notes

1 The term 'South' here refers to those countries which are less economically developed (also termed 'developing countries' or 'the Third World').
2 Participatory Needs Assessment and Participatory Rural Appraisal are participatory planning approaches described more fully in Millican's, Fiedrich's and Attwood *et al.*'s chapters.

References

Archer, D. and Cottingham, S. (1996) 'Action research report on REFLECT', ODA Serial No. 17, London: ODA

Bown, L. (1990) 'Preparing the Future: Women, Literacy and Development', ActionAid Development Report 4, London: ActionAid/ODA

Chambers, R. (1994) 'The origins and practice of Participatory Rural Appraisal', *World Development*, 22 (7): 953–69

Cooke, B. and Kothari, U. (eds) (2003) *Participation: The New Tyranny?* London: Zed Books

DfID (2002) 'Improving Livelihoods for the Poor: the Role of Literacy', Background Briefing Paper, London: Department for International Development

Oxenham, J. (2003) 'Review of World Bank Operations in Support of Adult Basic Education with Literacy in Indonesia, Ghana, Bangladesh, Senegal, and Cote d'Ivoire, 1977–2002', Washington DC: Human Development Education Network, World Bank

Rogers, A. (1999) 'Improving the quality of adult literacy programmes in developing countries: the "real literacies" approach', *International Journal of Educational Development*, 19: 219–34

Street, B.V. (1993) *Cross-cultural Approaches to Literacy*, Cambridge: Cambridge University Press

—— (2001) *Literacy and Development: Ethnographic Perspectives*, London: Routledge

UNESCO (2002) *Education for All: is the World on Track?* EFA Global Monitoring Report 2002, Paris: UNESCO

World Bank (2001) *Engaging with Adults: the Case for Increased Support to Adult Basic Education in Sub-Saharan Africa*, Africa Region Human Development Working Papers, Washington DC: World Bank
—— (2003) 'Enhancing the Contribution of Adult and Non-formal Education to Achieving Education for All and Millennium Development Goals', HDNED EFA Adult Outreach paper, Washington DC: World Bank

Part I

Questioning women's literacy

New research approaches

This part of the book explores how researchers are now approaching the area of women's literacy. A movement can be traced historically, from a quantitative research paradigm focused on statistical measurement of literacy to an alternative paradigm influenced by feminist and 'ideological' approaches to literacy. Rather than taking the starting point of evaluating and measuring the effectiveness of a literacy intervention, the researcher focuses attention on the literacy practices (of men and women) – both inside and outside the classroom, the process of learning and the relationship of the researcher to the researched, and of researcher to the written text. Written by researchers who have developed their approaches from wide-ranging practical experience in the field, this part offers an overview of the research methods and methodologies they have developed, theoretical concepts evolved and an alternative reading of earlier research findings on women's literacy.

Challenging the conventional research paradigm and the 'autonomous' model of literacy (see Brian Street's chapter) is not just a matter of changing research methods: substituting participant observation and discourse analysis for questionnaires and structured interviews. It is about asking different questions in ways that may enable people who do not normally have a voice in policy discussions to express their viewpoint. In the first chapter, I trace the different kinds of questions that have been posed by researchers on women's literacy: from *How can women's contribution to development be enhanced through literacy?* to *What does 'empowerment' mean to individual women in this literacy class?* Even today, many policy makers are more concerned with the first question than the second, as the literacy research agenda is still influenced by donor priorities. But the different kinds of question being posed are perhaps an indication of the broader spectrum of people becoming involved in literacy research. As Priti Chopra illustrates, researchers can attempt to create an opportunity for women through their narratives to 'speak back' to the dominant literacy policy discourse. In Shirin Zubair's chapter too, the women in the

Siraiki community 'speak back' but in a less direct way, through their construction of literacy as being around personal expression and escaping from the mundane routine of domestic life, 'creating an alternative culture ... to male culture'. The personal literacy practices explored in this chapter (diary writing and reading women's magazines) could present a dilemma for policy makers who seek to promote 'functional' literacy in very narrow terms, yet bring out important issues around the differing literacy practices (and implied needs) of younger and older women.

The representation of 'illiterate' women in all these chapters (and the book as a whole) counters the conventional passive stereotype – a woman who lacks the necessary skills to avoid being cheated or dominated by men, educated or otherwise. Naj Jamal Khatoum (see Chopra) is typical of many women presented in this book: 'a confident and "empowered" woman' who has become active 'in public and community activities without "literacy"'. How to negotiate the representation of such women within their own text is a dilemma discussed by several writers in this part. For Chopra, there are ethical issues about protecting anonymity, yet she considers that she too is constructing a narrative 'for' these women, in the same way as the Indian policy makers she critiques: 'my ethnographic writing, though claiming to be the outcome of "participatory research" intentions remains implicit in denial of voice as my research subjects ... are spoken for'. Chizu Sato's chapter is a detailed exploration of this power of the researcher, analysing her role within a women's literacy programme in Nepal. She analyses various 'components' of her identity within this research context – as a Japanese feminist researcher from the 'First' World – and how this influenced power relationships during the fieldwork process and writing up.

Several chapters share the idea that we need to shift away from an initial focus on 'literacy' to understand what literacy means in the lives of the people researched. The 'rich and varied gender text' constructed by women in the Usulután community of El Salvador illustrates how literacy is just one way in which relationships and identities are negotiated (see Julia Betts's chapter). In her conclusion, Betts states strongly that 'in contrast to the discourses of literacy as power, women's stories revealed here that they are not suffering primarily through lack of reading and writing skills. Rather, the sites of their struggle are those of poverty, scarcity and the forces of hegemony ...' The concept of 'communicative performances' provides Betts with a new lens for analysing literacy practices such as signing one's name (in contrast to its more usual simplistic representation by development agencies as a benefit of 'literacy'). Brian Street, in discussing the contribution of the New Literacy Studies for researching women's literacy programmes, similarly looks more deeply at what is behind policy makers' reports on the 'disappointing results' and poor 'efficiency' of adult literacy. Clues as to why people drop out of literacy programmes may, he suggests, be revealed through ethnographic research, and he relates the problems of gender insensitivity in programmes to the broader issue of 'cultural insensitivity'. Street's chapter challenges the divisions often set by planners and policy makers, questioning both the boundaries between literacy and education (how far are we talking only about 'acquisition'?), and between development and literacy (is this debate just about the 'use' of literacy?).

This part of the book thus moves us directly into the policy arena, by illuminating the ways in which research can help define what literacy and development is about. Through providing a more holistic view of literacy practices in the wider context of development and social relations within communities, these researchers and the 'illiterate' women whose voices are represented here challenge the stated and implicit agenda of many development agencies to promote a certain kind of literacy intervention.

1 'The illiterate woman'

Changing approaches to researching women's literacy

Anna Robinson-Pant

> The priority attention given to women's literacy is justified not only by the gravity and extent of their inferior position, but also by a recognition of the responsibilities they have for the survival and well-being of their children and the key role they play in transmitting knowledge to upcoming generations.
>
> (UNESCO 1988: 2)

This statement from a UNESCO briefing on 'Literacy for girls and women' gave the justification for a policy focus on women's literacy during the International Literacy Year (1990). The document presents the worldwide statistics on the gender gap between male and female illiteracy (20.5 per cent for men as compared with 34.9 per cent for women), as well as relating the story of an Ethiopian woman:

> At 27, Birke enrolled in a literacy centre and, after six months' conscientious and courageous attendance, despite her family and domestic obligations, she began, she said, 'to be aware of many things. It is like being reborn, like a blind person recovering his or her sight. I had never dared hope something like that could happen to me.'
>
> (UNESCO 1988: 1)

When I read this document again after fifteen years, I was struck by how little the dominant policy discourse on women's literacy had changed. The emphasis on women as mothers who need to be better educated to improve their families' lives, the metaphors of rebirth, gaining sight through literacy and the 'distress of the several hundred million' illiterate (ibid.: 1) can also be commonly found in most aid agency policy documents and reports today. Whilst I was working as a researcher in Nepal, I was often requested by NGO staff to 'give a case study' for their proposals or annual reports. The term 'case study' had come to mean a story told by a previously illiterate woman about the benefits of literacy (like Birke above). From a policy perspective, then, the main reason for promoting women's literacy (and girls' education) is still to contribute to their efficiency in their roles as mothers and workers: 'to improve the family's sanitary and dietary conditions ... to improve production, particularly agricultural production ... to follow up their children's school work more adequately' (ibid.: 2). Even today, the argument that women should have the opportunity to participate in literacy programmes as a human right, for their own individual development, is rarely heard. Since the Fourth UN World Conference for Women in 1995, the 'rights' perspective on women's education has however occasionally been added as an appendage to discussions of the economic and social benefits of women's literacy (see World Bank 1999: 3).

The relationship between research and policy is a complex one, which cannot be reduced to a simple equation, such as 'Does research drive policy or does policy drive research?' As Barton (1995: 464) points out, the issue also relates to questions around 'From whose perspective should it be done?' (policy maker or literacy implementer?) and 'Who owns the research?' Certainly, the research agenda on women's education and development has been largely determined by the World Bank (as the major sponsor of educational research) and appears to have focused exclusively on the economic benefits of educating women and girls. However, as I hope to explore in this chapter and in the book as a whole, when it comes to women's literacy (as distinct from women's 'education'), the dominant research approaches are increasingly being brought under scrutiny. The challenge is being posed both on methodological and ideological grounds, from 'within' the dominant discourse outlined above and from those researchers who work with an alternative theoretical model of literacy, gender and development.

> A better educated mother has fewer and better educated children. She is more productive at home and in the workplace. And she raises a healthier family since she can better apply improved hygiene and nutritional practices ...
>
> (King and Hill 1993: 12)

This well known quotation from King and Hill's book *Women's Education in Developing Countries* (1993) serves to illustrate just how approaches to researching women's literacy have changed. When first published, the statements reflected established statistical correlations between women's literacy and child mortality, fertility and health knowledge – research which was presented in that book[1] and was regarded as indisputable research 'evidence' for the World Bank's policy direction on women's education. More recently, however, this same statement and others from

Hill and King's (1993) overview have been quoted in research studies critiquing the dominant approach to researching women's literacy. The above quotation has been used to illustrate assumptions about women's role in development, such as the exclusive focus on their reproductive role and family welfare (Leach 2000: 340), and to question the assumed links between literacy or school education and health behaviour (Robinson-Pant 2001a: 1). Basu (1999: 279) goes a step further by rewriting a quotation from King and Hill to illustrate how the 'stylised representation' of both women and men in the book (for example the assumption that women are powerless and always follow their husband's lead in key decision making, such as whether to use contraceptives) can mislead us into believing that this characterisation is based on empirical evidence.

Thus, critical attention to the discourse, which has both influenced research approaches and provided the framework within which findings are presented, is one way in which researchers now approach the subject of women's literacy. As well as critiquing the dominant research and policy discourse, researchers (particularly those based outside aid agencies) have begun to offer new methods and research perspectives, and most important, to ask new questions about women's literacy. The aim of this chapter is to trace these challenges to the traditional approaches to researching women's literacy, and the move away from the previous focus on 'the illiterate woman'.

The dominant policy and research discourse on 'the illiterate woman'

I will begin with an overview of the prevalent approaches to researching women's literacy, with the idea of identifying some of the assumptions that have been challenged over the past decade. As I discussed above, this is not necessarily an historical perspective since many of these traditional assumptions still influence the nature of research undertaken in NGOs and government programmes today. This is particularly true in the case of programme evaluation: for example, Carr Hill *et al.*'s (2001) evaluation of adult literacy programmes in Uganda analyses answers to questions such as 'Did you eat fruit last week?' in terms of how many 'two years literate', 'literate' and 'illiterates' give 'the modern answer' (ibid.: 67).

The majority of studies in the 1970s and 1980s focused on the measurement of female and male illiteracy, with the aim of correlating female literacy rates with indicators of development, such as child mortality (Caldwell 1979), fertility (Cochrane 1979) or income and employment (Schultz 1988). Cochrane's 1979 *Fertility and Education: what do we really know?* is perhaps the best known of these studies, which attempted to investigate 'how education acts through other variables to bring about reductions in fertility' (ibid.: 5). It is significant that many of these studies were commissioned by the World Bank and were used to justify its policy direction on women's education – notably the promotion of girls' schooling in order to ensure greater efficiency in women's role in development. The assumption was that women's education should be proved to have tangible economic benefits (in terms of improved family health or income or reduced family size) if policy was to be promoted in that area. Researchers attempted to draw direct policy implications from their findings of a correlation between literacy and development indicators. For example, Caldwell stated that each extra year of maternal education was associated with a 9 per cent decrease in under-five mortality (see Sweetman 1998: 4). Most of these researchers identified with Summers's influential statement in 1993 (as chief economist of the World Bank) that the 'vicious cycle' of poverty could easily be transformed into a 'virtuous cycle' through the intervention of women's education (Summers 1993: vii).

The assumption that women's literacy (often used synonymously in the literature with 'education') could change behaviour influenced most research in the 1970s, which followed the World Bank lead in talking of literacy in depoliticised terms as a technical input. As Stromquist (1999: 2) points out in relation to the formal sector, the official discourse of women's education is still cast in 'apolitical terms', 'leaving the ideology of schooling totally unquestioned'. Rather than looking at what kind of literacy was being promoted, the research agenda was concerned with issues such as access, gender gaps in literacy rates, enrolment and retention and analysing barriers to women's participation (see Ballara 1991; Lind 1990). Literate women were assumed to have different attributes from illiterate women (LeVine *et al.* 1991), and attention was focused on 'women's failure to become literate' (Horsman 1996: 65). Illiteracy was regarded as the reason for women's lack of status or progress: as Horsman comments in the Canadian context, 'the illusion that illiteracy creates women's problems obscures the violence of many women's lives' (ibid.). The excuse of illiteracy provided the opportunity for researchers to follow the policy makers' lead in exploring how to make more women literate (whether through schools for girls or literacy classes for adult women), with the aim that literacy should enable women to be better mothers. From the early 1970s, literacy programmes focused exclusively on women's reproductive role, with curricula around child health, family planning and nutrition, and developments such as 'family literacy' reinforcing the assumption that women should learn to read and write largely for their children's benefit (see Bulman, this volume).

This policy focus on the 'illiterate woman' as the cause, rather than a symptom, of underdevelopment has influenced the kinds of questions that researchers decided to address. Assuming that literacy had cognitive effects on people,[2] researchers asked primarily, *What is the impact of literacy on women?*, seeking to document evidence to answer the question: *What differences do illiterate and literate women display?* The statistical investigations into significant correlations between women's literacy and development sought to provide policy makers with the answers to questions such as: *How can women's contribution to development be enhanced through literacy?* This quantitative approach to researching women's literacy dominated the literature for many years and reflected an unshaken belief in the 'great divide' hypothesised by Goody (1977) between literate and illiterate communities and individuals. Ironically, opposition came from within this same research approach, as the amount of statistical evidence grew and began to reveal inconsistencies and variation across countries and continents. In the next section, I will look at the challenge presented to these early studies from within the same paradigm and in particular, the methodological critiques of the assumed women's literacy/fertility relationship.

The challenge: issues around research methodology

Within the growing body of research on the links between women's literacy/education and health indicators, evidence began to emerge in the 1970s that these linkages might be more complex than was previously believed. As Eloundou-Enyegue commented (1999: 288), 'the education–fertility discourse has become more diffident as the facts accumulated and analytical methods have improved', reinforcing Jeffery and Basu's (1996: 13) statement that 'the causal link between female schooling and fertility change has had a high profile in policy making but a weak theoretical and empirical basis'. Though in several policy documents evidence of correlation had been readily taken as a causal relationship, researchers had begun to explore other factors that might account for literate women having, for example, smaller and healthier families. Studies looking in more depth at the different ways in which literate mothers interacted with their children or how they used health services began to identify variations in statistical patterns according to context (LeVine *et al.* 1991). Factors such as the presence of mass education or an active family planning programme were shown to influence the behaviour of illiterate women – whether or not they learned literacy (Diamond *et al.* 1999). The question *Is there a link between women's literacy and fertility?* changed in emphasis to *Under what circumstances can a relationship between education and fertility exist?* (Bledsoe *et al.* 1999: 2).

Questions were also raised about how far women's literacy rates could be used as an indicator of the impact of becoming literate, as compared with the effect of having been to school. As Bown (1990) pointed out, the measures of literate women were not disaggregated in terms of who had become literate as an adult, and in most cases were indicators of how many women had been to school as children. Using these statistical correlations between literacy and health to justify policy interventions in adult literacy made little sense when the statistics were based on girls' schooling. This question of whether researchers were comparing like with like turned attention to the nature of education: does non-formal education (NFE) have the same effect as schooling? The assumed negative relationship between women's education and fertility may in some cases become a positive one, depending on the values and behaviour that girls are encouraged to adopt in school: 'in most of South Asia, schooling, whether secular or religious in orientation, is dominated by the ideals of rote learning and submissive respect to the teachers, and seems as likely to reduce as to increase the creativity and self-confidence of girls' (Jeffery and Basu 1996: 20). Jeffery and Jeffery (2000: 5) attack the tendency of demographers to 'treat both "education" (usually glossed as "years of schooling") and "autonomy" as black boxes that are simple variables consistently and causally linked to one another and to fertility'. Carter similarly identifies the problem as lying in 'our notions of the universal cognitive consequences of education' (1999: 74), and disputes the idea that the same model of education will be transformative in any situation. He suggests that researchers within literacy studies, as compared with those working on girls' schooling, have been more ready to challenge this assumption through analysis of the kind of education being provided.

Recent research on the relationship of education and fertility has also highlighted the dangers of focusing on women's behaviour in isolation from men's. Basu (1999) in a chapter subtitled 'Do men really not matter?' argues that there is no reason why women's and men's reproductive goals should differ and that the links between female education and fertility need to be analysed in relation to marriage – that the kind of men educated women choose to marry is also significant. Basu presents an alternative reading of the statistical data on education and fertility, suggesting that female education is in fact a 'proxy' for the husband's characteristics as well, and their 'united ability to manipulate the environment' (ibid.: 282). The importance of bringing men into the picture is stressed here from the perspective of methodological rigour. This supports the ideological arguments for a focus on gender relations – as opposed to women's status – put forward by many feminists in this field (see White 1992; Kabeer 1994).

These critiques also suggest new methods of investigating women's literacy, influenced by the wider changes taking place in disciplines informing this area of research, notably demography and anthropology. Both

Carter and LeVine stress the need for collecting educational life histories of adult learners (in the same way that reproductive life histories are taken in population studies) in order to move away from the idea that education will have the same impact on all women, regardless of context. Thus the critiques made on methodological grounds assume that women's literacy does have a positive effect on health behaviour, but seek to move the debate forward by looking at the subtle differences between contrasting country contexts and educational systems. The recent body of research in this area still belongs within a quantitative paradigm but from asking *Are there any correlations between women's literacy and health?* researchers are more interested in finding out: *How does literacy affect women?* (Jejeebhoy 1995) *Why are there correlations? Why are there variations?* (Caldwell and Caldwell 1993), as well as asking *What other factors need to be taken into account?*

Changing development paradigms

Many of the research studies referred to above belong firmly within a modernisation paradigm of development, where education and literacy are seen purely in terms of building up human capital. As Schultz (1993) demonstrates in the context of schooling, research should focus on calculating the economic returns of educating women and girls. Seen from a gender policy perspective, this kind of research could be said to be based on what Moser (1993) terms an 'efficiency' approach – where the aim is to increase women's efficiency in their existing roles for the benefit of the economy, rather than for education to transform gender relations or lead to greater gender equity. From the Women in Development (WID) approaches of the early 1970s, which aimed to target 'women', there has been a gradual change in much development policy towards a Gender and Development (GAD) perspective, where the impact of development on gender relations is the focus. Such interventions have been accompanied by a greater understanding of the roles that women currently play (for example, that many women in the South are farmers, not full-time housewives) rather than adopting Western stereotypes or preconceptions. Changes in overall development policy approaches have thus influenced not just which questions researchers decide to explore, but how they situate themselves within the research study and the methods they choose to adopt (see Sato's chapter).

As questions arise about what kind of development approach should be adopted, attention is drawn to whether and how literacy fits into a particular paradigm. Horsman notes that 'literacy is easier to advocate than other solutions' (1996: 65), and there is increasing scepticism about why and how women's literacy is being promoted in countries as diverse as Nepal (Robinson-Pant 2001a) and Canada (Horsman 1990). Since the 1980s, approaches to development have evolved to encompass participatory action research, where women are regarded as the actors rather than the beneficiaries or objects of development. Participatory approaches to both planning and research have enabled researchers to explore women participants' views of literacy programmes, not simply quoting stories of their transformation to being 'literate' (like Birke), but to analyse women's own theories of development and literacy. Methodological advances in discourse analysis have allowed researchers to take a new perspective on the literacy/development relationship, analysing the inter-weaving of literacy and development policy discourses (see Betts and Chopra in this volume) rather than attempting to measure development indicators, such as the uptake of family planning.

As the earlier critiques showed, literacy could not be viewed in isolation from other development inputs, and researchers needed to take a more holistic approach to investigating change. Significant changes have taken place over the 1990s in the way that poverty and development are concep-tualised – influenced greatly by Sen's 'capabilities' framework (see Sen 1999). Within this development paradigm, literacy is seen in terms of how women's capabilities are enhanced and their choices widened to enjoy more 'freedoms'. Within the education sector (as compared with other development sectors) there is less direct evidence of Sen's theoretical influence on research and policy: however, the EFA Global Monitoring Report 2002 (UNESCO 2002) marked a shift to a 'rights' perspective (replacing an instrumental approach) on women's education, through referring to Sen's conceptual framework. Looking at the implications of these new theoretical developments for researching women's literacy, there seems potential for expanding the scope of previous research into 'women's empowerment' and exploration into how literacy learning and other kinds of human development strategies interact. Specific policy on adult literacy, such as DfID's 'literacy for livelihoods' approach, has also indicated the need for more multi-sectoral research into how and when women (and men) use literacy in their everyday lives.

The new poverty agenda of the 1990s has thus given weight to earlier statements by feminist researchers on the need to 'deconstruct women as a homogeneous group' (Mohanty 1991). Researchers, now more sensitive to the differences between poor and middle-class 'illiterate' women, strive to find ways of reflecting and representing their differing perspectives on literacy. Yates (1997) refers to the 'composite illiterate woman', suggesting the need to move away from stereotyped images of the sort of women who study in literacy classes, or as Basu (1999: 281) discusses, assumptions that illiterate women do not participate in decision making are equally mis-leading. There is increasing understanding of the differences between women literacy learners, according to age, ethnicity and occupation, and how these factors may influence decisions within the classroom such as language choice, curriculum design and teaching methods. However, feminist approaches do not necessarily entail participatory approaches to research and policy: poor women are sometimes portrayed as being unable to comment on educational interventions for themselves or their children until they become educated. For example, Stromquist's (1997a) booklet assumes different roles for educated and uneducated parents, stating: 'while educated parents could participate in teams to examine the gender fairness content of textbooks, fathers and mothers with no or little education can help ... making sure their daughters arrive at school on time and are physically clean' (ibid.: 75). This tension (between wanting participants to express their views, yet concern that they may not choose what is good for them!) becomes more explicit when participatory research into women's literacy practices is related to the policy context, as I will discuss later.

Looking at how the word 'empowerment' has been used in relation to women's literacy over the past three decades gives an indication of the ways in which research approaches and development paradigms have changed. Within the quantitative surveys of many aid agencies, 'empowerment' is taken as a development benefit that can be measured in the same way as child mortality or family size. Burchfield's (1996) USAID survey conducted in Nepal correlates forty measures of empowerment in relation to women's participation in literacy classes – including control over income, participation in public protest and actions to improve children's future. As Longwe (1998) points out, the word 'empowerment' can be used in a conservative rather than a radical sense, and in the literacy context the objective of empowerment is confusingly often used to suggest more functional aims, such as learning to keep written accounts. Within the literacy/fertility literature, the term 'autonomy' is used in a similar sense to that of 'empowerment' in aid agency reports. For example, Jejeebhoy's (1995) analysis of the ways in which women's education affects their behaviour hinges on five levels of 'autonomy', which overlap with indicators of women's empowerment: knowledge autonomy, decision-making autonomy, physical autonomy, emotional autonomy, economic and social autonomy (self-reliance).

Thus in these statistically based studies of women's literacy and education, the words 'empowerment' and 'autonomy' are based on a static view of power relations, where women are able to gain the power to challenge men's authority through literacy education. Sharing a WID approach, interventions and research are focused on women as a group, in contrast to the 'gender empowerment' policy approach identified by Moser. As I will explore later in relation to theoretical models of literacy, the term 'empowerment' takes on a more dynamic meaning in the political context of 'critical literacy' approaches (Lankshear and McLaren 1993). This contrasts with these technicist attempts to quantify women's empowerment through literacy or to break it down into measurable elements.

These shifts in the way that 'development' has been conceptualised and carried out have influenced women's literacy research in several ways. Participatory development approaches, emphasising the value of local knowledge and action research, can be linked with researchers' attempts to listen to women's views of their own learning (as in Mace 1998), to find out more about 'indigenous' literacy practices (Street 1993) and to use research as the basis of participatory curriculum and programme development. Asking questions such as *What do women want from literacy? What are their experiences of literacy learning? What are their views of literacy programmes?*, Dighe (1995) for example, explored the social dimensions associated with women's literacy in India – that they enjoyed the opportunity to interact as much as the chance to learn new skills. Assumptions about the goal of women's literacy being to enhance productivity have also been challenged through participatory research which asks instead: *What is the purpose/goal of literacy learning for these women? What kind of development is being promoted through this educational intervention?* The theoretical framework of 'development discourse' (Escobar 1995; Grillo and Stirrat 1997) has encouraged researchers to look more critically at why women's literacy is a focus of their research, to ask: *How far is the focus on gender or 'women' driven by policy? Or how does the labelling of this group as 'illiterate women' influence the kind of literacy activity undertaken? Are there ways of recognising the diverse perceptions and needs of individual women within development projects, rather than addressing them as a homogeneous group?* Finally, Sen's 'capability' approach has provided a new model of 'human development', moving away from what Carter (1999) terms the 'productionist' discourse of education, and enabling a more complex exploration of how literacy, gender relations and poverty are interlinked.

Policy and research directions in formal education for girls

In tracing the ways in which women's literacy has been researched, I have found myself using the words 'literacy' and 'education' interchangeably in this chapter. This is partly because within the literature analysing the links between women's literacy and health, literacy rates are used as a proxy indicator for women's education. The overwhelming policy attention to 'quantity' rather than 'quality' of education – increasing enrolments in literacy classes or schools as a measurement of success – has for many years meant that any distinction between 'education' and 'literacy' went unnoticed. However, recent recognition of 'quality' as an issue affecting dropout in schools (particularly in sub-Saharan Africa) has led the Education for All initiative to shift emphasis to consider the kind of curriculum being used in schools and the quality of teacher training. As Heward (1999) comments, there was a recognition of the need to move beyond the gender gap to analyse the content of education and the way that education is organised. Within the formal sector, research now looks at the kind of curricula, including vocationalisation and the need for a 'broader' curriculum (Afenyadu *et al.* 2001), as well as differing modes of delivery. In the field of girls' education, there has at last been more attention to what goes on inside the classroom – rather than assessing variables outside which affect girls' attendance, such as school fees or distance from school. Research conducted in Zimbabwe by Leach and Machakanja (2000) has revealed the extent to which girls encounter discrimination and are even sexually abused in many schools, and has brought a new dimension to the assumption that school is necessarily a 'good thing' or an uncontested area (Leach 2000).

These research findings and investigations within schools are paralleled within the non-formal sector: researchers have focused on the way in which the 'hidden curriculum' in literacy programmes can reinforce rather than challenge women's traditional roles (Ramdas 1990). Primers and materials used in women's literacy classes have been analysed to reveal gender stereotypes in stories and illustrations. As literacy research has broadened to take account of everyday literacy practices, materials that women read or write outside the classroom have also been analysed in terms of 'gendered literacy practices'. Stromquist's (1997b: 209) research in Brazil revealed that women were choosing to read magazines which 'reinforced their subordinate role'. Translated into a policy arena, these findings proved problematic, as Stromquist suggests that women should be encouraged to read more emancipatory literature!

Above all, research in formal education – particularly within the literature on gender and education – has contributed to new understanding about the interaction of formal and informal learning. Much research on women's literacy previously assumed that all learning was directed by the teacher and discounted peer group or self-directed learning. There was also an assumption that all education was promoting Western values, particularly the importance of the individual, and that this would account for any changes in behaviour due to literacy (see LeVine *et al.* 1991). However, many researchers in this field now pay more critical attention to the process of literacy learning, asking questions like: *What messages around gender roles and relations do literacy textbooks convey? What kind of learning environments do women prefer? How far are educational programmes promoting 'Western' gender roles and values?* Through looking in detail at how curricula are constructed, researchers have also begun to distinguish more clearly between literacy and other kinds of education, as well as between different approaches to women's literacy learning. This will be the focus of my next section.

Changing assumptions about literacy

Throughout the previous sections, I have hinted at how new theoretical models and assumptions about literacy have had great implications for the way in which women's literacy is researched. The greatest shift has been from what has been termed the 'autonomous' model – where literacy is regarded as a technical input with cognitive benefits for the way 'illiterates' think. As I suggested earlier, these assumptions lie behind many of the attempts to correlate women's literacy with health indicators – a divide between literate and illiterate women is taken for granted, simply in the calculation of literacy rates. The ideological approach to literacy, by contrast, proposes a continuum of orality and literacy and multiple literacies/languages (Street 1984): at different times in our lives we may all need to learn new literacies (e.g. ICT), linking also with the current policy discourse on lifelong learning. This shift in thinking about literacy has particular relevance for research on the links between women's literacy and health behaviour. For example, LeVine *et al.* (1991) assume that literacy imparts the ability to understand decontextualised information which enables women to communicate better in health centres. By contrast, the concept of 'practices' (both literacy and oral) within the New Literacy Studies brings into question how far interaction in a health centre would be similar to that in a literacy class, and whether 'decontextualised literacy skills' would be useful to either literacy or health learning. Heath's (1983) seminal ethnographic research in two communities in the United States, which centred on researching 'speech events', specifically the ways in which home interaction supported or provided alternative patterns to teacher–pupil interactions, has informed much of the current debate. Whether women's everyday literacy practices are acknowledged within the classroom is now considered key to understanding how literacy interventions might contribute to improving women's lives.

The distinction between literacy and education has increasingly been acknowledged in policy documents on adult education – recent World Bank papers have chosen to talk about 'adult basic education' in preference to literacy (see Introduction). More significant is perhaps the distinction now made between 'literacy' and 'knowledge'. The assumption that illiterate women are necessarily less knowledgeable than literate women has been countered by ethnographic research into the strategies that non-literate women use (see Kell 1996 and examples in Street's chapter) and the findings that in many contexts, illiteracy does not carry the stigma assumed in most Western societies. The recognition that illiterate women can also have knowledge of health practices or family planning presents a challenge to researchers investigating the linkages – how far is any difference between literate and illiterate women's health due to literacy, or even to new knowledge?

An ideological approach to researching women's literacy begins from the understanding that literacy practices are embedded in relationships of power and inequality. Viewing literacy as a 'political' intervention can enable researchers to identify the objectives and values conveyed through particular approaches, whether Freire's 'critical literacy', which aims to transform relationships of power, or the apparently apolitical 'functional literacy' approach (see Rogers *et al.*'s chapter). The influence of feminist pedagogies has enabled researchers to look more critically at notions of 'power' within Freire's work (Weiler 1994) and examine how literacy interventions may challenge class inequality yet reinforce unequal gender relations. Taking this further and taking the view that 'literacy is a feminist issue' (as Horsman 1996: 65, has put it), Rockhill (1993) used the concept of multiple languages and literacies to explore the 'gendering' of literacy practices in immigrant communities in Los Angeles. Analysing how literacy practices are embedded and reflected in gender relationships, Mace (1998) and Horsman draw on in-depth life history accounts of women's literacy practices, particularly in relation to motherhood. In all these studies, the emphasis has shifted from how we should teach or organise literacy programmes to finding out how women (and men) use and view literacy outside the classroom. Within this feminist approach, the division between public and private spheres is a central concept, often challenging the idea within the dominant development policy discourse that literacy can enable women to take a more active part in the public sphere. In many cases, women have been shown to value literacy for the space it gives them to reflect in the private sphere, for example, through writing personal journals (Horsman 1990; Robinson-Pant 2000).

From the above review of a body of work known as the 'New Literacy Studies' (see Street 1993, 2003) it is apparent that the focus of much research is still on women's literacy rather than gender and literacy. However, a change has taken place in how women's literacy is conceptualised: no longer the notion of the 'illiterate woman' who has to be schooled in order to adopt better health practices, the attention has turned to women (both literate and non-literate) and how they live, regardless of literacy skills. Emerging theoretical concepts such as literacy practices, multiple literacies and speech events have enabled researchers to explore literacy outside the classroom, asking: *How do literacy practices in the classroom relate to women's and men's everyday literacy practices? How are literacy practices in the home gendered? How do women make choices about which language to speak, inside the classroom and outside?* Within this paradigm, researchers are increasingly turning to ethnographic and life history approaches to explore women's individual experiences of literacy and to question: *What does 'empowerment' mean to individual women in this literacy class?* Such methods allow researchers also to critique the policy framework within which they work, asking: *How does the dominant development discourse construct 'illiterate women' and how do the 'illiterate' women themselves interact with this discourse?*

Leaving 'the illiterate woman' behind

In the course of this chapter, we have moved far from the opening image in a UNESCO briefing paper of Birke, the illiterate Ethiopian woman who was 'reborn' (her words) through a literacy class. By contrast, the contributors to this book all share a starting assumption that women are not powerless because they cannot read or write. As I have traced above, changes taking place in development and educational policy approaches, particularly the introduction of participatory development methodologies and policy attention to quality issues within formal education, have influenced the direction of women's literacy policy. From a research perspective, the dominant quantitative paradigm correlating women's literacy rates with health indicators has been challenged by researchers drawing on feminist and post-colonial theoretical frameworks (see Sato and Chopra in this part of the book). Above all, new concepts and understandings of literacy emerging from the New Literacy Studies have shaped how women's literacy is being researched (see Street's chapter). No longer regarded as a 'technical fix', women's literacy interventions are being analysed in terms of how they affect or reflect power relations between aid agencies and local communities. Rather than measuring the impact of literacy on women, researchers have been exploring how women 'take hold of' literacy within the classroom and their everyday lives (Kulick and Stroud 1993).

Within these alternative research methodologies, the terminology of the dominant research on women's literacy has also been challenged. Concepts that were taken for granted – such as 'motivation', 'drop-out', 'literacy' and 'empowerment' – have been problematised within the new paradigm and become the focus of research. For example, 'motivation' can be seen as an umbrella term to cover the range of reasons (often ideological) for which women decide not to attend the class regularly. Drop-out may be linked less with 'motivation' than with findings about the ways in which women find a programme inappropriate or irrelevant to their needs. Both these concepts have been used as an entry point for in-depth discussion of the interface between participants and literacy programme implementers.

As I discussed earlier, women's literacy has now been defined more precisely to bring out distinctions between literacy and other kinds of adult
education, as well as between adult literacy and schooling. The term 'literate' is no longer used synonymously to mean 'knowledgeable', nor 'illiterate' to mean 'ignorant'. Similarly, there has been a move away from the
tendency to use 'empowerment' as a term to describe all the less tangible
effects of participating in a literacy or development programme. As several
writers in this book suggest (see Khandakar in India, Zubair in Pakistan,
Flores-Moreno in Mexico), the meaning of 'women's empowerment'
varies greatly between cultural contexts.

The sites of research investigation – as will be apparent in this book –
are very different from those found in traditional evaluations of women's
literacy programmes. Whereas studies tended to focus on measures of
drop-out, enrolment rates and success in the final tests, research in the
area of women's literacy now encompasses literacy practices in communities – not just of women, but the study of how literacy practices are gendered. Where research is focused on women alone, ethnographic
approaches have allowed researchers to explore their differences as a
group, no longer starting from the assumption that their primary role is
reproductive, or that their main educational needs are for health.

The new approaches to researching women's literacy presented in this
part illustrate the complexity of what was previously assumed to be a
simple matter of calculating an equation between women's literacy and
health. Whilst we researchers may welcome the challenge of engaging
with more complex understandings of 'empowerment' or even 'literacy',
from a policy perspective, these developments can however be viewed by
many as disturbing! As I discussed at the beginning of this chapter, these
changes in research approaches cannot be seen as a linear movement
forward in time, from 'traditional' quantitative surveys based on statistical
data on women's literacy and health to the new research approaches in
this book. In fact, in many aid agencies and development programmes on
the ground, you are far more likely to come across the assumptions and
methods of the traditional paradigm. This may be because statistical data
– whether of national literacy rates or on a micro-level, of links between
women participating in literacy classes and attendance at family planning
clinics – translate more readily into policy objectives and strategies than
the more dense and lengthy ethnographic findings on gendered literacy
practices.

As Rogers (2001) comments in his Afterword to Street's edited volume,
Literacy and Development, the challenge is now for researchers within the
New Literacy Studies to recognise the importance of placing their
research findings in the policy arena. When conducting research on
women's literacy and health in Nepal for an American aid agency (see

Robinson-Pant 2001b), I discovered that it was a matter not simply of introducing new research methods for programme evaluation, but of encouraging policy makers to think more critically about established relationships with 'women participants' and their own starting assumptions, such as 'the illiterate woman'. The difficulty lies partly in persuading policy makers to take this research approach seriously. Because much of the research has been undertaken outside the major development agencies, such studies can be dismissed as of only of academic interest. A greater danger is that, on discovering that women's literacy has become more 'political', funders of research may turn their attention to areas which are still defined in more technicist terms, such as lifelong learning.

The diversity of approaches documented in this chapter is evidence of the energy and ideological commitment of researchers within this field. Implicit in this discussion are issues around the changing relationship between research and policy – from a situation where donors commissioned mainly research on women's literacy and health to a more ambiguous relationship where policy makers are beginning to take note of research generated from outside their own programmes. It is still being argued by some that this new research on women's literacy does not answer the right questions (particularly the need to measure the impact of innovative approaches to literacy teaching, like REFLECT). Yet, as I hope this chapter has illustrated, the attempts of researchers within this paradigm are as much around encouraging policy makers to ask different questions as around providing the answers. Rather than simply critiquing dominant research and policy discourses on the 'illiterate woman', this book as a whole intends to offer an alternative agenda and to suggest the practical ways in which recent research on women's literacy can help to improve and develop new programme directions.

Notes

1 See, for example, Cochrane and Caldwell in Hill and King's (1993) overview chapter, and Schultz's (1993) chapter on 'Returns to women's education'.
2 See Ong and Ong (1982) analysing the differences between the ways literate and illiterate people think.

References

Afenyadu, D., King, K., McGrath, S., Oketch, H., Rogerson, C. and Visser, K. (2001) *Learning to Compete: education, training and enterprise in Ghana, Kenya and South Africa*, DfID Research Report 42, London: Department for International Development

Ballara, M. (1991) *Women and Literacy*, London: Zed Books

Barton, D. (1995) 'Whose research? Conflicting agendas for development education research', *International Journal of Educational Development*, 15 (4): 461–5

Basu, A. (1999) 'Women's education, marriage and fertility in South Asia: do men
really not matter?' in C. Bledsoe, J.B. Casterline, J.A. Johnson-Kuhn and J.G.
Haaga (eds) *Critical Perspectives on Schooling and Fertility in the Developing World*,
Washington DC: National Academy Press

Bledsoe, C., Johnson-Kuhn, J.A. and Haaga, J.G. (1999) 'Introduction' in C.
Bledsoe, J.B. Casterline, J.A. Johnson-Kuhn and J.G. Haaga (eds) *Critical Perspec-
tives on Schooling and Fertility in the Developing World*, Washington DC: National
Academy Press

Bown, L. (1990) *Preparing the Future: Women, Literacy and Development*, ActionAid
Development Report 4, London: ActionAid/ODA

Burchfield, S. (1996) *An Evaluation of the Impact of Literacy on Women's Empowerment
in Nepal*, report for USAID ABEL project, Cambridge MA: Harvard Institute of
International Development

Caldwell, J.C. (1979) 'Education as a factor in mortality decline', *Population Studies*,
33: 395–413

Caldwell, J.C. and Caldwell, P. (1993) 'Women's position and child mortality
and morbidity in less developed countries' in N. Frederici, O. Mason and
S. Sogner (eds) *Women's Position and Demographic Change*, Oxford: Oxford University Press

Carr-Hill, R. with Oketch, A., Katahoire, A., Kakooza, T., Ndidde, A. and
Oxenham, J. (2001) *Adult Literacy Programs in Uganda*, Washington DC: Human
Development Africa Region, World Bank

Carter, A.T. (1999) 'What is meant, and measured, by "education"?' in C. Bledsoe,
J.B. Casterline, J.A. Johnson-Kuhn and J.G. Haaga (eds) *Critical Perspectives on
Schooling and Fertility in the Developing World*, Washington DC: National Academy
Press

Cochrane, S.H. (1979) *Fertility and Education: What do we really Know?* Baltimore
MD: Johns Hopkins University Press

Dighe, A. (1995) *Women and Literacy in India: a Study in a Re-settlement Colony in
Delhi*, Education for Development Occasional Papers, Series 1, No. 2, Reading:
Education for Development

Eloundou-Enyegue, P.M. (1999) 'Fertility and education: what do we now know?'
in C. Bledsoe, J.B. Casterline, J.A. Johnson-Kuhn and J.G. Haaga (eds) *Critical
Perspectives on Schooling and Fertility in the Developing World*, Washington DC:
National Academy Press

Escobar, E. (1995) *Encountering Development: the Making and Unmaking of the Third
World*, Princeton NJ: Princeton University Press

Goody, J. (1977) *The Domestication of the Savage Mind*, Cambridge: Cambridge University Press

Grillo, R. and Stirrat, R.L. (1997) *Discourses of Development: Anthropological Perspectives*, Oxford: Berg

Heath, S.B. (1983) *Ways with Words*, Cambridge: Cambridge University Press

Heward, C. (1999) 'Introduction: the new discourses of gender, education and
development' in C. Heward and S. Bunwaree (eds) *Beyond Access to Empowerment*, London: Zed Books

Hill, M.A. and King, E.M. (1993) 'Women's education in developing countries: an overview' in E.H. King and M.A. Hill (eds) *Women's Education in Developing Countries: Barriers, Benefits and Policies*, Baltimore MD and London: Johns Hopkins University Press

Horsman, J. (1990) *Something in my Mind besides the Everyday: Women and Literacy*, Toronto: Women's Press

—— (1996) 'Thinking about women and literacy: support and challenge' in C. Medel-Anonuevo (ed.) *Women, Education and Empowerment: Pathways towards Autonomy*, Hamburg: UNESCO Institute of Education

Jeffery, P. and Jeffery, R. (2000) '"We five, our twenty-five": myths of population out of control in contemporary India', Charles Leslie *Festschrift*, July. Available HTTP: www.ed.ac.uk/socio/Research/Staff/pjeffery5.htm (accessed 15 January 2003)

Jeffery, R. and Basu, A. (1996) *Girls' Schooling, Women's Autonomy and Fertility Change in South Asia*, New Delhi: Sage

Jejeebhoy, S.J. (1995) *Women's Education, Autonomy and Reproductive Behaviour: Experiences from Developing Countries*, Oxford: Clarendon Press

Kabeer, N. (1994) *Reversed Realities: gender hierarchies in development thought*, London: Verso

Kell, C. (1996) 'Literacy practices in an informal settlement in the Cape Peninsula' in M. Prinsloo and M. Breier (eds) *The Social Uses of Literacy: Theory and Practice in Contemporary South Africa*, Amsterdam: Benjamins; Johannesburg: SACHED Books

King, E.H. and Hill, M.A. (1993) *Women's Education in Developing Countries: Barriers, Benefits and Policies*, Baltimore and London: Johns Hopkins University Press

Kulick, D. and Stroud, C. (1993) 'Conceptions and uses of literacy in a Papua New Guinean village' in B.V. Street (ed.) *Cross-cultural Approaches to Literacy*, Cambridge: Cambridge University Press

Lankshear, C. and McLaren, P. (1993) *Critical Literacy: Politics, Praxis and the Postmodern*, Albany, NY: State University of New York Press

Leach, F. (2000) 'Gender implications of development agency policies on education and training', *International Journal of Educational Development*, 20 (4): 333–47

Leach, F. and Machakanja, P. with Mandoga, J. (2000) 'Preliminary investigation of the abuse of girls in Zimbabwean junior secondary schools', *DfID Education Research Series* 39, London: DFID

LeVine, R.A., LeVine, S.E., Richman, A., Uribe, F., Correa, C. and Miller, P.M. (1991) 'Women's schooling and child care in the demographic transition: a Mexican case study', *Population and Development Review*, 17 (3): 459–96

Lind, A. (1990) 'Mobilising women for literacy', International Bureau of Education, Paris: UNESCO

Longwe, S. (1998) 'Education for women's empowerment or schooling for women's subordination?' in C. Sweetman (ed.) *Gender, Education and Training*, Oxford: Oxfam

Mace, J. (1998) *Playing with Time: Mothers and the Meaning of Literacy*, London: UCL Press

Mohanty, C. (1991) 'Under Western eyes: feminist scholarship and colonial discourses' in C. Mohanty, A. Russo and L. Torres (eds) *Third World Women and the Politics of Feminism*, Bloomington IN: Indiana University Press

Moser, C. (1993) *Gender Planning and Development: Theory, Practice and Training*, London: Routledge

Ong, W.J. and Ong, S.J. (1982) *Orality and Literacy: the Technologizing of the Word*, London: Methuen

Ramdas, L. (1990) 'Women and literacy: a quest for justice', *Convergence*, 23 (1): 27–40

Robinson-Pant, A. (2000) 'Women and literacy: a Nepal perspective', *International Journal of Educational Development*, 20: 349–64

—— (2001a) *Why Eat Green Cucumber at the Time of Dying? Exploring the Link between Women's Literacy and Development in Nepal*, Hamburg: UNESCO Institute of Education

—— (2001b) 'Women's literacy and health: can an ethnographic researcher find the links?' in B.V. Street (ed.) *Literacy and Development: Ethnographic Perspectives*, London: Routledge

Rockhill, K. (1993) 'Gender, language and the politics of literacy' in B.V. Street (ed.) *Cross-cultural Approaches to Literacy*, Cambridge: Cambridge University Press

Rogers, A. (2001) 'Afterword', in B.V. Street (ed.) *Literacy and Development: Ethnographic Perspectives*, London: Routledge

Schultz, T. Paul (1988) 'Educational investment and returns' in Hollis Chenery and T.N. Srinivasan (eds) *Handbook of Development Economics* I, Amsterdam: North-Holland

—— (1993) 'Returns to women's education' in E.H. King and M.A. Hill (eds) *Women's Education in Developing Countries: Barriers, Benefits and Policies*, Baltimore MD and London: Johns Hopkins University Press

Sen, A. (1999) *Development as Freedom*, Oxford: Oxford University Press

Street, B.V. (1984) *Literacy in Theory and Practice*, Cambridge: Cambridge University Press

—— (1993) *Cross-cultural Approaches to Literacy*, Cambridge: Cambridge University Press

—— (2003) 'The implications of the "New Literacy Studies" for literacy education' in S. Goodman, T. Lillis, J. Maybin and N. Mercer (eds) *Language, Literacy and Education: a Reader*, Stoke on Trent: Trentham Books

Stromquist, N. (1997a) *Increasing Girls' and Women's Participation in Basic Education*, UNESCO Fundamentals of Educational Planning, Paris: UNESCO

—— (1997b) *Literacy for Citizenship: Gender and Grassroots Dynamics in Brazil*, Albany NY: State University of New York Press

—— (1999) 'What Poverty does to Girls' Education: the Intersection of Class, Gender and Ethnicity in Latin America', keynote speech presented at the Oxford International Conference on Education and Development

Summers, L.H. (1993) 'Foreword' in E.M. King and M.A. Hill (eds) *Women's Education in Developing Countries: Barriers, Benefits and Policies*, Baltimore MD and London: Johns Hopkins University Press

Sweetman, C. (1998) 'Editorial' in *Gender, Education and Training*, Oxford: Oxfam

UNESCO (1988) 'Literacy for Girls and Women', briefing paper for International Literacy Year (original in French: EDF/ILY/88-02/FEM), Paris: UNESCO

—— (2002) *Education for All: Is the World on Track?* EFA Global Monitoring Report, Paris: UNESCO

Weiler, K. (1994) 'Freire and a feminist pedagogy of difference' in P. McLaren and C. Lankshear (eds) *Politics of Liberation: Paths from Freire*, London: Routledge

White, S. (1992) *Arguing with the Crocodile: Gender and Class in Bangladesh*, London: Zed Books

World Bank (1999) *The World Bank and Girls' Education*, Washington DC: World Bank

Yates, R. (1997) 'Literacy, gender and vulnerability: donor discourses and local realities', *IDS Bulletin*, 28 (3): 112–21.

2 Distorted mirrors

(De)centring images of the 'illiterate Indian village woman' through ethnographic research narratives

Priti Chopra

> Identities are about questions of using the resources of history, language and culture in the process of becoming rather than being: not 'who we are' or 'where we came from', so much as what we might become, how we have been represented and how that bears on how we might represent ourselves. Identities ... are constituted within, not outside representation.
>
> (Stuart Hall, in Hall and Du Gay 1996: 4)

Ethnographic research: reflecting women as objects of knowledge?

The authors of this book, through research in several different countries, have provided critiques of dominant research and policy discourses on 'illiterate' women. These critiques suggest a complex variety of agendas more pertinent to the lives of adult education learners. They offer policy makers and practitioners alternative perspectives on meaning making through researching learners' lives and adult education practices. Travelling across their experiences and voices, I hear echoes of similar 'ethnographic realities' located in the particular context of my research. My writing also explores the practice of ethnography as a means of 'listening' to learners' experiences and realities in order to 'speak back' to the policy and practice of adult education programmes.

Striving to imagine the possibility of speaking back raises insights into 'ethnographic realities' which question the validity and legitimacy of 'empowering' relationships assumed between literacy, gender and development. Context-specific cultural, socio-economic, political and institutional practices, defining the relationship between literacy, gender and development, are articulated through specific modalities of power which construct and exclude the 'illiterate' woman as Other. The created product 'illiterate women' appears homogeneous, lacking but without difference.

I try to explore the discursive practices which create symbolic boundaries between 'literate' and 'illiterate' women. Through ethnographic research I attempt to 're-claim' 'illiteracy narratives' about women. A feminist and 'participatory' research engagement with the notion of 'dialogue' endeavours to listen to how the seamless 'illiterate woman-as-Other' creates and is created out of particular patterns of power within the context of 'literacy'.

'Illiterate' women already have knowledge of their conditions. Forms of knowledge held and expressed by them have been blocked, invalidated and forbidden through institutional practices that legitimise the desire of particular 'literacy for women's development' discourses to govern and dictate their behaviour. Ethnographic research may enable us to trace how the 'illiterate woman-as-Other' is stabilised in the specificity of these inscriptions. It could provide us with an analysis which attempts to move away from interpretations of women as 'illiterate and powerless' to recognition of multiple contexts of representation engaging different women's voice, visibility and agency. This may make discernible possibilities of renewal and transformation in the gaps, influencing the network of power, within which the named 'illiterate' woman, as a subject and object of knowledge, speaks (un)silenced.

In my first section entitled 'Developing the "illiterate woman": imposing fantasy of self in dreams of (m)Other(s)' I focus on how the 'illiterate' woman figures as a reproducer, producer and disempowered 'body' in Indian adult education policy perspective, through four periods marked as: (1) Appearance (1882–1947), (2) [Dis]appearance (1948–67), (3) Reappearance (1967–88) and (4) (In)visible (m)other of the nation (1988 to date). I do not here provide a detailed explanation and analysis of government adult education policy, processes of programme implementation and non-government adult education initiatives (see Chopra 2005). Instead, I concentrate on reinstating the resonating global 'image' of the 'illiterate' woman through a brief national policy overview.

Having signalled representations of a 'Women's Literacy and Development' grand narrative within a policy overview, I explore the (in)visible voice and agency of different 'illiterate' women. Through four ethnographic narratives[1] I imagine the possibility of 'speaking back' in a politics of interpreting 'illiterate' women. The following section, 'Speaking back: other stories-in-becoming 'literate', is based on a focus group discussion, during one visit, in a Hindu village in north Bihar. I was invited by the District Literacy Society to interview a few women in this village about their experiences of the Total and Post Literacy campaign that took place several years ago. I used this opportunity to gain an understanding of people's perspectives on 'illiterate'/'literate' women and on themselves as 'literate'/'illiterate'.

Tulsibai, a non-programme participant and 'self-declared illiterate', refutes a fantasy of 'illiterate' women as lacking in knowledge about cleanliness. She draws attention to socio-economic day-to-day realities as much more powerful concerns in 'narratives of cleanliness' than 'images' of becoming dirt-free through 'literacy'. Naj Jamal Khatoum's story of her 'illiterate' self participating in *panchayat*[2] elections is narrated in English in the voice of the first person. Her story is based on extracts from a series of interviews, conducted on different days, in Hindi. Naj Jamal Khatoum resides in a Muslim village in a different district of north Bihar from Tulsibai. She has very strong links with a women's non-governmental organisation (NGO) working in the area and is participating in several of its income generation and 'women's development' programmes. Naj Jamal Khatoum's narrative speaks about her self-perception as a confident and 'empowered' woman becoming an active participant in public and community activities without 'literacy'.

Ajimun Khatoum resides in the same village as Naj Jamal Khatoum. Her story is narrated, in English, directly through my voice. As I was visiting and living in this village, for several days at a stretch, over a period of eight months, my conversations with Ajimun took place, in Hindi, at a variety of times on different days. Ajimun has been an 'irregular' participant in the non-governmental organisation's 'literacy' programme in her village. She, however, does consistently participate in several other programmes run by the same organisation. In her narrative on 're-claiming' the 'illiterate' woman, Aijimun shares her practices and experience of becoming an entrepreneur. She shares her experience of communication practices learnt during her childhood, informally, through her father and formally at the local *madarsa*.[3] She shares her knowledge of mental arithmetic as a part of numeracy practices involved in her shop management and in 'teaching' and guiding her children.

The narrative of Sakina Khatoum as the 'housebound undergraduate' is based on one visit to her home and was conducted in Hindi. Sakina Khatoum lives in the same village as Ajimun and Naj Jamal. During the course of my research in this village I visited 139 houses in order to meet and speak to women who may be living in purdah.[4] I met Sakina during one of these visits. Sakina's narrative 'speaks back' to the 'illiterate' woman to say that notions of 'empowerment' and 'development' attached to representations of 'literacy' are inadequate. There are many gendered context-specific class, caste and religious communication practices, influencing different women's expression of voice, visibility and agency. She, in English and through the voice of the first person, speaks back to the policy of literacy, development and gender empowerment to claim that absolute distinctions between 'literate' and 'illiterate' women are unstable and exclude ways of understanding how women are constructed and construct themselves through multiple discourses and subject positions. For instance, she lives in purdah to maintain boundaries of respectability but she negotiates these boundaries, e.g. by opening the back door, once her father leaves the house, and allowing people in to socialise with her.

In the section 'Denunciation and annunciation: refuting denial of voice, visibility and agency' I construct 'ethnographic narratives' not as straightforward descriptions – transparent and analysed – but rather as stories suggesting readings and representations of the voice, visibility and agency of 'illiterate' women. Stories which struggle to problematise representations of the 'underdeveloped', lacking 'illiterate', requiring the 'fix' of 'literacy'.

I conclude with 'Preconceptions, prejudice and prejudgement: miming the route of how I could not "know" her stories'. This section involves a synopsis of reflections on my process of creating 'ethnographic accounts'. I have worked with two languages, Hindi and English. I have occupied different positions of enunciation (representing voice through the use of the first and third person) to create false linearity and progression – in a series of non-linear interpretations and translations – in order to recognise and validate a cohesive narrative, that remains, in itself, a fantasy.

Developing the 'illiterate woman': imposing fantasy of self in dreams of (m)Other(s)

> Illiterate women are at the lowest level of the social strata and gender inequality ... Illiteracy deprives them from all opportunities and prospects of leading a meaningful life and enjoying a good standard of living ... Literate women have a progressive outlook enabling them to handle family and other matters in an effective manner. Educating a woman expands the horizon of education in the whole nation, as the home is the first school ... A mother is not only the first teacher but also the mentor ...
>
> (Sonali Kumar, National Literacy Mission 2001: 6–7)

In this section I write about (re)productive 'images' of the 'illiterate Indian village woman' emerging through Indian adult education policy. I outline a brief historical overview of the 'illiterate woman' as she [dis]appears in Indian adult education policy through four periods: (1) Appearance (1882–1947), (2) [Dis]appearance (1948–67), (3) Reappearance (1967–88), (4) (In)visible (m)other of the nation (1988 to date). Ways of figuring the 'illiterate woman' as [re]producers of the home, village and nation emerge as a repeated chorus throughout

Plate 2.1 Campaign poster on 'Women's Literacy' displayed at the Bihar Literacy
fair in Patna, Bihar, 2001 (source: Priti Chopra).

different policy periods. During 1995, when I first became involved as a
literacy volunteer in a women's adult education programme in Gurgaon,
Haryana, I started collecting articles about literacy in Indian newspapers.
Selected glimpses from a melange, spanning a period of seven years,
recreate the fantasy of Indian 'illiterate' women. A powerful fantasy
reiterating international 'literacy, gender and development' discourse
and practice promoting Women in Development (Kabeer and Subrahmanian 1996) approaches for 'empowering' the 'illiterate' woman
(see Ballara 1991; Bown 1990; Sato this volume; Robinson-Pant this
volume).

Not much priority in Indian government policy and programme planning was given to 'women's literacy' until the 1986 National Policy Document on Education which proposed the 'removal of women's illiteracy
and obstacles inhibiting their access to and retention in elementary education ...' (Kumar 2001: 7). Vimala Ramachandran (1998: 79) provides a
succinct summary:

> Government policy has kept pace with developmental thinking, ...
> From the early seventies the focus shifted to reducing fertility, improv-
> ing infant and child mortality, encouraging better child rearing prac-
> tices ... women's education was linked to national demographic goals

... the eighties onwards have not only accommodated the 'demands' of the women's movement, but simultaneously retained both the early welfare orientation and the later mother–wife–reproducer rhetoric.

Appearance (1882–1947)

'Developing the illiterate woman', in a reproductive vision, imagined women as sites of maternal power. Women became (m)others of the family and the nation. Indian nationalists such as Iswar Chandra Vidyasagar, Sashipada Banerjee and Keshub Chandra Sen made organised attempts to support the 'social development' of 'illiterate' women (Paul 1991: 66). During the nineteenth century, Keshub Chandra Sen established the Bama Hitaishini Sabha (Society for the Welfare of Women) where 'literate' women read newspapers and led discussions to develop social awareness among Indian women so that they would be 'receptive' to reform schemes for their 'upliftment' (Chatterjee 1983: 178–80).

During the twentieth century, adult education was mainly promoted as a non-government initiative through night schools. Indian academics, nationalist leaders, social, religious and political organisations placed emphasis on 'teaching' literacy through Laubach's 'Each one, Teach one' method (Shah 1999). Literacy, as an autonomous skill (Street 1995) was believed to 'empower' 'illiterate' men and women. Shukla (1991: 5), sharing his experience, explains:

> When I first heard of literacy as a schoolchild in the late 1930s the Congress government had just made their first try at governing and we all went out in a procession under the slogan 'Each one, Teach one' ... considering it a sacred task to free our compatriots from ignorance.

As a part of this process, eradication of the 'illiterate' woman signalled progress for the family and the nation. As Mahatma Gandhi's much quoted slogan reverberates, 'One step for a woman, ten steps for a nation ...' (Kumar 2002: 1).

[Dis]appearance (1948–67)

> The low value attached to female education in much of India links with some deep-rooted features of gender relations ... First, the gender division of labour ... Second, the norms of patrilocal residence and village exogamy ... Third, the practice of dowry and the ideology of hypergamous marriage ...
>
> (Dreze and Sen 1998: 134–5)

Immediately after Independence, universal primary education became the main focus of Indian education policy. On the margins of central government initiative, a few short-lived adult education programmes such as the Gram Shikshan Mohim – a village literacy movement in Maharashtra – (1959) and the Farmers' Functional Literacy Project (1967–8) took place. These adult education programmes mainly concentrated on defining and developing the socio-economic 'education needs' of 'illiterate' men and women (Shah 1999). As an effort to challenge and reduce discriminatory practices, from the sidelines of a reproductive and productive vision, 'illiterate' women were encouraged to access education and 'become equal' in enabling national socio-economic development (see Ramachandran 1988).

Re-appearance (1967–88)

> We do not equate literacy with the mere ability to read and write. Literacy, if it is to be worthwhile, must be functional. It should enable the literate [*sic*] not only to acquire relevant knowledge which will enable him [*sic*] to pursue his [*sic*] own interests and ends.
>
> (Indian Education Commission, quoted in Shah 1999: 23)

During 1977, government education policy prioritised both universal primary education and adult education. The National Adult Education Programme (NAEP) was formally launched in 1978. The structure and contents of the NAEP were contributed to significantly by the Gram Shikshan Mohim and Farmers' Functional Literacy Programme (Awasthi 1993; Saraf 1980). According to Anil Bordia (Bordia and Carron 1985: 64), NAEP was conceptualised as:

> Literacy and numeracy at a level which would enable learners to continue to learn in a self-reliant manner. Functional development . . . viewed the role of an individual as a producer and worker, as a member of the family and as a citizen in the civic and political system
> . . .

'Women's literacy' did not emerge as a distinct area of focus within NAEP. Educating the 'illiterate' was linked with the wider project of national human resource development. Within this process 'illiterate' women continued to exist as a site of national socio-economic regeneration. Emphasis was placed on strengthening woman's productive role as a wage earner, contributing to poverty alleviation and the national economy, and her reproductive role as a mother, positively impacting on national demographic goals.

(In)visible (m)other of the nation (1988 to date)

Write woman to read power: ... eradicate illiteracy among adult
women ...

(*The Times of India*, New Delhi, 31 May 1996)

Care has been taken to have educational material which is both life
oriented and gender sensitive. So along with lessons on nutrition,
hygiene, and environment, the lessons shall also be revealing their
sensitivity to the female gender.

(*The Times of India*, New Delhi, 23 October 1995)

Secondary Education Minister Mr Ram Lakhan Ram Raman opined
that since a child learns his or her first lessons of life in mother's lap
therefore it was imperative for mothers to be literate. He exhorted the
educated to propagate their knowledge to illiterate people of the
State.

(*Hindustan Times*, Patna Live, Bihar, 16 June 2001)

*Ashikshit samaj kabhi bhi vikas key sopanpar nahin char sakta hai ...
Mahilan rashtri ki mukhya dhara sey mukamal roop sey nahin joor payi hai
... mahilan ko agey aney ke liye usey shikshit hona avashak hai ... mahila
kalm utakar unguta chap ko telanjel dey. Jo lok hastakshar karna sikh lengey
aur sakshar hongey unhey hi Indra Awas anv Vridvastha pension ka labh
diya jayega.*

  Illiterate society can never climb the ladder of development ...
women have not been able to completely join mainstream national
development ... for women to come forward it is necessary for them
to be literate ... women pick up the pen and reject the thumbprint.
Only those people who learn to sign and will be literate will be given
the benefits of Indra Awas and old age pensions. [My translation]

(Dainik Jagran, Begusarai, Bihar, 1 September 2001)

During 1988, the National Literacy Mission (NLM) was established
by the Indian government to provide functional literacy to 80 million
'illiterates' by 1995 (Athreya and Chunkath 1996: 90–1). Once inaugu-
rated, NLM was transformed by the mass campaign efforts of the
Kerala Sastra Sahitya Parishat [KSSP] and the Bharat Gyan Vigyan
Samithi [BGVS] two non-government facilitators of literacy campaigns as
people's movements. KSSP with its success story in Eranakulum district,
Kerala, became a 'guiding light' for the national Total Literacy Campaign
(TLC) (see Joseph 1996). The Eranakulum district campaign began in
1989 as an initiative to make the entire district literate. The success of the

Eranakulum District programme led to TLC's being initiated all over Kerala, making it the first 'literate' state in 1992. Following this, under the Government of India Education for All Declaration, the TLC was launched throughout the country. The Total Literacy campaigns were followed by Post-literacy campaigns and then Continuing Education programmes. The BGVS was organised in 1990 to politicise literacy and motivate people at grass-roots level to become involved in 'literacy'. Developing 'literacy' as a mass movement rather than a government programme placed the emphasis on mobilising people to collectively address and act upon their issues and concerns, e.g. the anti-arrack movement in Nellore (see BGVS 2002). Emphasis was placed on the role of 'literacy' as a tool for 'empowering' women (Dighe and Patel 1997). A gender dimension incorporated in the NLM vision stated a commitment to 'enable women to make informed choices in areas like education, employment and health (especially reproductive health)' (Ramachandran 1998: 79). According to Sonali Kumar, a senior bureaucrat in the National Literacy Mission:

> Empowerment ... not only refers to economic liberalisation but also to access to opportunity, right to decision making and access to education and information ... literacy ... is a very important factor towards the attainment of the intellectual, moral and social upliftment of women. It equips them to fight against injustice, exploitation, inequality and corruption.
>
> (Kumar 2001: 6)

The 1986 National Policy on Education included a section entitled 'Education for Women's Equality' which placed emphasis on developing women's (re)productive roles through vocational education, technical education and education on early childhood care (Shah 1999). A revised policy in 1992 aimed to extend 'education' for 'illiterate' women beyond the realms of reproductive engineering and international population control policy, by including a gender dimension in all aspects of policy planning and administration. This was implemented through a pilot project called Mahila Samakhya which 'in the course of time became an accepted "component" of some basic education projects ... as an effective means of meeting donors' gender checklist requirements' (Ramachandran 1998: 81).

Through international Women in Development anti-poverty and efficiency approaches (Moser 1993) to literacy, the Indian 'illiterate' as the rejected daughter, the lost self-as-wife, the ignorant mother and oppressed worker becomes (in)visible within the 'donor checklist' fantasy of Others.

Ethnographic narratives: the politics of interpretation

My stories-as-her-stories emerge from ethnographic research in two villages, TDK and DCB, located in north Bihar. TDK village is situated 1 km from the roadside and the district administration offices. This village has approximately 167 houses belonging to a total population of 1,342 people. All the people in the village are Muslim and a majority of them work as construction and agriculture labourers. DCB village is situated 110 km from the town area where the district administration offices are based. This village is approximately 0.5 km from the roadside. There are 247 houses in the village holding a total population of 1,305 people. The majority of people in this village belong to Dalit[5] 'communities'.

In re-creating the fantasy of interpreting representation I hope that these ethnographic narratives establish that a village is not an insular cohesive geographical space 'fixed' in time and devoid of a history of communication practices involving reading and writing. The 'illiterate' woman is not a homogeneous 'entity'. There are many different women whose (un)successful engagement with communication practices is interlinked with their socio-economic, political, cultural and religious realities. Engagement that is influenced by a history of power relations maintaining gender, class and caste divisions. These ethnographic narratives work towards disrupting a fantasy of the 'illiterate Indian village woman'. I hope my 'stories-as-her stories' make visible voice and agency 're-claiming' the 'illiterate' woman through the hybrid nature of her communication practices.

Speaking back: other stories-in-becoming 'literate'

As a part of my research, I tried to broaden my understanding of how policy representations of the 'illiterate' woman are constructed within 'literacy' discourses appropriated and re-created by literacy programme participants. During my 'ethnographic' travels, in 2000 I visited a village in BP district, Bihar, where the Total and Post-literacy campaigns were a claimed success. My visit took place six years after the programmes had ended. I was invited by the District Literacy Society to interview some of the women who had participated in the programmes. At a central meeting place in the village, I was introduced to four programme participants and then considerately left on my own to spend the night in their homes. I sat on the ground talking to them, surveyed by a few inquisitive men, women and children standing over and around us. After listening to a series of 'personal testimonies' about their transformation through 'literacy', I wondered if it would be acceptable to draw. I had brought some chalk powder, cardboard and marker pens. Using chalk powder, we became engrossed in drawing the outline of an 'illiterate' and a 'literate' woman on the ground. Initially I got confused – could both women be drawn as the same? This prompted a discussion. Fifteen women, standing as onlookers, gradually involved themselves in different ways. I was told that the 'illiterate' woman would be drawn as 'thin and sick' and the 'literate' woman would be 'plump and healthy'. On the two drawings we placed labelled cards with phrases and descriptions from the personal testimonies – adding some more along the way. Some shared representations that emerged, during the activity, were 'illiterate' women:

- *safiye nahin karti* (do not do cleaning)
- *patre nahin likhti hai* (do not write letters)
- *dosrey par nirbar rahti hai* (stays dependent on others)
- *murakh hoti hai* (is ignorant)
- *kuch nahin janthi hai* (does not know anything)
- *apney bachchey ko nahin parathi hai* (does not teach her children)
- *siraf apna ghar sambalti hai* (only manages her house)
- *bahar ka kaam nahin karti* (does not do work outside the home)
- *uski soshan hoti hai* (is exploited).

Using the labelled cards as prompts, I asked questions. I selfishly appropriated the District Literacy Society's agenda for 'knowing' 'illiterate' women, to discover why and how the 'illiterate' woman was 'conceived'.

Plate 2.2 Labelling the 'illiterate women', BP district, Bihar (source: Priti Chopra).

Did she recognise herself differently? What 'other stories' could her knowledge and lived experience create? I started to hear different 'testimonies'. Tulsibai, insulted, refused the fantasy of 'becoming clean through literacy':

> *Main unpar hun. Lok kehtey hain unpar mahila safiye nahin karti. Ghar saf nahin rakhti. Bachey saf nahin rakhti. Kaprey nahin dhoti. Merey panch bachey hain. Ab roj nahlaney dohlaney key liya kitna pani jama karoon, kitna sabun sarf karchun. Pani ka samasya, paisa kitna, mangey kitna isko dekhtey nahin. Kahli ajatey hain sikhaney unpar mahila safiye karo, safiye karo . . .*

I am 'illiterate'. People say that the 'illiterate' woman does not clean. She does not keep the house clean. She does not keep her children clean. She does not wash clothes. Now for washing and cleaning everyday how much water should I collect? How much Surf and soap should I spend? They don't see the problem of water, the amount of money and the cost. Just come and teach 'illiterate' woman do cleaning, do cleaning . . .

Naj Jamal Khatoum becomes the panchayat election candidate

I don't know my exact age. I think I am between thirty-six and thirty-eight years old. I married when I was six or seven years old. I came to this village, after my marriage, thirty years ago. I am the mother of seven sons and five daughters.

I am campaigning to become a *panchayat* member. My election activities involve frequent visits to the block development office. I interact with a lot of government officials in the office. This helps me to access information. I believe that as a *panchayat samithi* member my work will be to make sure that government funds for village development reach the *mukhiya*[6] and public in Madhuban *panchayat* area. As part of my campaign, I promise to make sure that government funds and other resources for women's development reach women. I have been making door-to-door campaign visits, accompanied by women in my village, to neighbouring Muslim and Hindu villages. I have also been going to the town area to have my campaign banners, posters, and loudspeaker cassettes made.

My campaign pamphlet says that I am a *soygya, karmth anvm shiksit mahila.*[7] I have studied Urdu in my village *madarsa* and can sign my name in Urdu and write my address in Hindi. Why should I not claim to be educated? My children will help me to read all the *panchayat* and government papers. In the election papers it is written that a person can help you if you cannot read and write. People should not think if

ग्राम पंचायत मधुवन से पंचायत
समिति के सुयोग्य, कर्मठ एवं
शिक्षित महिला **उम्मीदवार**

नाज खातुन

के चुनाव चिन्ह

''नारियल''

''नारियल'' छाप पर मुहर
लगाकर भारी मतों से
विजयी बनावें।

मुद्रक : हाई सॉफ्ट कम्प्यूटर एण्ड प्रिंटर, राजेन्द्र भवन गली सीतामढ़ी। फोन :- 20311 संख्या 200

Plate 2.3 Naj Jamal Khatoum's *panchayat* election campaign pamphlet (source: Priti Chopra).

a person cannot read and write they have no brains. I am 'illiterate' but that does not stop me from doing my work. I use my brain to move forward.

Ajimun Khatoum becomes the entrepreneur

Ajimun Khatoum lives in TDK village. She estimated her age to be between thirty-five and thirty-six years. Ajimun was born in PCM district. She belongs to a family of three sisters and one brother. They used to live with their mother in the village and visit their father, a shopkeeper, in Calcutta. She said that she must have been seven or eight years old and her husband fifteen or sixteen years old when their marriage was arranged. Ajimun said that she came to this village, as a bride, when she was approximately ten years old. Her husband worked as a daily wage labourer and earned Rs 4–5[8] per day. Today he can earn Rs 100 a day working as a construction labourer. He also migrates to Gujarat and other states, for three to four months a year, to do construction labour work.

Her brother, sisters and herself studied in the village *madarsa* during their childhood. They did not access any other formal schooling. Her husband did not access formal schooling during his childhood. She says that she remembers learning prayers from the Koran, the Urdu script and mental arithmetic, from the *madarsa* and her father, during her childhood. She can still write her name in Urdu, recite prayers and do arithmetic calculations. Ajimun has three daughters and two sons. She has encouraged all her children to study at the village *madarsa*. However, owing to corporal punishment from the teacher, none of her children continued their studies on a regular basis. She has taught all her children to recite prayers from the Koran. Through involving them in her shop activities she has also taught them to keep accounts. Her eldest daughter, now nineteen and the mother of two sons, was married at the age of fifteen. Her eldest son, now fifteen, has been working as a daily wage labourer for the past three years. He also migrates with his father to different parts of the country for construction labour work. Her other two daughters (aged twelve and six) and son (seven years of age) help her with her shop.

Ajimun started her shop eighteen years ago with a loan. She said initially she used to sell *bidis*,[9] firecrackers and a few other small things. Three years ago she took a loan of Rs 1,000 from a non-governmental organisation for women and bought more items such as rice, spices and salt to sell in her shop. She repaid this loan and saved Rs 250 from her earnings. She then took a loan of Rs 2,000 and added wheat, biscuits and children's games to the items she sells. She repaid this loan and has now taken a loan of Rs 3,000 to invest in her shop. She bought some chickens and ducks with the money to sell their eggs and now sells the following items in her shop: rice, wheat, vegetables, lentils, spices, toffees, savoury snacks, needles, *bidis,* eggs, dolls, costume jewellery, *bindis,*[10] candles, kerosene oil, cooking oil, bread rolls, *paan,*[11] *paan parag,*[12] children's games and soap. During festival periods she also keeps items commonly used for the festival in her shop. She has a small piece of land near her home where she grows vegetables and lentils. She also sells the produce from this in her shop. She does all the marketing herself at seven different types of market. Sometimes her husband helps her and at times she has shop items delivered to her home. There are no fixed hours for her shop. She says that she generally opens at 6.00 in the morning and closes at 10.00 at night. Her daily routine normally consists of waking at 4.00 a.m., cleaning the house and feeding her goats, chickens and ducks. Then she cooks for her family and feeds them. Her son and husband go to work and then she and her children eat their morning meal. She then sits in her shop. During the day she may also take care of the vegetables grown on her land and visit any one of several markets in the town area. She cooks in the afternoon and in the evening and feeds her family.

Ajimun says that she does not keep accounts of her income and expenditure. Most people do not spend large amounts of money per day, so it is easy for her to keep an account of what is bought and who owes the shop

Plate 2.4 Ajimun in her shop (source: Priti Chopra).

money. However, it can at times be difficult to collect money that customers owe. She said that if things sell well she can make a profit of Rs 700 in a month.

Ajimun recognises money but cannot write and recognise written numbers or do written calculations. I asked Ajimun questions to understand some processes for her mental calculations. For instance, I asked if she had Rs 328 and somebody made purchases of Rs 21 how much money would she have. She promptly said Rs 349. I asked her to explain to me how she did this calculation. She said, 'I took 2 from 21 and joined it with 28, which made it 30. Then I joined 19 to 30, which made it 49, and then I joined 300, which made it 349'. While we were doing other similar mental arithmetic calculations related to money, her seven-year-old son was sitting outside the shop and running his own business of cooking and selling *papads*.[13] Ajimun had lent him Rs 13 to buy *papads*. He was selling each *papad* for Rs 1. Ajimun told me that so far he had returned Rs 7 and she reminded him that he still owed her Rs 6. Her son got very angry. Ajimun told me that she sold items for Rs 49 and her son sold a *papad* for Rs 1. The customer gave her a Rs 100 note and she forgot about her son's Rs 1 and returned Rs 50 to the customer. Her son was angry that she did not cut his Rs 1 from the customer and was refusing to return all the remaining Rs 6 he owed her. Even though he had been listening to all of Ajimun's precise mental calculations, he said, 'She does not know how to do *hisab-kitab* [accounts].' Ajimun laughed and said, 'I am illiterate but I am still teaching all my children to manage money and the shop.'

Sakina Khatoum becomes the 'housebound undergraduate'

I am twenty. I live in purdah. I only go out to give my exams. Women who have enough status need not go out of their homes. They can stay in purdah. I have never been out of the house unaccompanied. Even to my college, the hospital or when I visit relatives. I have not walked around this village or the town area. I have never even been to a train station. Once or twice I travelled with my family, by bus, to visit relatives in other districts. I spend the day in the house doing housework, studying and helping my mother. I read magazines in Urdu and teach children Urdu at home in the evening. When my father leaves I open the back door and talk to people and invite them in to talk with me. I study via correspondence. I am doing a BA in history. I only go to college to give the exams.

My father has a postgraduate degree in Urdu literature. He works in the Bihar Education Project training college. He does training for literacy workers in the *mahila samakhya* project. He also teaches educational psychology in the local women's training college. My father says

Plate 2.5 Ajimun's son selling *papads* outside her house (source: Priti Chopra).

that we live in a slum and he does not want me to mix with the public here. It is an issue of respectability.

You should talk to my father. Ask my father if you can take a photo of me. (Sakina's father said that I could not take a photo as it was against muslim practice. He said that I could take a photograph of the newspapers, she reads, in his home.)

Denunciation and annunciation: refuting denial of voice, visibility and agency

Literacy, development and gender empowerment international and Indian policy narratives speak about 'transforming' the 'illiterate' woman who lacks ability in performing 'efficient' reproductive and productive roles and about 'empowering' her to participate in national development plans. The 'spoken for' 'illiterate' woman is represented in a space marked by the dominance of a false dichotomy creating the 'literate'. The 'illiterate' woman, in this discursive practice of subordination, becomes a commodifiable object, digesting donor 'checklist' demands. Ethnographic narratives interpreting resistance on the part of the 'illiterate' woman make visible a 'claimed' voice and agency of women as ways of 'speaking back' and imagining her intervention in the 'literacy' world. These narratives do not suggest that 'illiteracy' has been transcended. They aim to suggest 'images' of difference calling into question a discursive practice of 'illiteracy' which has a significant impact on the representation of women.

The politics of 're-claiming' 'illiteracy', through the four ethnographic narratives, may open and strengthen spaces for grassroots level planning

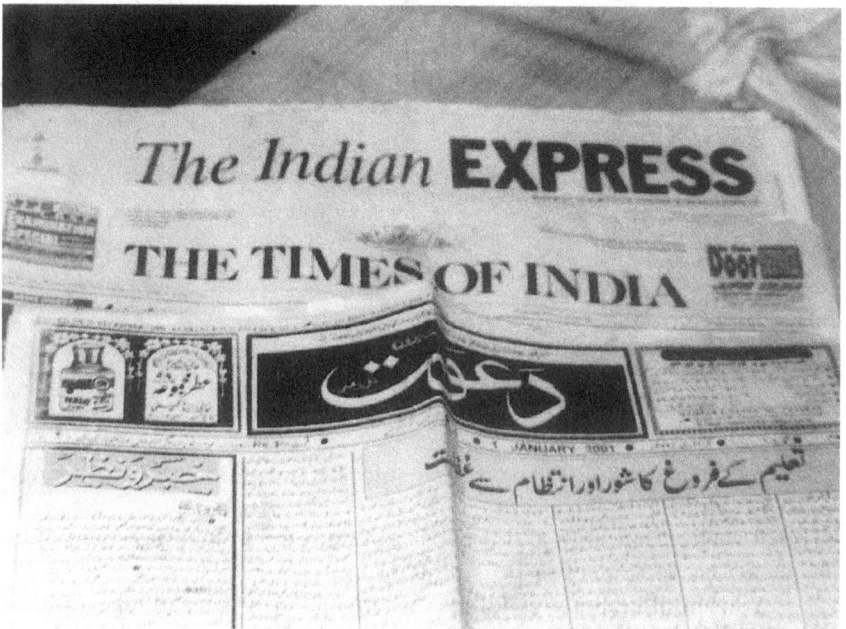

Plate 2.6 Newspapers that Sakina's father brings home for her to read (source: Priti Chopra).

through which people themselves engage with and influence the process within which 'images' of their 'needs' become understood and internalised. Thinking about how the 'illiterate Indian village woman' is constructed and represented through metanarratives on gender, literacy and development, influencing Indian adult education policy, enables reflections on how 'illiterate' women feature as objects/subjects of knowledge. Ethnographic narratives do not transcend processes of objectification. Nevertheless, ethnographic 'accounts' do provide insights into 'other' realities which form a part of subjective processes through which women, as different, understand, use and create knowledge to write themselves into multi-layered representations. 'Other' stories critiquing grand narratives on 'women's development through literacy' suggest processes for redefining the constructs and relationships between gender, literacy and development that impinge on fantasies of the 'illiterate' woman. Describing local knowledge is not simply a process for encouraging policy to redefine relationships with the 'illiterate' woman but rather to review how constructs of the 'illiterate' woman are shaped through pre-existing relationships influencing donor-validated institutional outcomes and interventions (Mosse 2002, 2003). Redefining constructs also entails reinterpreting how 'success' in literacy programmes is produced and re-reading the absence of gaps between literacy policy and literacy rates, such as the Eranakulum literacy campaign in Kerala. The reinterpretation of outcomes appearing to be the consequence of policy intentions opens up possibilities for recognising and legitimising different women's voices and agency expressed and made visible through communication practices embedded in their realities.

Preconceptions, prejudice and prejudgement: miming the route of how I could not 'know' her stories

> sweep away individuality in representation and man [*sic*] becomes the trace of a reflection.
>
> (Derrida 1997: 224)

Claiming to portray ethnographic narratives is by no means a shared vision, a shared narrative or a shared fantasy. It is an interpretation of a returned gaze to master narratives examining representations and conceptualisations of women as 'illiterate'. To create ethnographic narratives that are not just descriptive of 'other realities' but productive in 'speaking back' to relationships of negotiations, between different agencies, and the constructs of gender, literacy and development that inform practice, policy and planning has been a shared and dynamic research agenda.[14] As an ethnographer I do not claim to 'know' the 'illiterate-as-literate' (Chopra 2001), but rather am attempting to contribute to conversations questioning discursive practices legitimising representations of the 'illiterate' woman – as representations of 'needs' for the 'illiterate'. This engagement in itself 're-claims' a process of naming and of imparting knowledge, as an accumulative resource, that renders (in)visible the voice and agency of 'illiterate' women.

My ethnographic writing, though claiming to be the outcome of 'participatory research' intentions, remains implicit in denial of voice as my research subjects – Naj Jamal, Ajimun, Tulsibai and Sakina – are spoken for. Their interviews have become 'my stories-as-her stories'. Their Hindi words have become English words and their voice, in the first person, becomes third-person, as the linearity created to project a 'complete' ethnographic narrative is based on a series of interpretations and translations of brief research encounters. Shared encounters, however brief, have created a strategic purpose of speaking back to education practice through which different women develop, use and create knowledge, to write (act) in their voices on their realities. In positioning myself, as an interpreter, translator and ethnographic researcher, I also construct 'illiterate' women as excluded by these ethnographic practices. My writing, in itself, becomes a secondary source, resulting from interpretation – open to interpretations. For me, this is an account of historical practices not possessing a 'knowing' of women but rather miming the route of how I could not 'know' (Spivak 1999: 241) without her voice – which leaves me to wrestle with the (im)possible perspective of the *'native informant'* (ibid.: 49).[15]

Notes

1 Apart from the names of Ajimun Khatoum and Naj Jamal Khatoum all the names of places and people mentioned in these ethnographic narratives have been changed to protect people's identity. Ajimun Khatoum and Naj Jamal Khatoum would like their orginal names to be used in any research writing about them. During my ethnographic research I was engaged in a constant process of translating interviews into English and then reading back in Hindi what I had written about people as well as requesting consent to the use of this information in research writing.
2 Grassroots level democratic organisation.
3 Muslim school.
4 Literally meaning 'curtain' but signifying a practice of seclusion.
5 Lower castes.
6 *Panchayat* leader.
7 Capable, hardworking and educated woman.
8 There are Rs 78 to £1 sterling.
9 Handmade cigarettes.
10 An Indian cosmetic.

11 Betel leaf.
12 Chewing tobacco.
13 An Indian crispbread.
14 On writing ethnographic narratives see Coffey (1999), Visweswaran (1994) and Wolcott (1999).
15 I refer to myself as 'native informant' as I am a Hindi-speaking Indian doing research work based in 'Hindi-speaking' regions of north India.

References

Athreya, V. and Chunkath, S. (1996) *Literacy and Empowerment*, New Delhi: Sage

Awasthi, O. (1993) 'Educational development in India', *Journal of Education and Social Change*, 7 (1): 73–80

Ballara, M. (1991) *Women and Literacy*, London: Zed Books

BGVS (2002) 'Impact of Post-literacy', a report sponsored by UNESCO, New Delhi: UNESCO

Bordia, A. and Carron, G. (eds) (1985) *Issues in Planning and Implementing National Literacy Programmes*, Paris: UNESCO

Bown, L. (1990) *Women, Literacy and Development*, ActionAid Development Report 4, London: ActionAid/ODA

Chatterjee, R. (1983) *Impact of Raja Mohan Roy on Education in India*, New Delhi: Chand

Chopra, P. (2001) 'Betrayal and solidarity in ethnography on literacy' in B.V. Street (ed.) *Literacy and development: Ethnographic Perspectives*, London: Routledge

—— (2005) 'Parody and Power in the Gaze', unpublished PhD thesis, King's College, London

Coffey, A. (1999) *The Ethnographic Self*, London: Sage

Derrida, J. (1997) *Writing and Difference*, London: Routledge

Dighe, A. and Patel, I. (1997) 'Gender Issues in Literacy Education', Working Paper 108, New Delhi: Institute of Rural Management

Dreze, J. and Sen, A. (1998) *India: Economic Development and Social Opportunity*, New Delhi: Oxford University Press

Hall, S. and Du Gay, P. (eds) (1996) *Questions of Cultural Identity*, London: Sage

Joseph, P. (1996) 'The Total Literacy Project of Eranakulum', *Convergence*, 29 (1): 11–19

Kabeer, N. and Subrahmanian, R. (1996) *Institutions, Relations and Outcomes: Framework and Tools for Gender-aware Planning*, Discussion Paper 357, Brighton: Institute of Development Studies, University of Sussex

Kumar, S. (ed.) (2001) *Literacy Empowers the Indian Woman*, New Delhi: National Institute of Adult Education

Moser, C. (1993) *Gender Planning and Development*, London: Routledge

Mosse, D. (2002) 'People's knowledge, participation and patronage: operations and representations in rural development' in B. Cooke and U. Kothari (eds) *Participation: the New Tyranny?* London: Zed Books

—— (2003) 'Good Policy is Unimplementable? Reflections on the Ethnography of Aid Policy and Practice', paper presented at EIDOS conference, London, 26–28 September

Paul, M.C. (1991) 'Women and development of adult education in colonial Bengal: a sociological exploration', *Indian Journal of Adult Education*, 52 (1&2): 64–71

Ramachandran, V. (1998) *Bridging the Gap between Intention and Action*, New Delhi: ASPBAE

Saraf, S. (1980) *Literacy in a Non-literacy Milieu*, Paris: International Institute of Educational Planning

Shah, Y. (1999) *An Encyclopaedia of Indian Adult Education*, New Delhi: National Literacy Mission

Shukla, S. (1991) 'Literacy and development', *Indian Journal of Adult Education*, 52 (3): 5–11.

Spivak, G. (1999) *A Critique of Postcolonial Reason*, London: Harvard University Press

Street, B.V. (1995) *Social Literacies*, London: Longman

Visweswaran, K. (1994) *Fictions of Feminist Ethnography*, Minneapolis MN: University of Minnesota Press

Wolcott, H. (1999) *Ethnography: a Way of Seeing*, London: Sage

3 Implications of the New Literacy Studies for researching women's literacy programmes

Brian V. Street

As other chapters in this volume unpack the problems associated with traditional approaches to women, literacy and development, this chapter will focus on the implications of the New Literacy Studies for researching women's literacy programmes. In particular, I examine problems with current approaches, putting issues of gender in the broader context of adult literacy policy as articulated amongst international organisations, such as the World Bank; and the problems associated with cultural insensitivity that have been highlighted by more ethnographic approaches to the uses and meanings of literacy in context. An 'ethnographic' perspective involves making the invisible visible; theorising 'context'; paying greater attention to local meanings and uses; and describing real practices in everyday life, in the context of literacy involving such 'real' materials as credit slips, notes, notices, water slides. Rather than just considering 'educational' material, ethnographic approaches, then, lead to a focus in teaching and learning on 'Real Literacy Materials' (RLM) (cf. Rogers 1994). Such approaches also entail pre-programme research that starts from social practices, not necessarily from literacy itself: this includes, for instance, looking at subjects' engagement with markets, religion and political relations between the local and the global, within which literacy may take on different priority for different participants. I draw on the theoretical foundations of these approaches, in what have come to be termed the 'New Literacy Studies'. An account of literacy in this tradition begins with social theories and research. I describe my own personal history in this field and how my experience in Iranian villages in the 1970s, later reinforced by work in South Africa, Ghana, Nepal and elsewhere, made me aware of the remarkable contrast between what an ethnographic approach was telling us about people's uses of literacy and how it was viewed from 'outside' as it were by agencies and formal institutions. Such experience, both my own and that of other ethnographers of literacy, has led to a new theoretical framework for conceptualising what counts as literacy and how we might design programmes to address people's literacy needs and desires.

I describe the distinction between autonomous and ideological models of literacy; explain what is involved in the notion of 'social literacies' and community literacies and develop a conceptual distinction for research purposes between literacy events and literacy practices. Starting from recent theories of learning as situated or distributed, the approaches described here attempted to build on people's knowledge and prior experience of literacy, to facilitate them to 'take hold' of their own and new literacies rather than treating them as empty vessels or 'illiterates' as in Freire's critique of the 'banking' theory of literacy work. It is in this larger account of literacy and learning that the present volume's concern with the 'illiterate woman' can be located. I provide brief examples from three parts of the world and three different research projects that detail the uses women make of real literacy materials in their lives and the problems that arise when 'autonomous' perspectives on literacy lead to these same women being labelled 'illiterate' despite their facility with actual social practices of literacy. A social as opposed to an 'autonomous' approach can help provide explanations for the high drop-outs and low take-up of formal literacy programmes that, as we shall see below, the World Bank and other agencies are worried about. The approach suggests alternative strategies for literacy learning that are tailor-made rather than off-the-peg (cf. Newsletters for the Community Literacies Project in Nepal, clrc@wlink.com.np). I suggest that an understanding of the particular problems associated with women's literacy programmes can usefully be located within this larger framework which indicates ways in which gender, development and ethnography can be brought together to both research literacy as we find it and to develop programmes that will enhance literacy for ordinary people.

Problems with current approaches

I begin with an earlier comment by this volume's editor, Anna Robinson-Pant. She argued in favour of 'gender planning' as a means of enabling the needs of both men and women to be incorporated into strategic planning. She wrote:

> Male needs and consequently the framework in which these have been met are generally perceived as the norm. Most planning is 'gender blind'. Experience has shown that if specific constituencies within the majority, such as women and cultural minorities, are not identified at the planning stage, their requirements will be subordinated to those of the dominant minority.

(Robinson-Pant 1997: 6)

In this chapter, I take my cue from this analysis to link gender insensitivity to the broader issue of cultural insensitivity raised by ethnographic approaches to literacy. I argue that such insensitivity may provide a significant level of explanation for the lack of success in many adult literacy programmes. This problem was raised by Helen Abadzi in a position paper for the World Bank in 1996. In Chapter 1, which she entitles 'Adult literacy: a problem-ridden area', she states:

> It was once believed that if the illiterate poor learned to read they would have access to information that would improve their lives. For that reason many countries undertook large literacy campaigns in the 1950s, 1960s, and 1970s with the help of international organizations, and the World Bank included literacy in thirty education projects between fiscal years 1963 and 1985. In contrast to children's education, however, adult literacy programs have yielded disappointing results worldwide. They generally fail to teach stable literacy skills to the intended beneficiaries, who thus cannot access useful information. About 50 per cent drop out during the course and about 50 per cent of those who stay fail to meet performance criteria at the end. Not only are dropout rates inordinately high, but relapse into illiteracy seems widespread, particularly among populations with few opportunities for daily reading. In campaigns conducted during the 1970s, efficiency could be as low as 12 per cent (UNESCO/UNDP 1976).
>
> (Abadzi 1996: 1)

She is surprised that such a 'disappointing performance' seems not to have been extensively researched and calls for a rigorous research programme. Whilst her own approach is based in experimental psychology, which has contributed major insights into this 'problem', I am here concerned with a more qualitative approach located in ethnographic studies that might also offer us some clues to the low take-up and high drop-out that so exasperate Abadzi and her colleagues. A close ethnographic account of how people actually engage in literacy in their daily lives might help explain why they are reluctant to enter literacy programmes, for reasons that will become apparent as we pursue the experience of a number of such women in different parts of the world. I take as indicative cases the experience of Oum Fatima in Morocco (Wagner 1993), Señora Ana in Mexico (Kalman 1999) and Winnie Tsotso in South Africa (Kell 2003). In all these cases, the 'feel' of the experience with literacy that is afforded by such an ethnographic account can help us understand the strengths and limits of the formal programmes available to them and indicates pointers for future programme development.

Some ethnographic accounts of women's experience with literacy

Oum Fatima in Morocco (Wagner 1993)

In his account of literacy practices in Morocco, Wagner commences with a story that we find repeated in its general principles across the world and that characterises the difficulties new researchers are having in challenging the dominant accounts of 'illiteracy' in the world:

> Oum Fatima has labored virtually every day of her 55 years. With four children and a chronically ill husband unable to help financially, she could only hope to bring in money by doing housecleaning in the wealthier homes of the labyrinthine *medina* (or old city) of Marrakech.
>
> Beyond regular washerwoman duties, it was normal for Oum Fatima to handle a gamut of contacts between the 'outside world' and the home and children for whom she worked so hard. Such activities varied enormously. On some days the mailman would arrive with letters; Oum Fatima would deliver each to the addressee, knowing simply by the type of handwriting or script used – Arabic or French – who should receive which letter. Once a month the 'electric man' would arrive to collect money for the month's charges; Oum Fatima handled this affair with just 'a question or two', drawing money from an earthenware jar in which she stashed odd coins and bills in anticipation of his visits. At the souk (market), Oum Fatima's skill in mental arithmetic and bargaining was legendary. Not only could she switch effortlessly between the several parallel currency units in use – dirhams, francs, and riyals (a base-five system) – but her ability to negotiate the lowest possible price made her a well-known figure in the derb (quarter). To those of her social class, as well as to those 'higher up', Oum Fatima was a woman worthy of great respect.
>
> Never having gone to school, Oum Fatima could neither read nor write in any language, nor could she do simple arithmetic on paper.
>
> (Wagner 1993: 1)

Oum Fatima, then, became one of the many women described as 'illiterate' in dominant terms – because they could not pass the tests imposed on them from outside and because outsiders failed to see the literacy work they were actually engaged in that closer ethnographic accounts bring to view.

Señora Ana in Mexico (Kalman 1999)

A similar story is told by Judy Kalman in her account of literacy practices in Mexico:

> Two or three times a week, Señora Ana attends a basic education class held in a spare room at her neighbour's house. She lives in Aguazul, a working class community on the eastern edge of Mexico City made up of native residents and rural immigrants like herself. As a child in the state of Vera Cruz, she never went to school because her father believed that school was only for boys; according to her father, girls who went to school inevitably ended up in trouble. Ana considers herself to be illiterate, alienated from the uses of written language and the ways of schooled people.
>
> However, the concept of illiteracy becomes questionable when Ana describes or demonstrates how she deals with written language. When encouraged to reveal herself, she shyly confesses that she can follow the numerical instructions published in knitting magazines, review her children's report cards, and make lists of merchandise to order for her little neighbourhood store. She receives bills and commercial advertisements in the mail, interprets neighbourhood announcements painted on walls, and keeps important papers in a special place. Ana displays a series of written language practices neatly tucked away in her everyday life, almost invisible to the untrained eye. Her uses of written language do not correspond to the more publicly recognized signs of literacy: reading newspapers, extensively reading and writing documents at work, sending and receiving correspondence, reading literary works such as novels, poetry or stories. Yet she is competent at resolving the paperwork demands of her every day life. She had no formal schooling as a child, so reading and writing have crept into her life little by little over the years, one way or another. This is not to say that Ana could not benefit from enhancing her knowledge and understanding of the use of writing; but what this does imply is that she is in fact knowledgeable about many written language uses. Furthermore, her literacy practices suggest that the dominant uses of reading and writing do not necessarily define literacy for everyone.
>
> (Kalman 1999: 1)

Kalman goes on to cite the shifts in theory and research that have enabled us to 'see' what Ana can do in a new light and that rejects the dominant 'autonomous' model of literacy, with its demeaning accounts of such women:

The idea that literacy is a multiple construct, shaped by context, history and communicative necessity has gained widespread acceptance over the last twenty years ... a growing body of specific reading which was followed by a growing body of qualitative studies of specific reading and writing practices situated in community life, a new interdisciplinary study of literacy has emerged, a research trend that Street (1993) has dubbed the new literacy studies. These studies have made important contributions to our understanding of literacy as a collection of possibilities rather than a single construct. Working in a variety of cultures, languages, and situations (vernacular literacy, second language literacy, immigrant literacy, religious literacy, workplace literacy, and so on) what these studies have collectively shown time and time again is that it is difficult for people living in lettered societies to be without knowledge of written language. What knowledge they have, and how they make use of it, varies widely and is more a consequence of social relations and power than the result of individual abilities or personal drive. As illustrated by Señora Ana ... people tend to develop a working understanding of literacy to the extent that they have access to written language and its use, to opportunities to interact with other readers and writers, and to the degree that they have a need to use reading and writing.

Underlying these findings are important implications for literacy education, particularly in the realm of adult and youth education in poor nations where underschooling is still widespread. In Mexico, for example, there are currently 35 million adults who have not finished the nine years of required basic education, a population equal in size to the number of students registered in primary and junior high school (SEP 1999). The message to be gleaned here is that adults often labeled as illiterate have a wealth of knowledge about reading and writing and develop ways to use it when there is a personal or societal need to do so. This is a pedagogically significant finding, given the importance that the current literature on teaching and learning gives to starting with what a learner knows (Archer and Costello 1990; Cendales 1996; Kalman 1996; Soifer 1990). Despite the growing body of knowledge about everyday literacy and what people know about reading and writing, it seems that this information has not made its way on to the adult educator's or policy maker's desk. Even though current international educational policy underlines the need for programs that capitalize on learners' existing knowledge, few programs seem put this into practice. Garcia Huidoro, a recognized expert on adult education policy in Latin America, wrote in 1994 that adult education 'must find its starting point and base itself on the culture and daily lives of the learners' (p. 29). However, all over the

world many of the programs offered to adults mimic primary school
for children.

(Kalman 1999: 2)

Winnie Tsotso in South Africa (Kell 2003)

Finally, I cite a further example from South Africa where again a woman
actively involved in local life – and in this case the struggle politics of the
apartheid era – is recognised and valued by her companions but misun-
derstood and misrepresented when viewed through the lenses offered by
the dominant literacy theory embedded in literacy programmes. Cathy
Kell, a literacy researcher like Kalman and Wagner, attempts to redress
the balance in her account of the powerful activist Winnie Tsotso:

> Winnie Tsotso has been one of the key community leaders living in an
> informal settlement in the Cape Peninsula over the past twelve to
> fifteen years. I conducted an ethnography of literacy practices within
> her community, Masiphumelele, over a number of months in the
> early 1990s, just prior to our first national democratic elections. As
> one part of this study I interviewed Winnie in the rambling shack
> which she had built for herself and her family. I observed her partici-
> pation in literacy classes over around twenty-four evenings, at a
> number of community meetings and for a while I visited her daily.
> This process of data collection resulted in an account of Winnie's day-
> to-day life and literacy practices at a time of dramatic change in South
> Africa. In the account I focused on understanding the different and
> multiple roles that Winnie played, and what resources she could draw
> on in the accomplishment of these roles.
>
> I found that within her family she played the role of mother, grand-
> mother and partner. Within her immediate neighbourhood and
> community, she played the role of friend, member of a sewing group,
> member of the Baptist Church and member of the Catholic Welfare
> and Development (CWD) Creche Committee. She worked sporadic-
> ally as a domestic worker in the homes of neighbouring white families.
> She ran a soup kitchen for pensioners for CWO and was active in the
> local Civic Association on the Youth and Development Committees.
> She had played an important role in co-ordinating a Supreme Court
> case whereby the members of Masiphumelele (who had been classi-
> fied 'illegal' and were constantly hounded and harassed by apartheid
> authorities) won the right to permanent residence in the area. Winnie
> had also completed a First Aid course and was often called out if
> people were injured in the community. She was an active member of
> the recently established Development Forum as well as the organiser

for the local branch of the African National Congress, for which she attended both regional and national meetings. Perhaps most importantly she played the role of local advice office worker, helping people get their pension cards, sorting out funerals, assisting people in their welfare grant applications, helping people to get their identity documents and so on. And finally she played the role of literacy learner in the adult literacy night school that had recently been set up, classified as a 'beginner', where I watched her night after night slowly spelling out her name and reading short sentences in isiXhosa like 'Ndingu Winnie Tsotso' (I am Winnie Tsotso), 'ndihlala eKapa' (I live in Cape Town). Winnie had never spent a day in school, and saw herself as totally 'illiterate'.

(Kell 2003)

Winnie's story continues as South Africa makes the shift from apartheid to the ANC government, intent on redressing the wrongs of the previous era, among which was lack of formal education for such women. The new situation, however, although intended to make up for that loss by providing her with classes and with access to formal literacy, served in practice to marginalise her more than she had been in the previous era. In a story similar to many across developing societies, where well intentioned literacy policy appears to be offering women a way out of oppression, Kell demonstrates the problems that arise when a narrow view of literacy is imposed on such 'empowerment':

I tracked Winnie through the various institutions and organisations to which she belonged. It appeared that Winnie had some difficulties participating in the development agencies and that she was starting to be left out of meetings. She herself expressed frustration; she felt she was excluded from getting a job as a community worker by the fact that she was not literate. It was for this reason that she had enrolled in the adult literacy classes, which were run by what was seen as one of the most professional, progressive and dedicated literacy agencies in South Africa. But over the months of my research I observed that Winnie was slowly withdrawing and had more or less stopped going by the time I left.

(Kell 2003)

We might ask how many more Winnies, Anas and Oum Fatimas are to be found in societies apparently being given the benefit of 'modern' education and literacy. The chapters of this book attempt to address the myopia of these dominant views and to offer more sophisticated models and theories that enable us to see their already existing womanhood and their literacy. Once we understand these we might be in a better position to offer enhancement, support and facilitation in developing the kind of literacy skills that will be appropriate for the new worlds these women are entering but that build upon what they already know and have achieved rather than ignoring or demeaning it.

A personal perspective

My own research in Iran during the 1970s, and in other countries since, brings out this point from a personal perspective. Indeed, this experience explains why I, like many researchers in this new tradition, took on research in this area. I went to Iran during the 1970s to undertake anthropological field research. I had not gone specifically to study 'literacy' but found myself living in a mountain village where a great deal of literacy activity was going on: I was drawn to the conceptual and rhetorical issues involved in representing this variety and complexity of literacy activity at a time when my encounter with people outside the village suggested the dominant representation was of 'illiterate', backward villagers. Looking more closely at village life in the light of these characterisations, it seemed that not only was there actually a lot of literacy going on but that there were quite different 'practices' associated with literacy – those in a traditional Koranic school; in the new state schools; and among traders using literacy in their buying and selling of fruit to urban markets. If these complex variations in literacy which were happening in one small locale were characterised by outside agencies – state education, UNESCO, literacy campaigns – as 'illiterate', might this also be the case in other situations too? I have kept this image in mind as I have observed and investigated literacy in other parts of the world – urban Philadelphia, South Africa, Ghana, Nepal, the United Kingdom. In all these cases I hear dominant voices characterising local people as 'illiterate' (the media in the United Kingdom are full of such accounts, cf. Street 1997) whilst on the ground ethnographic and literacy-sensitive observation indicates a rich variety of 'practices' (Heath 1983; Barton and Hamilton 1998). When literacy campaigns are set up to bring literacy to the illiterate – 'light into darkness', as it is frequently characterised – I find myself asking first what local literacy practices are there and how do they relate to the literacy practices of the campaigners? In many cases, the latter fail to 'take' – few people attend classes and those who do drop out, precisely because they are the literacy practices of an outside and often alien group. Even though in the long run many local people do want to change their literacy practices and take on board some of those associated with Western or urban society, a crude imposition of the latter that marginalises and denies local experience is likely to alienate even those who were initially motivated.

Research, then, has a task to do in making visible the complexity of local, everyday, community literacy practices and challenging dominant stereotypes and myopia. This indeed has become a major drive in my own research, teaching and writing, both in the research community and in the public arena. Following through its implications for programme design, including pre-programme research on local literacy practices and for curriculum, pedagogy and assessment/evaluation are major tasks that require first a more developed conceptualisation of the theoretical and methodological issues involved in understanding and representing 'local literacy practices'. Viewing the gender issues involved in literacy pro-grammes through this lens may offer a different, more culturally sensitive view than that derived from a more traditional 'external', perspective.

References

Abadzi, H. (1996) *Adult Literacy*, Washington, DC: World Bank

Barton, D. and Hamilton, M. (2001) *Local Literacies*, London: Routledge

Heath, S.B. (1983) *Ways with Words*, Cambridge: Cambridge University Press

Kell, C. (2003) 'Accounting for not Counting: Ethnography and Literacy in South Africa', paper presented at National Research and Development Centre (NRDC) conference 'What Counts as Evidence for what Purposes in Research in Adult Literacy, Numeracy and ESOL?' Nottingham, March

Prinsloo, M. and Breier, M. (eds) (1996) *Social Uses of Literacy: Theory and Practice in Contemporary South Africa*, Amsterdam: Benjamins

Robinson-Pant, A. (1997) 'The Link between Women's Literacy and Develop-ment', PhD thesis, University of Sussex

Rogers, A. (1994) *Using Literacy: a New Approach to Post-literacy Materials*, London: ODA

Street, B. (1984) *Literacy in Theory and Practice*, Cambridge: Cambridge University Press

—— (ed.) (1993) *Cross-cultural Approaches to Literacy*, Cambridge: Cambridge University Press

—— (1996) *Social Literacies: Critical Approaches to Literacy in Development, Education, and Ethnography*, London: Longman

—— (1997) 'The implications of the New Literacy Studies for literacy education', *NATE*, 32 (3): 26–39

Recent works on literacy from an ethnographic perspective

Aikman, S. (1999) *Intercultural Education and Literacy: an Ethnographic Study of Indigenous Knowledge and Learning in the Peruvian Amazon*, Amsterdam: Benjamins

Barton, D. and Hall, N. (1999) *Letter Writing as a Social Practice*, Amsterdam: Benjamins

Barton, D. and Hamilton, M. (1998) *Local Literacies: Reading and Writing in one Community*, London: Routledge

Barton, D., Hamilton, M. and Ivanic, R. (eds) (1999) *Situated Literacies: Reading and Writing in Context*, London: Routledge

Besnier, N. (1995) *Literacy, Emotion and Authority: Reading and Writing on a Polynesian Atoll*, Cambridge: Cambridge University Press

Brandt, D. (2001) *Literacy in American Lives*, Cambridge: Cambridge University Press

Collins, J. (1998) *Understanding Tolowa Histories: Western Hegemonies and Native American Response*, New York: Routledge

Doronilla, M.L. (1996) *Landscapes of Literacy: an Ethnographic Study of Functional Literacy in Marginal Philippine Communities*, Hamburg: UNESCO Institute of Education

Gregory, E. (1997) *One Child, Many Worlds: Early Learning in Multicultural Communities*, London: David Fulton

Hornberger, N. (ed.) (1998) *Language Planning from the Bottom up: Indigenous Literacies in the Americas*, Berlin: Mouton de Gruyter

Kalman, J. (1999) *Writing on the Plaza: Mediated Literacy Practices among Scribes and Clients in Mexico City*, Cresskill NJ: Hampton Press

King, L. (1994) *Roots of Identity: Language and Literacy in Mexico*, Stanford CA: Stanford University Press

Prinsloo, M. and Breier, M. (1996) *The Social Uses of Literacy*, Amsterdam: Benjamins/Sacched

Robinson-Pant, A. (2001) *Why Eat Green Cucumbers at the Time of Dying? Exploring the Link between Women's Literacy and Development: a Nepal Perspective*, Hamburg: UNESCO Institute of Education

Sheridan, D., Street, B. and Bloome, D. (1999) *Ordinary People Writing: Literacy Practices and Identity in the Mass-Observation Project*, Cresskill NJ: Hampton Press

Street, B. (ed.) (2001) *Literacy and Development: Ethnographic Perspectives*, London: Routledge

Wagner, D. (1993) *Literacy, Culture and Development: Becoming Literate in Morocco*, Cambridge: Cambridge University Press

Yates, R. (1994) 'Gender and Literacy in Ghana', PhD thesis, University of Sussex

4   Creating the gender text

Literacy and discourse in rural El Salvador

Julia Betts

In the village of San Cristobel, high in the mountains of rural El Salvador, a woman and her partner sit at the only table in a small wooden and corrugated iron house with a dirt floor. They wave their hands to guard their meal of beans and tortillas from flies. They are engrossed in a discussion which ranges from this year's maize harvest to the price of dried beans, from strategies for accessing aid grants to their community to the morning's events in a neighbour's household. Local and national concerns, history, politics and gossip are intertwined in a narrative of struggle, survival and hope.

This couple have no access in their home to electricity or potable water, minimal contact with newspapers, television and books, and in terms of social conditions their life remains largely materially unchanged since the civil war. They are disparagingly described by the local mayor, and by members of a local NGO, as *analfabetos* – illiterates. Yet the lunchtime talk within their house, as in many other rooms that day, in fields, on coffee plantations, on the shady verandas and under the mango trees of Usulután, is of 'progress', of 'moving forwards'.

This chapter explores the relationships between dominant constructions of the 'illiterate female peasant' in El Salvador and actual gender constructions and processes within rural communities. During a year's ethnographic fieldwork in Usulután, I met women who, on one hand, appeared to concur with the labels pasted on them as 'unknowing illiterates', and who behaved with demureness and almost submissiveness in front of their male partners, and who on the other acted creatively and cleverly to contest and subvert these constructed images of themselves both inside and outside the home. I learned how, in this situation of struggle and scarcity, many women knowingly 'took hold of' the dominant discourses of the landscape, co-opting these and literacy practices in pursuit of their own determined livelihood strategies, aims and aspirations. The result is a rich and complex gender 'text', constructed by women and men out of a patchwork of new and old literacies and discourses.

Locating this text

Literacy, as Rockhill puts it so succinctly, has been constructed as power in discourses of power (Rockhill 1993). The Freirean vision of disempowerment in particular has been critiqued for its unidimensional model of social power, and by its tendency to conflate women's realities into one oppressive experience (see Mohanty 1991; hooks 1993; Moser 1993; Stromquist 1997). Ethnographic approaches to literacy and communication, as evidenced by the other chapters in this book, have become almost ideological movements in themselves, embedded within modern emphases on diversity and the politics of difference.

This chapter takes, as do the others in this book, an ideological approach to a study of gender and literacy. The approaches of and justifications for ethnographic/ideological methods have been too thoroughly discussed elsewhere to need further words here, but it is worthwhile stressing that, in Usulután, I found discursive practices to be rooted in the rhythms and discourses of people's lives, in the quiet patterns of daily movement and talk that so often stay uncaptured and unknown. Reading, writing and orality are integrally related and intertwined within the frame of discursive practice. This starting point helps us explore how women labelled as being oppressed through gender[1] structures or 'illiteracy' cope. And how do they manage and control the structures which form their social context while pursuing their own hopes?

Usulután

In Usulután, as everywhere, people manage as best they can in a situation of struggle and challenge. They seek out humour and happiness, and are constantly looking out for the next rung of the ladder that will take them 'onwards'. But Usulután is a challenging environment today, one which even the most determined and resistant of people finds at times overpowering.

Usulután county lies in the far east of El Salvador. It is one of the poorest and most rural areas of the country, having been a bitterly and violently contested arena during El Salvador's recent civil war, with control fluctuating between the army and the guerrilla forces. The fundamental social, psychological and spiritual unit of many Usulutecos' lives, the family, has experienced major changes with the upheavals of the civil war and the post-war transformation of the rural political economy. During the conflict, rural families were often destabilised by the necessity of the male leaving the family for long periods in the face of political repression or in order to search for work. Thousands of families became headed by women, causing them to look desperately to the so-called informal sector of the economy as a means of survival.[2] During the war years, women increasingly organised and participated in grass-roots popular organisations, as well as fighting as combatants. Many writers examining this phenomenon have applauded the apparent gains made by Salvadoran women during wartime.[3] But inside Usulután today, economic necessity among other factors has meant there has been little opportunity to build on any wartime social change.

Male absence and the subsequent dislocation in family life continue to be a major factor in the shaping of Usulután society, owing to the uncertain nature of seasonal employment and the culture of emigration to the United States, with temporary absence frequently ending up as permanent abandonment. These pressures are greatest among the landless and the land poor, who live in the most precarious economic circumstances. For such households, much crucial additional household income comes from 'women's work' such as the selling of bread, or engaging in other forms of petty commerce. What an economist might call the 'informal economy' is too innocuous a term to describe the range of activities to which people resort in Usulután's long and continuing crisis. The 'informal economy' here is simply this: people do whatever they can to survive.

Within the broad gender constructs of Usulután, it is generally men who hold the primary power of household decisions: whether to send the children to school, for example, or whether to sell animals or land. Similarly, it is men who can travel 'outside' the community to engage in external business, while women remain at home. This arises from the dominant patriarchal discourse; men are constructed as the 'real' breadwinners, with their wage being regarded as real income, while women's is merely supplementary. Women's identities are not primarily constructed as workers or decision makers, but as the domestic experts.

A sense of identity: different voices

Traditionally, the 'silencing' of women is located, especially in the feminist and emancipatory traditions, within doctrines of oppression. Their concordant doctrines of participation and empowerment, as Fiedrich notes in this volume, have become orthodoxies in themselves. It is certainly true that many women living in rural communities in Usulután do not openly contest the dominant discourses around them. When it comes to literacy, for example, the voices of the large number of women who opted against attending free classes, provided by the local NGO, were almost a chorus. 'What for, at our age?' 'We've always lived like this and we'll die like this.' It was these voices that led literacy promoters in Usulután to characterise women as 'too oppressed by their husbands', or 'unmotivated', or 'unwilling to learn'. Yet the ways of silencing female voices in Usulután, as Zubair also found in Pakistan, are in fact highly complex processes, bound up in multidimensional webs of free-flowing power dynamics and communicative strategies.

Had I been able to spend time only within the NGO responsible for running the literacy classes, or talking to local and national leaders, I might well have struggled to get past the traditional, unidimensional characterisations of oppression. Yet I was fortunate in being able to slowly develop conversations and relationships in communities which revealed tensions and dissonances not easily reconciled. Theories of oppression and silencing did not sit well with the deliberate, tangible ways in which women went about creating their lives. While strong structural, social and cultural barriers clearly surrounded them, there was also dissonance between women's words and their actions. 'I'm too old to learn [to attend literacy classes] . . . what do I want to do that for now?' said many women, *but* they wanted, and tried, to read the Bible, *and* they practised in private signing their name. 'Nobody listens to us, women are the silent ones,' said Maria Leocardia, but she instructed her cousin, the village leader, to apply for a grant to mend the dam across the river, and offered to write the official letter.

How then to account for this tension between voices being silenced, and yet women simultaneously taking control of their destiny, negotiating relationships and resources through discourse for personal advantage? This was clearly no simple matter of 'silencing'. It gradually became clear that what outsiders constructed as passivity or conformity was in fact a form of artful resistance and perhaps the creative pursuit of happiness. Women were constantly engaging in negotiations of power and struggles over resources and relationships, interacting with and reshaping the gender text around them.

A theoretical approach

As is evident from the other chapters of this book, the notion of communicative practices is central to modern literacy research, reflecting the general cultural ways in which literacy and discourse are used (Street 1993). Communicative practices are cultural texts, created through discourse. The emphasis on agency within the concept of communicative practices allows us to focus on what has been called dominant literacies (Street 1994) revealing how discursive practices become sites of contestation and negotiation.

The concept of practices in this ideological sense was very useful as a basis on which to explore the nature of social processes in Usulután. But it did not seem to capture the most striking aspect of interactions between men and women: the potent and subtle agendas, and the ways that power dynamics – in conversations within households, on coffee plantations, under trees and on the shady streets of Usulután – were negotiated with an often tangible undercurrent of agency. At these moments, the emphasis seemed to lie less on the event or practice itself than on its creation – its enacting as a moment of theatre – less an event formed by ideology than one carefully directed at shaping it.

One route down which to travel here is that of anthropologists and folklorists, who view culture itself as social discourse, comprised of meanings and expressions of experience that are negotiated in instances of social interaction, or performances (see Hymes 1964, 1981; Bauman 1986; Basso 1985). Communicative processes are in this vision treated as literary texts, representing at least one view of experience to society. For Bruner, for instance, culture is negotiated through the public performance of the individual apprehension of experience. The text stands in a dialogical relationship to the individual and society; its public performance both constructs the text and accomplishes culture, or society, while each of these processes shapes the other. 'It is in the performance of an expression that we re-experience, re-live, re-create, re-tell, re-construct and re-fashion our culture' (Bruner 1986: 11).

So in theoretical terms we can combine the notions of 'communicative practices' from the New Literacies approach with that of 'cultural performance' from anthropology, to arrive at a new concept of 'communicative performances'. This concept helps us understand how history, experience and ideology are combined with discourse, and how this intertextuality of discourses recreates history, meaning and social relationships anew. The performative act is a moment of meeting, the nexus of ideologies, values and experience – the creation of the social, cultural, political text. It is, to quote Bakhtin, an instant of 'dialogic encounter of two cultures' (Bakhtin 1986: 7), such as those of men and women – both collision and collusion between social worlds, in which meaning is both created and revealed.

This vision of 'communicative performance' seemed to resonate with the very powerful ways women in particular in Usulután are active agents in the historical process: both constructors and negotiators of the gender text. It also seemed to offer a way of capturing the range of diversity and difference in the social processes I watched. Silence, in the Bakhtinian view, is a communicative act in itself – part of the dynamic ethnopoetics of everyday life.

Constructing identities

As we have seen, in Usulután a striking dissonance exists between women's constructions of themselves as 'one who knows nothing' and 'one who cannot do [i.e. read and write] anything at all' and their capable, confident, actual practices. Usulutecas' frequent self-identification as 'illiterates' is both striking and dismaying: 'We are,' said the same Maria Leocardia, 'the blind ones. We don't know anything, in that condition one goes around blind.' Women in particular here often described themselves as unable to move around in the outside world. 'I can't leave the community ... I can't read the bus signs,' said many. But their practices in fact powerfully belied these self-constructions. Women who labelled themselves as 'one who cannot do anything' certainly did do things; they negotiated, for example, their way to the country's capital, a minimum of three hours away on three different buses, to sell their home-grown produce. During this process many engaged in a range of complex calculations; working out how long it would take to get home and therefore at what time they would have to leave; calculating their net income for the day, minus the bus fares, and deliberating about their budget for the week.

So how to account for this discordance? The construction of the self as one who cannot, yet being at the same time one who does? The point here is twofold. First, many of these practices remain concealed not only from powerful local figures and literacy 'experts' but from those same people who perform them. Second, for the women of rural communities in Usulután, literacy, or *alfabetización*, almost entirely consists in the practices around 'essay-text literacy'; that is, schooled literacy.[4] This goes some way towards telling us how successfully dominant discourses and ideologies around literacy have become integrated and assimilated into the landscape of Usulután.

Space as a communication strategy

The pattern of gendered symbolic capital described above can be well captured in the picture of social space constructed within Usulután communities. Space is a discursive resource, determined by the same structures of power and ideology and the same rules of negotiation as other commodities. Male space, as stated, is more extensive than that of married or accompanied women, whose physical limits are organised around the home. This factor is tied in with socially defined roles; to leave one's house empty and unguarded, much less one's children, is to attract negative comment and gossip for not fulfilling one's social role. This was one reason why so many women found themselves unable, or were unwilling, to attend literacy circles. Social roles and duties are a far greater imperative than attending an event organised by a local NGO, an agency with whom they, if married or accompanied, are within the patriarchal code supposed to have little to do except as relates to their role – with health or bread-making projects, for example.

So, spatial strategies are part of the social dialogue/communicative performances in Usulután; they are both symbol and signifier of the struggle where travel and knowledge, and thereby control over relationships and resources, are ingrained through discourse into the male role and position. This image is captured in any given momentary scene of local life; men of all ages are to be found on the outside, in yards, on porches, in coffee fields, while women are generally located firmly within walls. In such performances, men are perhaps unknowingly recreating their patriarchal ideology through its signification and reiteration.

It is by moving out into a broader social space that women can challenge this constructed ideology, and the ways in which this happened shed light on some of the subtle modes of challenge to the established gender text. Marlenis, for example, was the wife of a relatively wealthy household: her husband Ermis owned a few cattle and had a sideline producing hammocks as well as the traditional work as a daily waged labourer. Because of their improved circumstances, Ermis was reluctant to allow his wife to work. But Marlenis told Ermis that the family would benefit from enabling the children to wear uniforms to school; the teachers would look on the children with greater favour and they would be more likely to score high marks in tests. This was a sore point for Ermis, whose rival for the village leadership had four children who scored consistently high marks at school. Marlenis suggested that, while the children were at school in the morning, she could go around selling bread to pay for the uniforms. Ermis was reluctant at first to allow his wife to as he saw it neglect her social duty, but was won over by Marlenis' insistence that he would surely gain prestige – and possibly the village leadership – as a return.

Marlenis admitted in private that she did not really think the local teacher would be induced to give the children higher marks in school because of the uniforms, 'and in any case I'll never earn enough to pay for four!' But she had her own, strong reasons for wanting to sell the bread. 'Like that I'll get to go from house to house . . . I'll hear all the news and be able to tell the others. One has to manage things, no?' Information is a powerful commodity in Usulután: by being able to spread news and gossip, Marlenis is putting herself in a position of power, accruing her own social capital without alienating her husband. She is achieving her own ends while 'covering herself' in a cloak of respectability. She is using the resources available to her – relationships, the possibility of economic advancement, envy and hope – to resist her silencing, to subtly and cleverly weave her own version of the dominant gender text.

Negotiation within households

Glimpsing inside the houses of Usulután, into the private worlds of women, many hidden communicative practices go on. Behind doors and within walls, many married or accompanied women's lives are hubs of activity, filled with narratives of social activity in the community, with children's homework, with acquiring and using the mandatory identity documents. In Usulután such narratives have a powerful intertextual quality; stories, television, gossip and events all co-construct each other and the broader text. The written, the spoken, the overheard and the rumoured are performed as sites of negotiation within households; the contestation of private resource allocations, or Sen's co-operative conflicts (Sen 1992).

There were two key discourses within families in Usulután: one of survival, for oneself and one's family, and one of aspirations and hope for the future. Combined together, these discourses constitute the powerful metaphor of 'marching onwards' which represents, in Usulután, people's striving to achieve their longings and dreams. Within this single phrase lies a vision of the future, a challenging of history and an articulation of hope.

Engaging in communicative performances is often construed as 'helping the family', that is, as part of the survival discourse. But the process is firmly bounded within existing hierarchies and ideologies. 'If she can sign her name,' said José of his wife, 'she can sign when they [the local NGO] come to give seeds.' Yet while Juanita signed for the seeds, it was José who took control of them. 'I can sign at parents' meetings at the school,' said Juanita. 'Yes, you're right,' said José. But at the next school meeting, only Jose attended. His wife, he explained, 'had to stay in the house'.

Juanita used her social capital in this way as an act of co-operation, of support of the family relationship. Yet it still stands rooted within the text of male dominance. Certainly, few of the accompanied women I met ever explicitly went against their husband's values, or challenged the wider gender text – 'I conform to the usual [pattern]' was the majority refrain. All the women voiced their desire to learn as part of their discourse of hope, but several explained that they were prevented from attending literacy classes by the symbolic violence of patriarchal discourses; 'my husband is not willing . . .'. Three women participants did take the step of defying their husbands and came to the literacy circles in spite of opposition, although none of them lasted very long. Acts of explicit resistance therefore do occasionally take place.

But, whether private or public, whether undertaken as a co-operative act within the family or as one of open resistance, such communicative performances are subtle challenges to the common gender text. By

wanting to be the one who signs, Juanita was contesting both José's dominance and the wider discourses of patriarchy, even though she constructed this in terms of family support. Her private conversation revealed
this: 'He is my husband, we make decisions together ... I want to sign so
that they see that someone in our family can sign, so that I can go to the
meetings in the same way as him, if he is busy.' Embedded within the discourse of teamwork, then, is a striving for equality, for greater social space.
Literacy functions here not merely as a commodity but as part of the renegotiation of the gender text; as a tool for ideology within the social construct of the relationship.

Knowledge constructs in the external world

This limitation of social space for women, their tying to the inside – of the
home, of the community – is related to another resource, that of knowledge. 'Official' knowledge in Usulután is concerned with the external
world outside the household: information about and methods for negotiating the discourses of power – how to take money out of the bank, for
example, or how to deal with the transfer papers for animal sales. Such
'official' knowledge is often kept from women. Maria Alejandra, for
example, has a fifth-grade education and can read aloud her family's land
possession papers that sit in the mayor's office. Yet it was her husband Her-
mundo, who cannot decode written text, who went to the office to 'sign'
the papers using his thumbprint and thereby claim ownership of the land.

These knowledge constructs are both bound up with and themselves a
binding mechanism for the restriction of female social space within the
negotiation of relationships and the struggles for resources. Women are
both vulnerable since they don't *know anything* – 'One who doesn't leave
the house doesn't know anything' – while simultaneously the dominant
gender patterns prevent them from leaving the restricted domain in case
they do learn things, and go on to threaten male dominance over fields of
official, external knowledge. 'He never wanted me to go outside in case I
learned something; he didn't want me to learn' is a common epigraph
among female heads of household in speaking about their ex-partners or
husbands.

One way of resisting and challenging these dominant discourses is the
act of signing one's name. Doña Emilia tells a story about how the teller in
the local bank reached for the ink pad when she arrived at his counter:

> He looked at me and saw I was from the rural zone and he wanted me
> to ... with the thumb! But I can sign, I learned to sign, and I said to
> him, 'Listen, *señor*, I can sign my name,' and I signed my name. . . .
> 'Eh,' said the teller, 'you certainly do know how to sign, you!'

Such a narrative, recounted by Emilia in a tone of wonder and delight, reflects the inscription in discourse of a performance of resistance, and the challenging of the assumption of Emilia's identity as a poor unlettered *campesina*, or rural 'peasant'. It was a performance in which she took great pride, where new meaning was iterated in the communicative performance, hierarchies challenged and history and the gender text recreated anew.

Space and learning within female-headed households

These performances of resistance to the dominant gender text become much more explicit where the houses are headed by women, about 35 per cent of households in the five communities I spent time with during fieldwork. The community with the greatest proportion of female-headed households is that of Los Llanitos, also, surely uncoincidentally, the poorest, with a rate of nearly 70 per cent of households as single-mother-headed. The women here have few resources other than their own ingenuity and skill; most engage in some small production on rented land, and/or selling at a nearby road junction. Very few have any experience of reading and writing at all and none could sign her name, although two could print it. Yet these women were far from being constrained in their social practices by such conditions. Their mental arithmetic skills were far more advanced than mine, and they could engage in complex financial transactions with ease and confidence. Abilities such as these might be described by theorists as 'working intelligences', to distinguish them from 'literacy practices', yet in Los Llanitos at least these seemed not distinct from literacy but rather deeply embedded within the communicative practices of which literacy is a part. 'I don't work it out on paper,' said Elsa. 'What for? I can do it in my head. I always have done, since I was a child. Paper is only for those who can't do in their heads.' Written text, in Elsa's view, is not woven into the fabric of her life but rather stands as something additional, something distinct. Elsa rates her own ability and skill above that of 'paper'; her own performances, then, take place in the dominant and technically superior discourse medium of her orality; her primary resource is her own creativity and intelligence. One wonders how the planners of literacy campaigns and projects would respond to such clear and confident logic.

Yet a powerful tension exists between these frequently expressed attitudes of lone women towards literacy skills – that they were secondary in use within daily life to existing practices and abilities in which they were already confident – and their views about *learning* where this relates to something undiscovered, a goal envisaged. Women heads of household were often openly defiant in their desire to move outside the community.

'I need it [reading] to read the names of the buses, to be able to sign my name,' said Maria Elena. Yet this was related less to the processes of decoding than to the embodiment of hope. In fact Elena already did travel frequently to the capital city, managing the buses and other aspects with confidence. 'Oh! That's no problem. I can always ask,' she said, when we went together to San Miguel, a city to which neither of us had ever travelled. On this journey Elena acted as guide: she used tactics such as asking other women and locating herself by landmarks. 'I'm never afraid. The War was much worse that this; then one really never knew what would happen . . .' For women such as Elena, who have been forced by the economic desperation of abandonment to confront their restriction of social space, a new courage has been encountered which could have barely been conceptualised before. 'If you had said to me that I could have done this before he left, I would have said, never! Never, I would have said . . . it seems strange to [the other men] but what is one to do?' Such women have ventured alone beyond the community, and found the world something they cannot only face but creatively *manage*.

Literacy learning for such women as Maria Elena, then, operates mainly as part of an ongoing discourse of identity, bound up in lived reality. In wanting to facilitate the negotiation of greater space, Elena is expressing her desire to expand her *choices* – a term which literally means 'possibilities' and which is a powerful motif in Usulután, suggesting rights denied by history. Through circumstance and her own ingenuity and strength, she has engaged upon a path of challenge to the gender text; 'becoming literate' for her is not a source of social capital alone but rather the hope of a better life. Her choice to attend literacy classes is similar; by learning to read Elena *may* get a good job, or she *may* be able to move to another place.

Single women in Usulután, then, face almost an impossibly difficult struggle to survive, yet they also experience greater freedom to contest ideology because they have more opportunity to reshape the gender text through overt challenge than their sisters in male-headed households. Unfortunately, though, the dominant gender discourse still seems all-powerful in the 'official' arena. Despite these women's confidence in their own abilities and in many cases their more varied experiences, it was noticeable that in community affairs they almost without exception deferred to men. I watched while a group of people in Joya Grande worked out the details of a budget they were preparing to submit to the local NGO for the purchase of building materials. The discussion was led by the men, who then asked one woman, a head of household and member of the literacy classes, to calculate the final amount, an act which she performed with ease. Yet the formal request was signed only by the men, although these were neither members of the formal village Board of

Directors nor, in two cases, established co-operants with the agency, unlike the woman. In some arenas, therefore, where local structures of power and control remain dominant, the patriarchal discourse goes uncontested.

Women–women networks: resource struggles and literacy exchanges

It would be mistaken, though, to group all women together as if they unidimensionally set about challenging male patriarchy. In fact, communicative performances in Usulután were often used as tools to negotiate positions and resources between women themselves – creating a dynamic, shifting text of female relationships just as diverse as that of male–female relationships.

We can see this in the ways that literacy exchanges took place between women at different times. The notion of literacy exchanges is one that has been well documented (Fingeret 1983), yet it can be sometimes in danger of underplaying the role of power relations. In Usulután, the striking thing about these exchanges was their emphasis on strategy. They operated as calculated gestures of positioning, even between women. They were both deliberate and gainful performances.

An example of such an exchange process occurred when Rosa Maria received from her sister in the United States a money order for $15. Having neither the writing skills to be able to sign her name nor a bank account (both requirements for cashing the cheque), she approached her cousin, Laura. Rosa Maria is already to a great extent economically dependent on Laura, since she and her family are refugees from a flooded part of Usulután; they lost all their possessions in the flood and Laura loans them a small empty house next to their own.

Instead of asking Laura directly to help her cash the cheque, Rosa mentioned to Laura that the berries on Laura's fruit trees were in danger of decomposing before they could be picked. Rosa offered to pick them, to Laura's gratitude, since Laura had no other younger relatives to help her. But as she made this offer, Rosa mentioned the problem of the money order. 'That's no problem,' said Laura, and agreed to negotiate cashing it. When Rosa went to the town to pay the order into Laura's bank, added Laura, Rosa could pick up some materials needed to help build the turkey coop which was in the process of being constructed. Rosa consequently spent the following week, after her exhausting day clearing land with a scythe, picking the berries in the tree, having the previous week struggled back from town carrying several kilos of wire and nails.

The striking thing about this exchange is how creatively it was managed by both parties. Rosa, in fact, privately agreed that she had already known for two weeks that the berries on the trees were becoming overripe, and she also knew she was socially obliged to offer to pick them. However, she purposely withheld this offer, waiting until 'the right time came to mention it'. This right time came with the unexpected arrival of her money order, which presented an occasion to employ the bargaining chip of the berry picking to a specific, desired end. But Laura meanwhile recognised immediately in the performance that the bargain was being controlled by Rosa, and quickly capitalised on the situation to ask Rosa to fulfil another, more challenging task.

There were many examples of such resource struggles, or literacy exchanges, all as striking in their creative management as this story of Rosa and Laura. In establishing their own systems of support in this way, women are creating their own hybrid, shifting texts of obligation, relation and identity, away from the constructions of men. In artfully deploying these networks within social processes, individuals resist their characterisation by external agents as 'helpless' or 'blind' and iterate their own capabilities and 'power to', using literacy as part of commodity exchange to help them do so. So literacy becomes between women as much a tool of ideology as it does between women and men: an economic and social resource which can be employed to good effect within networks of survival and hope.

There was one striking moment when the diversity and richness of the female text were revealed in all their colours. This occurred in a bread-making demonstration aimed at income generation, given by the literacy promoter, Margarita, to women from five communities. Margarita began by laying out the ingredients and demonstrating how to mix the ingredients to create dough. She handed out written copies of the recipe, to which no one paid attention. Women and children crowded around the table, which stood under a tree. Children ran among the bright dresses of the women. As Margarita explained and modelled the procedure, the women watched attentively and talked among themselves as she shaped the dough into balls and then left it to rise on trays.

Two hours later, however, we were still waiting. The dough had risen little if at all and many women were becoming restless, with tasks to do at home and husbands due back from the morning's work. They crowded round the trays, debating the problem. Margarita offered her explanation that the yeast was old, although we had in fact bought it that morning. But one woman contested this. The reason, she said, lay in the fact that a woman who was menstruating had touched the dough; it was well known that this would prevent the mixture from rising. Margarita, in her authority as literacy promoter, rejected this explanation forthwith. 'That is just an old story. A menstruating woman can't prevent the dough from rising, the problem is the old yeast.' But now individuals were murmuring among themselves and suddenly a cacophony of voices broke out, heated discussions rising in groups, offering a wide range of explanations. The day was cold, it was windy, the paper on which the dough was resting was unsuitable ... someone who had recently given birth could prevent dough from rising. Each explanation was backed up with evidence from experience, proof cited from other authorities; stories, hearsay and witnesses. The clamour went on for a quite a few minutes, until Margarita, shouting to be heard above the melée, concluded that, whatever the reason, the dough was unlikely to rise further and should be placed in the oven. With this, everyone concurred.

This episode lasted only briefly, but within these moments of variety the women were asserting their own ideology and history, exerting the dominance of their knowledge, and backing it up through cited experience and expertise. A wide range of explanations all vied for space in the cacophony, a moment of true Bakhtinian heteroglossia where, for a brief moment, the varied anecdotes, folk sayings and songs of the rural communities, Bakhtin's 'rivulets and droplets' (1981: 263) of social polyphony, dominated and subdued those of power and, for an instant, created space for carnival.

Conclusion

This experience in Usulután has shown us, therefore, just as Zubair found in Pakistan (this volume), how a rich and varied gender text is constantly negotiated, renegotiated and reconfigured to create an ever changing pattern of social relations. Dominant discourses are taken up and co-opted, and sometimes overtly contested as part of the construction of this text. Just as language is no fixed entity but a shifting sea of meaning, so relationships, expressed as they are through language, shift and flux continuously, directed by the actors who imbue them with meaning.

The figure of the illiterate peasant woman who stands 'out there' in the land, waiting to be classified and 'made literate' in the name of the greater good – whatever model of good that may be – exists only as a phenomenon created through discourse. Difficulty with reading and writing certainly does constrain women from for example, constructing their identity at times in their preferred mode, as when they find themselves unable to sign their names. But in contrast to the discourses of literacy as power, women's stories revealed here that they are not suffering primarily through lack of reading and writing skills. Rather, the sites of their struggle are those of poverty, scarcity and the forces of hegemony, which reflect at them through discursive texts a view of themselves as subordinate, disempowered, a problematic 'other'.

So the discourses of 'literacy for empowerment' as they so often arise in

research and policy are here critiqued by the voices of women in Usulután. Literacy skills do not, in this local world, represent a direct means
to social status or a channel to dominant codes of communication; these
routes lie elsewhere, in experience, history, relationships and local constructions of social power.

Local communicative practices are often in Usulután conscious acts of
performance, moments of theatre in a complex, multidimensional and
shifting tapestry of discourses. Through this performative vision of discursive practices and texts, we reintroduce the notion of agency, an ideal
which lies at the heart of the ideological paradigm of the New Literacies
and a gesture which returns the creative act and the textual content, or
narrative event, to its author. By extending our notion of literacy practices
to include the dimensions of performance and text, we can expand our
conceptualisation of how communicative practices intertwine with lived
realities of power and control and simultaneously restore them to their
source.

In Usulután, therefore, divisive and arbitrary categories of 'literate' and
'illiterate' cannot capture the dynamics of individuals' practices and performances as they act out their own gender relations within the complex
world of Usulután. Communicative performances are fluid events which
are both shaped by and created for the demands of the moment and the
future. Written and read, uttered and left silent, such texts intertwine with
the wider patterns and histories of the gender text to create a fluid mosaic
of meaning.

Women as creators

The emphasis in this chapter on authorship portrays many women in Usulután as creative and shrewd, as consummate and ingenious dealers and, it
could be argued, cunning manipulators of people, discourse and ideology, just as Fiedrich found in Uganda (this volume). It may well offend
adherents of those discourses which view 'development' and 'literacy' as
part of the requirements for the salvation of a universally oppressed
community of people. But unproblematised discourses of liberation and
empowerment stand perhaps in contrast to human nature in the face of
daily struggles for survival; in the face of such battles, and surrounded by
such powerful forces, women here do only what they can. They turn to the
resources available to them, co-opting and remoulding these to create
sites of contestation and struggle, adaptation and change. Women's struggles for voice in Usulután reflect the fluid nature of language, where positions are negotiated, contested and reformed from moment to moment.

Language and literacy practices in Usulután therefore, do not merely
reflect social relations but rather are a major force in their construction;

they are constitutive of relationships rather than only indicating them. Assumptions that social actors are trapped in a system of their own making because they are unable to perceive the structures of domination with which their practice complies, come undone in Usulután – where women and men are constantly engaging in acts which involve conscious participation in recreating the world and their lives. It is through these careful and artful processes and performances, using the few resources available to them with consummate skill, that women in Usulután shape their identities, weave the gender text and, ultimately, find their hope.

Notes

1 The term 'gender' is used here according to Carver's definition as 'the ways that sex and sexuality become power relations in society' (1996: 120).
2 See Mason and Krane (1989) for a description of the effects of the war on family structure.
3 But these gains often relate only to the refugee camps outside the country, periods of suspension from the economic and other forces of daily life. See for example Maria Juliá's series of two studies in 1994 and 1995, the second of which concluded that the previously striking reconstruction of gender relations in the refugee camp had regressed to 'patriarchy and oppression' (p. 230).
4 As Mpoyiya and Prinsloo found in Khayelitsha (1996: 187).

References

Bakhtin, M. (1981) 'Discourse in the novel' in M. Holquist (ed.) *The Dialogic Imagination: Four Essays by M.M. Bakhtin*, Austin TX: University of Texas Press, pp. 259–422
—— (1986) *Speech Genres and Other Late Essays*, C. Emerson and M. Holquist (eds) Austin TX: University of Texas Press
Basso, E. (1985) *A Musical View of the Universe*, Philadelphia: University of Pennsylvania Press
Bauman, R. (1986) *Story, Performance and Event: Contextual Studies of Oral Narrative*, Cambridge: Cambridge University Press
Bruner, E. (1986) 'Experience and its expressions' in V. Turner and E. Bruner (eds) *The Anthropology of Experience*, Chicago: University of Illinois Press, pp. 3–30
Carver, T. (1996) *Gender is not a Synonym for Women*, Boulder CO: Lynne Rienner
Fingeret, A. (1983) 'Social networks: a new perspective on independence and illiterate adults', *Adult Education Quarterly*, 33 (3): 133–46
hooks, b. (1989) *Talking Back: Thinking Feminist, Thinking Black*, Boston MA: South End
—— (1993) 'bell hooks speaking about Paulo Freire – the man, his work' in P. McLaren and P. Leonard (eds) *Paulo Freire: a Critical Encounter*, London: Routledge, pp. 146–54
Hymes, D. (1964) *Language in Culture and Society: a Reader in Linguistics and Anthropology*, New York and London: Harper & Row

—— (1981) *'In Vain I tried to Tell You': Essays in Native American Ethnopoetics*, Philadelphia: University of Pennsylvania Press

Julia, M. (1994) 'The changing status of women: social development in a repopulated village', *International Social Work*, 37: 61–73

—— (1995) 'Revisiting a repopulated village: a step backwards in the changing status of women', *International Social Work*, 38: 229–42

Mason, T. and Krane, D. (1989) 'The political economy of death squads', *International Studies Quarterly*, 33: 175–98

Mohanty, C. (1991) 'Under Western eyes: feminist scholarship and colonial discourses' in C. Mohanty, A. Russo and L. Torres (eds) *Third World Women and the Politics of Feminism*, Bloomington IN: Indiana University Press, pp. 51–80

Moser, C. (1993) *Gender Planning and Development: Theory, Practice and Training*, London and New York: Routledge

Mpoyiya, P. and Prinsloo, M. (1996) 'Literacy, migrancy and disrupted domesticity: Khayelitshan ways of knowing' in M. Prinsloo and M. Breier (eds) *The Social Uses of Literacy: Theory and Practice in Contemporary South Africa*, Cape Town: SACHED/Benjamins, pp. 177–96

Rockhill, K. (1993) 'Gender, language and the politics of literacy' in B. Street (ed.) *Cross-cultural Approaches to Literacy*, Cambridge: Cambridge University Press, pp. 156–75

Sen, A. (1992) *Inequality Reexamined*, New York: Russell Sage Foundation; Oxford: Clarendon Press

Street, B.V. (1993) *Cross-cultural Approaches to Literacy*, Cambridge: Cambridge University Press

—— (1994) 'Cross-cultural perspectives on literacy' in L. Verhoeven (ed.) *Functional Literacy: Theoretical Issues and Educational Implications*, Amsterdam: Benjamins, pp. 95–111

Stromquist, N. (1997) *Literacy for Citizenship: Gender and Grassroots Dynamics in Brazil*, New York: SUNY Press

5 Qualitative methods in researching women's literacy

A case study

Shirin Zubair

This chapter draws attention to the emotive and personal uses of literacy among younger women in a rural Siraiki community in Pakistan. Emphasis is placed on the use of ethnographic methods in tapping the hidden literacy practices of women: the use of unstructured interviews, focus groups, participant observation, case studies reveal that literacy use is linked very closely and intricately not only with women's social roles but also with their feelings, and deepest identities. Through analyses of excerpts from women's diaries, informal conversations and interviews, the study captures their lived experiences, their subjectivities and the finer nuances in their speech, writing and behaviour. There are contestations of self and of gender relations: through their deeds and words they call into question the traditional gender ideologies. These literacy practices illustrate how they resist, challenge and negotiate change in the traditional gender ideologies. Hence the study goes on to argue that contrary to popular perceptions, these uses of literacy are significant in that they reflect women's subjugated position within patriarchy and a desire to find agency and voice through their literacy practices.

Research on women's literacy use, reading of popular fiction, women's magazines and television viewing is mainly focused on Western women (Ang 1985; Radway 1987; Hermes 1995, 1998; Horsman 1987; Finders 1997; Morley 1986; Mace 1998; Rockhill 1993; Stacey 1994). Finders' work (1996, 1997) on the 'underlife' and the 'hidden literacies' of junior high-school girls' literacy practices in the United States has shown how teenage girls tend to resist an official view of who they must be and what they must do. This chapter analyses the role of multiple literacies in the lives of women from a non-Western community. The analysis of excerpts from women's speech (focus groups, interviews) and writing (diaries) shows that these women's engagements with literacy are far from meaningless or trivial. Focusing on how women use literacy skills to make sense of their lives and worlds, this chapter strives to illustrate that younger women's uses of literacies in English and Urdu complement their search for a new identity as opposed to the traditional gender roles. These literacy practices are not only reflective of women's social and communal roles, they are also a means of resistance to and transcendence from the dominant traditional gender ideologies.

Ethnographic methods

Data for this chapter come from ethnographic fieldwork carried out in Pakistan, during my PhD research completed at Cardiff University, funded by the Ministry of Education, Pakistan, under the Central Overseas Training Programme for the university faculty.[1] The data were collected in various phases during June 1995–March 1998, in two adjoining villages (Mirpur and Basti) in the Siraiki-speaking area of southern Punjab, Pakistan.[2] This area, known as the Siraiki belt, is underdeveloped in terms of female literacy and education: the literacy rates for women were reported as low as 6.2 per cent in rural and 30.1 per cent in urban Multan (Punjab Social Services Board 1994). Contemporary anthropologists, social linguists and literacy researchers like Heath (1983), Baynham (1995), Barton and Hamilton (1998), and Street (1984, 1995) have argued that in order to capture the diversity and complexity of various literacies in such underdeveloped communities, the ideological issues and social practices that surround people's literacy practices need to be taken into account. During the various stages of fieldwork and data collection in the two Siraiki villages where I carried out my fieldwork, I felt that the research methods in social science research of this kind are best seen as an ongoing process of negotiation between the researcher and the researched. Methodologically, Spivak (1988) has problematised the necessity of speaking for people who have no voice, thus empowering the research subjects. One way of achieving this goal is to let the methods be open-ended or dialogic (Cameron *et al.* 1992). Initially I chose ethnographic methods for carrying out my research, which included participant observation and long interviews. This involved negotiating my own research agenda with that of my respondents. Owing to the unfamiliarity of my respondents with the one-to-one interview format, at times I had to abandon the tape recorder and use research tools other than I had planned. In using focus groups, I realised that research methods that may be successfully administered in qualitative research are determined not only by the nature of the research questions but also by the context of the research. Since some of my subjects were more at home with group discussions of a communal nature than with the Western format of one-to-one interview, I decided to interview fewer people in an intensive way.

My key informants Nazia, twenty-four, and Razi, fifty-eight – both women from the landowning class – led me through these villages, to spend time with different people and families in the houses, hospitals and schools. We were a team, and as I proceeded with the data collection some more people joined the team: young male relatives of my key informants who recorded focus and survey groups of men from the village. Some young women talked enthusiastically about literacy(ies), being very vocal in the focus group discussions as well as their personal interviews. Therefore I asked some of them to write diaries for my research during my stay in the villages.

My key informant, Nazia, was instrumental in my entire fieldwork phase. As the time passed she became more and more involved with my research, and by the time the fieldwork was drawing to a close she would herself talk to the village women and ask questions about literacies in their lives. She had spent so much time with me that towards the end of the fieldwork she was very familiar with my research and would give valuable comments and suggestions. I stopped data collection when both of us felt that a lot of repetition started occurring and new information stopped coming. I conducted forty-five interviews with men and women from the two villages, and led six focus groups; survey group data were recorded by the brother of my key informant. In this chapter I use data exclusively from women's interviews, diaries and group discussions. (For a fuller account see Zubair 1999.) I also took fieldnotes, and collected pictures and other literacy documents such as diary pages, termed 'literacy artefacts' by Barton and Hamilton (1998).

As the problem of finding a voice for themselves emerged as one of the main issues when the older women used the metaphors *silent birds* and *caged birds* to describe their lives and literacies (Zubair 2001), the research reported here focuses on women's *literacy needs* and *literacy practices* from their own perspectives in a community that remains relatively isolated from the mainstream Pakistani society. I have made a conscious effort to *research for* and *research with* these women rather than *research on* their lives and literacies. Participant observation, unstructured interviews, case studies and focus groups have been used in an attempt to achieve these objectives, thus empowering the subjects by giving them a voice. These participatory approaches enabled me to explore women's subjective involvement with literacy(ies), and their own aspirations as opposed to measuring development indicators; within this new research paradigm women are studied as agents of change rather than passive recipients of dominant literacy(ies). (See Introduction to this volume.) Researchers like Radway (1987) and Farah (1992) have also discussed these issues at some length. During their research they came to realise that the research issues and methods have to take account of the researched and at times are determined by them. Radway's research project changed from the way romances as texts are interpreted to an analysis of romance reading as a form of behaviour in the social life of actual social subjects, women who saw themselves first as wives and mothers. It happened so because the Smithton women repeatedly answered her questions by talking about the meaning of romance reading as a social event in a familial context. Similarly, in her doctoral research in a rural Pakistani community Farah found that the choice of research methodology is determined not only by the research questions but also by the context in which the research is done, and to some degree it is made by those among whom we intend to use the methods. Keeping their work in view, I deliberately kept my research methods open. Thus, drawing on theory and methods from the multidisciplinary and expanding field of the New Literacy Studies, in the following parts of the chapter I look at women's changing identities and social roles in relation to various literacies within the socio-cultural context of their families, homes and the wider community.

Literacy and social class

The community under study is predominantly agrarian. The socio-political structure of the community is based on the feudal system, with two classes of people, the landowning and the landless. These two classes are mutually interdependent for the smooth and effective functioning of the communal and social life. Women from the landowning class strictly observe *purdah*,[3] which restricts their mobility, thus perpetuating illiteracy and lack of awareness of their rights. This strict adherence to *purdah* leads to the exclusion of women from the public domain. However, some change is evident as more and more women from the younger generation are gaining access to literacy in Urdu and English in addition to the traditional Arabic. The notion of identity is inextricably tied to multi-literacies: gaining access to a code goes hand in hand with an individual's personal and social roles, as identities are partly constructed and forged through language(s). Thus gaining access to English literacy goes hand in hand with younger women's new concept of their identity – and they negotiate this change through their everyday (literacy) practices and through their talk and behaviour. This is illustrated with examples from the data in the remainder of the chapter.

Upper-class women's access to literacy is not hindered by lack of resources but due to the traditional, archetypal role models portrayed in religious teachings, textbooks, popular culture and the media, all of which emphasise that women must be confined to the domestic domain. These conditions are favourable to men, who view female literacy and education as a passport to economic as well as social autonomy and independence, and therefore a threat to their power and control. Lower-class women have even less opportunity to learn literacy because their problems are compounded by lack of financial and economic resources.

Women's literacy practices

Baynham (1995) defines literacy practice as 'a concrete human activity', involving not just the objective facts of what people do with literacy, but also what they associate with what they do, how they construct its value, and the ideologies that surround it. It involves the attitudes of people – what people think about what they do. It also involves the concept of values (Barton 1994; Barton and Padmore 1991); it focuses on the subjectivity and agency dimension of practice. In the remainder of the chapter follows an analysis of the patterns that cut across literacy practices of television viewing, diary writing and reading of women's magazines.

Reading women's magazines

The time women in these two villages can allocate to reading papers and magazines relates to the division of labour. Women read the paper in their leisure time, while it is an important daytime activity for men. The choice of paper also reflects a gendered preference. Women's leanings seemed to be towards left-wing papers like *Pakistan* and *Jang*; these papers are trendy and glamorous in that they give a lot of coverage to fashion, gossip and celebrities and have coloured pictures, especially in their weekly editions. Not surprisingly, in these papers and magazines, women tend to read more fiction than facts. The choice of particular sections read by women is also related to their prescribed social and familial roles. Some middle-aged women said they only read the headlines while others said they only read some particular columns, e.g. the religious column, in the paper. A pattern found in the data is that whereas the middle-aged group and young girls read various types of articles and world news in the newspapers, the religious columns and the headlines are read mostly by older women. Some of the younger women read news from across the world to remain well informed about the current happenings internationally. Some said they especially read news about the events and happenings in the lives of their favourite celebrities, like actors, sportsmen or politicians. Lady Diana, Benazir Bhutto and Imran Khan are a few names, news of whose personal lives is read with interest by younger women. However, it is significant that women have to choose times and spaces for reading and writing between heavily gendered home activities. Some women reported reading the newspaper at bedtime, as they do not get free time to read it during the day.

The younger and middle-aged women are generally more interested in romantic fiction and women's magazines. Writing about the practice of reading women's magazines, Hermes (1995) observes that everyday practices, far from being meaningless, are highly significant in that they can be a form of resistance to the mainstream cultural practices. She interprets the reading of these magazines as empowerment because the images in them portray the 'perfect selves' of women as opposed to the reality. It can therefore be argued that the young women's reading of romantic fiction and writing of personal diaries is significant in two respects: first as self-expression because women are denied a public voice, and second as a denial of and resistance to the dominant male culture. The act of reading, therefore, functions as a way of transcending the mundane through their literacy skills and practices and envisaging an alternative albeit imaginative culture of their own. As for Radway's readers (1987) the reading of romances was a declaration of independence: a kind of minor rebellion against the position accorded by the dominant patriarchal discourse, that of the caring housewife and mother. Similarly, these women through their reading and writing practices try to resist the dominant cultural practices by creating a world of their own and an alternative set of values as opposed to the male culture through romance reading and finding a voice through creative writing.

Writing diaries

Keeping a diary emerged as a very prominent literacy use in the Siraiki community under study. It exists across genders but there are differences in terms of its use, frequency and maintenance. Reading women's magazines and writing personal diaries emerge as two very distinct literacy practices that the young women engage in regularly. It was found to be common and very popular among younger, especially unmarried women. Almost all young and middle-aged women who were interviewed had kept a personal diary at some point in their lives. Some write in it every day. These diaries consist of pages of personal feelings, intimate thoughts and reflection. Some women also write quotable quotes which they call 'golden words', i.e. words of wisdom from religion, philosophy and famous scholars of the East and West.

Some women in their mid-thirties wrote diaries before their marriage but said that they had stopped writing them after marriage. They have however kept their old diaries as memoirs. Some women who write a diary do not let anyone else read or even have a peep into their personal diaries. The diaries are their private possessions and they are personal and somewhat sacred. Something very deep and subjective was discovered in their diary writing, as some of them had composed their own verses, poems and short stories and had preserved the diaries for a long time.

As Mace (1998) has argued, literacy engages our imaginations, intellects, emotions and memories, and is a matter of enormous mystery. These literacy practices are tied in to the availability of time and space in their lives, and simultaneously they serve as a means of excursions from the mundane into the realms of the imagination. These diaries are strictly personal, only to be read by the writer, but some women did volunteer to offer a few pages from their diaries to be used as documents in this research. These diary pages are intimate, uncensored expression of feelings and contain details about their day-to-day experiences.

While looking at the emotive aspects of literacy in Nukulaelae letters, Besnier (1995) argues that it is commonly assumed that spoken language is universally more *involved, emotional* and better suited to the representation of emotions than written language. He argues that these claims are supported with data from mainstream Western contexts where writing is viewed as being less 'subjective', less 'emotional'. However, Besnier's research and the present data suggest otherwise. In the following paragraphs, two excerpts from the personal diaries of young women show how literacy is linked with our deepest feelings and emotions. During the final stages of the fieldwork, I asked some younger women to make journal entries of their everyday literacies. These younger women were quite familiar with my research themes at the time of these journal entries. The diary excerpts that follow come from those journal entries.

> After dinner I took my radio and went upstairs on the terrace. I liked a drama which was on air. It was about an educated daughter-in-law who is a doctor. She wants to work but her husband and mother-in-law do not approve. They want her to remain domesticated. She feels suffocated. At last, she leaves her husband and takes up work. She earns her own living, has her own house and car. I thought strange thoughts after listening to this play, whether she made a right decision or not. I kept thinking until I dozed off.

Huma is twenty, single, lives with her mother and brother. She has completed school and First Certificate at college in town and has taught in a primary school. She writes diary pages, reads women's magazines for pleasure in Urdu, and can read headlines in English magazines. This extract provides evidence of the younger women's use of writing skills as an expression of the self and the conflicting ideologies regarding women's space and role in the community. The young woman's preoccupation with the issues of female education and employment, self-realisation through work rather than marriage, challenging and renegotiating the existing stereotypes regarding personal and social identity, are well illustrated through this quotation from her personal diary.

However, it is pertinent to note that this critical awareness of literacy – the use of literacy skills not only to read and write the word but also to read the world (Freire 1985) – was witnessed only among younger women. Although the older women described themselves as *caged* and *silent birds* in focus groups, unlike their younger counterparts they did not raise these questions. As these younger women become exposed to the Western and local media they are in the process of examining their own lives in relation to the new images of women portrayed through the media culture. They are gradually learning how to create and take up new opportunities and move into what had always been viewed as 'male jobs' or 'male spaces'. This is reflected through their literacy practices, their entry into public domains as well as adopting and envisaging new social roles for themselves. The pages of their personal diaries contain a mixture of personal and sociological insights. The quotations, short stories, poems, personal observations, all point to the fact that these women are not merely functionally literate but are able to understand and interpret the world from their own standpoint. They demonstrate the capability, as in the example quoted above from a personal diary, of critically analysing social expectations of women's roles. The problems and issues relating to the traditional roles and the conflict of resolving the personal aspirations with the expectations of their families and the larger community are often the focal points of their writings. The tussle between the contested and conflicting ideologies was also found in their interactions in focus groups. (For a fuller account see Zubair 1999, 2001.)

> Comparing myself with the village girls, I feel I am much better in a lot of ways compared with them. I thank God for that. I observed little knowledge is dangerous. Well! to some extent this applies to me as well *but* I try to improve my knowledge by reading and watching television . . .
>
> They were mixing Islam with their own old stupid traditions, e.g. the *purdah* system, for them wearing a *burka* was *purdah* whereas wearing a *chaddar* was not.[4] I think they have complicated their lives themselves. If they had changed their trends and mentality their lives would have been much more easier. If people of cities can digest certain things they belonged to the same country they would have digested it as well. Yes! The point is the same lack of education and lack of facilities, which is really a pity because village people are missing too much and suffering too much.

Nazia was my key informant. She was twenty-four. Separated from her husband, she lived with her parents and unmarried brother and worked part-time in town. She had been to a convent school followed by college education and held a degree in English literature, French, human and social biology. Here she seems to be questioning the dominant cultural practices by arguing for reading and watching television not only as leisure activities but to help her improve herself, improve her *knowledge*, presumably improve her knowledge of the world. This desire for self-improvement through both print and visual literacy is evident among younger women in my data. Whereas men use diary writing as a way of organising their records, and timetable, women use this literacy event for their emotional catharsis and self-exploration.

The use of literacy skills for personal satisfaction and for creative expression of the self is found mostly in relation to young women. Watching television programmes and listening to the radio in the late afternoons and evenings, after finishing the housework, is the most popular leisure activity among women. Younger women who are literate in English may watch American soaps like *The Bold and the Beautiful.*

Research on television viewing (Morley 1986; Ang 1985) shows that fictional programmes and soap operas are particularly popular among women. While *Dallas* and other soap operas present stereotyped and role-conforming images of women, they also give their viewers scope to construct their own meanings of the same images. This might imply that women watch fictional programmes for personal fulfilment; thus the significance they attach to personal relationships is realised through the vicarious pleasure they derive from television viewing as well as romance reading. Radway (1987) suggests that romance reading is a relaxing release from the tension produced by daily problems and responsibilities, it creates a time or a space within which a woman can be entirely on her own, preoccupied with her personal needs, desires and pleasure. Hence it seems logical to conclude that these women engage in romance reading and watching soaps on television because the experience offers them a welcome break from their mundane, day-to-day existence.

Stacey's (1994) study of the relationship between Hollywood female film stars and British female spectators revealed that American femininity was seen as transgressing British femininity. Therefore, the consumption of commodities by women audience, resulting from watching the films, was not merely an act of conformity to the stereotypical image of females as desirable objects but also a way to rebel against restrictive British norms. According to Radway (1987: 215), romance reading creates a fantasy world and a utopian state for women who read romantic fiction time after time, not out of contentment but out of longing and dissatisfaction and as an escape from and protest against their traditional roles. This may partly explain the popularity of American soap operas such as *The Bold and the Beautiful* and *Santa Barbara* in a country like Pakistan (in general and among younger women in this sample in particular) where American stereotypical images of femininity are received by women as liberating rather than restrictive.

McRobbie (2000: 146) has analysed the emergence of the fashion in *Jackie, Elle* in the 1980s and, 'the infinitely perfectible self and the clothes to go with that self'. The weekly magazine *Akhbar-e-Jehan*, published by *Jung* publications was found to be the most popular women's magazine in the village community. Although the cover image shows a traditional image of femaleness, for these women it is still new in that the woman shown in the picture is famous, attractive and powerful. This is a picture of a career woman – a famous model and actress – who unlike these women is independent, works in the public domain, and commands respect for her work. Hence for younger women who are themselves confined to their homes and restricted in their mobility, such images in women's magazines are liberating and new rather than restrictive or traditional.

Younger women who are married engage in literacy activities such as reading the Koran, offering prayers, looking after their homes and children, but unlike the old women (over sixty), they also buy young women's magazines and read them in their leisure time. They mostly read fiction and true stories, nothing that might be traditionally considered heavy or serious. The reasons Hermes's readers (1995) gave for reading women's magazines was that they could be 'easily put down'. Hermes emphasises the double meaning of the phrase in that while women use the phrase to refer to an activity which does not require concentration and can be done simultaneously with other household work, the reading of women's magazines is not regarded as serious reading at all by the highbrow. In fact, it is considered lowbrow. The women read glossy fashion magazines, read true stories, romantic fiction, cooking recipes, etc., during their leisure hours in-between domestic responsibilities.

Most of these women used to write personal diaries before they were married but do not find time to do so after their marriages. Nevertheless, they have kept their old diaries. For reading the women's magazines they do not have to set aside time. They can flick through these magazines simultaneously with other housework without applying their full attention. For diary writing, however, they have to allocate a specific time and place as this is a very personal activity and women need some personal space for writing their diaries. After marriage, most of the women from this age group seemed to have lost some of their personal time and space. Therefore they do not write in their diaries any more, but the fact that they have preserved their old diaries suggests that diary writing is not an 'easily put downable' activity – either literally or metaphorically, from their point of view. The preservation of their old diaries might be said to reflect a desire to retain their personal identity as individuals or to create another self as opposed to their identity as someone's daughter or wife in the community. The creation and preservation of an 'imaginative other self' through diary writing, again, could be a reflection of their dissatisfaction with the dominant system.

The denial of a public voice thus seems to have led to a denial of a personal voice too for these married women, who tend to lose whatever little room or space they had created for themselves in their youth. While recounting their literacy histories, some of the older women's comments on their early lives and literacy experiences were highly significant. For instance, 'We are like caged birds' (older women's focus group, 23 December 1996) and 'We remained indoors like silent birds – now there's freedom children are also being educated' (older women's focus group, 23 December 1996). In this context, speech stands for literacy and the ability to express themselves and thus achieve self-realisation. Silence, being the antonym of speech, stands for illiteracy or lack of literate abilities to enable people to participate and function fully in society. Lakoff (1995) and Kramsch (1998) have argued that silence is analogous to invisibility; that cultures resonate with the voices of the powerful, and are filled with the silences of the powerless. Only the powerful decide whose values and beliefs will be deemed worth adopting by the group, and whose voices will be heard. Similarly, Freire (1972) observed that learning to read and write ought to be an opportunity to know what *speaking the word* really means, i.e. a human act implying reflection and action. He went on to suggest that in the culture of silence the masses are *mute*, they are prohibited from creatively taking part in the transformations of their society and therefore prohibited from being. Hence it might be argued that these metaphors epitomise the older women's peculiar predicament in that they had neither any contact with the outside world nor access to literacy lest they find a voice for themselves through literacy and education. Although a *caged bird* is restricted in its movement it can still sing and its voice can reach out to ears outside its confines, whereas these women are *caged* as well as *silent* birds, as they are not even heard; *silent* here is equivalent to *silenced*.

The following is an excerpt from an older woman's interview:

> I must have been eight or nine when I started observing purdah . . . purdah was so strictly observed that even the air of the [male] servants was not allowed inside the houses, tongas[5] were covered with curtains . . . if you go out and about you stay sane . . . I'm beginning to lose my sanity.
>
> (Interview notes, 25 October 1997)

The use of such powerful images to describe their peculiar predicament and their childhood experiences reflects some kind of underlying complaint. These women see themselves and their peers as *caged* and *silent birds*, using a universal image for domesticated women deprived of their basic rights. They were shut indoors within the confines of their homes from very early on in their lives. Their voices were thus silenced. The women are using an apt image for their lifelong silence. Thus the women from the older generation were not active agents in decision making about their own lives but rather passive recipients of others' decisions.

The younger women in the community have far more varied and diversified literacy habits, preferences and practices, ranging from the traditional ritual prayers to the most modern and westernised. First of all, this group includes women in their early twenties and late teens, women who have been to English schools and colleges and women who have not received any formal schooling or education at all. The women in this group who have had English schooling are literate in English, Urdu and Arabic, and can fluently read and write in these languages, except Arabic, which they can only read and use for reading the Koran. As these women mostly come from the landowning class, they have access to English magazines, books, including novels, and also to dish channels like CNN and BBC Asia. Some of these women work or have worked, so they are not totally confined to the domestic domain, they have had some exposure to the public domain.

Conclusion

Feminist analysts of popular culture and women's magazines (McRobbie 2000; Radway 1987; Hermes 1995, 1998) have shifted their focus away from expressing concern to showing respect for magazines like *Jackie*, *Elle*, *Seventeen*, *Cosmopolitan* as women's magazines which have continued to thrive in the 1990s. Hermes (1995) emphasises the 'pleasure' these magazines offer to women since even after thirty years of feminist writing they remain popular, hence are not 'easily put downable'. Street (1998) has observed that research indicates that literacy practices are spreading in complex ways which the reductive discourses of mainstream educational paradigms fail to capture or choose to ignore. The low/high culture divide still prevails, implying that mass culture is bad culture. What happens in actual practice is that people actively and creatively make their own meanings rather than passively absorb pre-given meanings imposed on them. This process of renegotiation and conflicting ideologies becomes evident from the diary extracts of the younger women and from their arguments in focus groups and informal discussions (Zubair 2001). These young women are in their twenties and late teens. They question, challenge, resist and renegotiate values and their roles within patriarchy. Neilsen (1998) has argued that engagements with texts in everyday life help readers and writers to shape their identities and reshape them in an ongoing process; that adolescents engage in more fluid, intentional and often more passionate identity play in their encounters with texts.

Although, owing to the constraints on these women's time and space, their access to Urdu and English literacies is curtailed, diary writing and reading women's magazines in leisure time has special significance in their lives, as they choose times and spaces between gendered domestic activities to indulge in these little pleasures. With examples from the data, I have suggested that women create an alternative and imaginative culture as opposed to the dominant male culture. Quoting extracts from their diaries and talks, I have argued that these literacy practices are not merely temporal excursions, but imply that this alternative set of values is far more significant to women who are denied a public voice. Thus they endeavour to find a voice and carve an identity for themselves through creative writing. This is their way of establishing their own identity: these non-utilitarian functions of literacy fulfil their innermost needs of self-expression and self-realisation; the desire to find a voice and to be recognised as human individuals as opposed to the prescribed social roles of mothers, daughters and wives. Hence, for these women, literacy is a means of self-improvement and self-empowerment.

I found that younger women have a far more advanced approach to literacy than older women and men (see Zubair 2001). They are more willing to embrace social change, and a newer identity which goes hand in hand with the acquisition of secular literacy, because they have more to gain than older women and men. They are less committed to the traditionally male-dominated system of agriculture. In focus groups their language choices also hint at their desire to identify with the mainstream languages, Urdu and English, which symbolise social prestige and status. Women, especially the younger generation, aspire to wider education rather than literacy as a set of skills. I suggested that the younger women's desire for literacy and education complements their acquisition of English literacy and access to the Western media: the younger women negotiate this change through their talk and literacy activities whereas younger men seemed content with their existing roles.

The findings of this research show the inadequacy of quantitative paradigms to capture the values, subjectivities and aspirations of people regarding literacy(ies) in similar underdeveloped, multilingual communities. More studies like the present one with an ethnographic orientation are needed to challenge the rather reductionist view of literacy given by statistical studies, which stress a binary opposition between literacy and illiteracy. The study also presents a strong case for using qualitative methods in researching literacies since the emotive and personal aspects of literacy discussed here could not have been captured through quantitative methods.

Notes

1 Some of these data are discussed from a different perspective in Zubair (2001).
2 In the interest of privacy the names of villages and persons have been changed.
3 *Purdah,* screen; segregation of sexes at puberty.
4 A *burka* is a two-piece garment worn outdoors by women and a *chaddar* is a big shawl-like garment worn by women to cover themselves.
5 *Tonga* refers to a horse carriage.

References

Ang, I. (1985) *Watching Dallas,* London and New York: Routledge
Barton, D. (1994) *Literacy: an Introduction to the Ecology of Written Language,* Oxford: Blackwell
Barton, D. and Hamilton, M. (1998) *Local Literacies,* London: Routledge
Barton, D. and Padmore, S. (1991) 'Writing in the community' in D. Graddol, J. Maybin and B. Stierer (eds) *Researching Language and Literacy in Social Context,* Clevedon, Adelaide and Philadelphia: Multilingual Matters
Baynham, M. (1995) *Literacy Practices: Investigating Literacy in Social Context,* London and New York: Longman
Besnier, N. (1995) *Literacy, Emotion and Authority,* Cambridge: Cambridge University Press
Cameron, D., Frazer, E., Harvey, P., Rampton, B. and Richardson, K. (1992) *Researching Language: Issues of Power and Method,* London: Routledge
Farah, I. (1992) 'Literacy practices in a rural community in Pakistan', unpublished PhD thesis, University of Pennsylvania
Finders, M.J. (1996) 'Just girls: literacy and allegiance in junior high school', *Written Communication,* 13 (1): 93–129
—— (1997) *Just Girls: Hidden Literacies and Life in Junior High,* New York: Teachers College Press
Freire, Paulo (1972) *Cultural Action for Freedom,* Harmondsworth: Penguin
—— (1985) *The Politics of Education,* Hadley MA: Bergin & Garvey
Heath, S.B. (1983) *Ways with Words,* Cambridge: Cambridge University Press
Hermes, J. (1995) *Reading Women's Magazines,* Cambridge: Polity Press
—— (1998) 'Cultural citizenship and popular fiction' in K. Brants, J. Hermes and L. Zoonen (eds) *The Media in Question: Popular Cultures and Public Interests,* London, Thousand Oaks CA and New Delhi: Sage
Horsman, J. (1987) *Something in my Mind besides the Everyday: Women and Literacy,* Toronto: Women's Press
Kramsch, C. (1998) *Language and Culture,* Oxford: Oxford University Press
Lakoff, R. (1995) 'Women and silence' in K. Hall and M. Bucholtz (eds) *Gender Articulated: Language and Socially Constructed Self,* New York: Routledge
Mace, J. (1998) *Playing with Time: Mothers and the Meaning of Literacy,* London: UCL Press
McRobbie, A. (2000) *Feminism and Youth Culture,* New York: Routledge
Morley, D. (1986) *Family Television: Cultural Power and Domestic Leisure,* London: Comedia

Neilsen, L. (1998) 'Playing for real: performative texts and adolescent identities' in D. Alvermann *et al.* (eds) *Reconceptualizing the Literacies in Adolescents' Lives,* Hillsdale NJ and London: Erlbaum

Punjab Social Services Board (1994) 'NGO's Literary Movement'

Radway, J.A. (1987) *Reading the Romance,* London and New York: Verso

Rockhill, K. (1993) 'Gender, language and the politics of literacy' in B.V. Street (ed.) *Cross-cultural Approaches to Literacy,* Cambridge: Cambridge University Press

Spivak, G.C. (1988) 'Can the subaltern speak?' in C. Nelson and L. Grossberg (eds) *Marxism and the Interpretation of Culture,* Urbana IL: University of Illinois Press, pp. 271–313

Stacey, J. (1994) *Star Gazing: Hollywood and Female Spectatorship,* London: Routledge

Street, B.V. (1984) *Literacy in Theory and Practice,* Cambridge: Cambridge University Press

—— (1995) *Social Literacies: Critical Approaches to Literacy in Development, Ethnography and Education,* New York and London: Longman

—— (1998) 'New Literacies in Theory and Practice: What are the Implications for Language in Education?' inaugural professorial lecture, King's College London

Zubair, S. (1999) 'Women's Literacies in a Rural Pakistani Community: an Ethnographic Study', unpublished PhD thesis, Cardiff: University of Wales

—— (2001) 'Literacies, gender and power in rural Pakistan' in B.V. Street (ed.) *Literacy and Development: Ethnographic Perspectives,* London: Routledge

6 A self-reflexive analysis of power and positionality

Toward a transnational feminist praxis

Chizu Sato

This chapter is concerned with two interrelated issues taken up in this volume: representations of 'illiterate' 'Third World' women and research for policy advocacy within the context of international development, particularly that of adult literacy education. It engages with the former in so far as dominant discourses of adult literacy education, international development as well as some feminisms tend to constitute non-literate people in the 'Third World', and in particular women, in three distinct ways: liberal modernisation discourse represents them as 'ignorant' or 'ignorant mothers who need to be enlightened' (Betts, Chopra and Robinson-Pant in this volume), leftist underdevelopment discourse as 'victims' (Mohanty 1991) and neoliberal development discourse as 'potentially rational economic agents' (Rankin 2001). Though divergent in composition, these three representations have a common troubling effect. The representations make it possible to conceive of and therefore engage with 'illiterate' 'Third World' women as if they are somehow abstracted from the specificities of the contexts within which they live their lives and within which their agency necessarily finds its specific expression. Turning to the second point, this chapter explores questions of research for political advocacy in its critique of those critical researchers who, albeit countering the dominant positivistic research paradigm and/or the dominant representations of 'illiterate' 'Third World' women, express no need to negotiate research processes with their research subjects or extend their political interventions beyond the texts they author. Though these critical approaches are important, they can be exploitative: in failing to extend their engagement, such exercises may confirm their subjects' subordinated position.

This chapter is built around a feminist-informed self-reflexive analysis of the research I undertook in 1997–8 in Nepal. The original research was intended to assess the impact of the literacy component of a health improvement project funded jointly by a major international governmental organisation and a private association. This research proceeded through semi-structured interviews with individuals and focus groups that were supplemented with field observations. The original research is revisited with a special focus on power relations between the female and male research subjects and myself. These power relations are explored through various aspects of the positionalities we embodied, such as gender, age and nationality, during and after my fieldwork within our situated local/global contexts. Today we live in a world where hegemonies of economic, political, cultural and/or legal structures are interconnected yet scattered on multiple levels (Grewal and Kaplan 1994: 17). In order to be more accountable, this chapter argues, researchers must attempt to build a transnational feminist praxis that links the views and voices of our selves and our informants with others who share partially overlapping perspectives in different locations (cf. Haraway 1988). The strategy offered in this chapter is to provide scholars and practitioners in the field of adult literacy education with an opportunity to explore the processes of knowledge production in which the partial, fluid and contradictory positionalities of the researcher and, by extension, the possible partial, fluid and contradictory positionalities of the informants are formed during research. In so doing, it suggests a means to challenge the master narrative of development which subordinates the 'illiterate' and 'Third World' women by recognising such women as active agents in complex processes of mutual, albeit unequal, knowledge production.[1] Recognition of this mutuality may go some way to securing a condition necessary to be able to imagine a larger community in which the commitments of the researchers and their informants partially connect in pursuit of overlapping political struggles.

Analytical framework

How was power manifested in the process of the original research? When, with whom, in what context and why? Wolf (1996) helps answer these questions. She proposes that 'the most central dilemma for contemporary feminists in fieldwork . . . is power and the unequal hierarchies or levels of control that are often maintained, perpetuated, and re-created during and after field research' (1996: 2). To analyse power during and after field research, she divides power into three interconnected dimensions (ibid.):

- Power differences stemming from different positionalities of the researcher and the researched (race, class, nationality, life chances, urban–rural backgrounds[2]).
- Power exerted during the research process, such as defining the research relationship, unequal exchange and exploitation.
- Power exerted during the postfieldwork period – writing and representing.

Whilst her proposals identify dimensions through which it is important to examine power in the research process, I have had to elaborate on this framework. My first concern is that her framework only operates from the position of the researcher. That is, I also ask questions of whose definitions of the spheres and significance of power in research relationships are to be employed in analysis. Second, Narayan, drawing on the work of Rosaldo, claims that '*every* anthropologist [and I would argue every researcher and researched] exhibits "multiplex subjectivity" with crosscutting identifications' (1997: 28). I understand this multiplex-ness of one's subjectivity to be due to the multiple discourses in which one is differentially positioned as a subject at any given time. I link this understanding of 'multiplex subjectivity' with the non-universal, non-essential, historical and relational notion of positionality (Alcoff 1988). Following Lal's observation that researchers are 'constantly being situated into [the research contexts] by the micropolitics of the research interactions and the macropolitics of societal inequality' (1996: 197), this vision enables researchers to ask how ever-shifting local/global relations of power shape which facets of the subjectivities of both researchers and researched are differentially illuminated (cf. Narayan 1997) in the mutual constitution of their positionalities. Understanding power as an exercise of shaping the ability of both researchers and researched to know in a network of relations (Foucault 1980), both parties are thought of being able to construct knowledge only within their context specific positionalities. Further, by going beyond Crenshaw's exemplar examination of the intersection between gender and race (1997), I deploy intersectional analysis to explore how different facets both within myself and in relation to my *imagined* others intersected to delimit the context within which we were positioned and we produced knowledge. In employing these theories within Wolf's framework, I will examine the situated cultural construction of knowledge through mutually negotiated local/global relations of power during and after my fieldwork in Nepal.

Representing multiplex subjectivity in research context

In reflecting upon my positions in my research I identified a range of facets of my multiplex subjectivity which seemed to be differentially highlighted and/or silenced in the range of research contexts within which I found myself (see Figure 6.1). To be sure, this diagram is inevitably static, biased and utterly silent on the complexity introduced by the contextually specific intersections between this mapping and those with whom I engaged. Each facet has in-depth meanings whose intersection with other facets through my body is context specific. It also does not describe how my ways of knowing and their meanings were historically constituted and

within the circle:

working with a
Japanese male boss   part of the Japanese
donor organisation

assistant

inexperienced   young   researcher

single

volunteer/paid   heterosexual   working-class

(naive) feminist   **Chizo Sato**   Japanese/Western-educated

female   佐藤　千寿   Japanese

being in Nepal   **Chandani[a]**   foreign

from non-Western but so-called 'First World'

historically, culturally, socially linguistically and/or politically in-/outsider
within the research and/or fieldwork context

my partial knowledge of some Nepalese cultures

looked like a Gurung[b]   being able to speak some Nepali

student of the native Nepali interpreter

representative of the informants
to the Japanese donor org.

Figure 6.1 'Facets' of multiplex subjectivity in a research context.

Notes
a Nepali name given to me by my Nepali language teachers.
b A hill tribe in Nepal who have similar features to those of the informants (Magar).

shifting. The border of my subjectivity and all its facets were always fluid
and ever changing in relation to others and my environments.

Three dimensions of power

First dimension

Wolf's first dimension of power takes up power differences resulting from
different positionalities of the researcher and those engaged as the
researched. In the fieldwork period, power circulated between my informants and myself in complex ways, depending on the varying intersections
of our shifting positionalities. For example, consistent with Papanek's
argument that 'foreign women may gain more license and flexibility to
cross boundaries' (summarised by Wolf 1996: 8), in relation to the
Nepalese female informants of various ages with various sexual histories

and marital statuses who were the beneficiaries of the organisation for which I worked, my being a young, single, yet female Japanese researcher with the Japanese donor organisation enabled me to do things (such as ask about gynaecological issues in public) that would have been culturally inappropriate for many others to raise. The recognition of micro-level specific intersections of my positioning in relation to those of the informants within a global structure supported by both parties' historically learned recognition of me as part of the powerful donor organisation and of them as its subordinate recipients made this knowledge production possible. Were I a young single Western-educated Nepalese female researcher, the knowledge produced between the researched and myself would have been quite different. Such differences are noted by Chopra, who, positioning herself as an academic researcher and an Indian national Hindi-speaking female in her 'home' community, found her ability to discuss issues that did not interest her informant to be quite limited (2001).

In comparison with my positionality as constituted in relation to the Nepalese female informants, I found that my positionality had different effects when I was relating to the male family members (spouses and fathers) of the female informants. I, as a young feminist foreign researcher, acknowledged the authority of the local patriarchy perhaps because it paralleled that found during my own socialisation within a patriarchal Japanese household. That ascription of patriarchal authority made it more difficult for me to engage older men in the sorts of conversations I found possible with female interviewees. For example, I could not ask what types of contraception they knew and used. In other words, our compatible though historically very different positioning of me in a relative subordinate position – that of junior femaleness – seemed to modify the effects of our shared recognition of me as an educated Japanese researcher with a Japanese donor. Here the junior foreign femaleness that facilitated discussion of the taboo topics which interested the donor with female subjects worked against me. Thus the same identifications as manifested through contextually specific positionalities produced different effects. My experience, contrary to Papanek's argument above, is consistent with Wolf's statement that 'because of their foreign "otherness", they [female researchers] may indeed receive and feel more pressure than men to adhere to gender role behaviors' (1996: 8). I, as a young foreign feminist researcher, followed the example of the female informants and accepted culturally constructed rules, such as accommodating and not offending their male family/community members. This could be seen as reinforcing patriarchy, which contradicts my feminist convictions. However, I rationalised this by saying that I needed to build and maintain a credible subjectivity, which, I thought, required that I respect my understanding of their positionalities, such as the female informants' (and by extension my own) possible subordinate positions in relation to their male family members, in this specific cultural context.

Second dimension

Wolf's second dimension addresses power exercised during the research process. Owing to context-specific illumination of some facets of my subjectivity, especially my recognition and acceptance of my being part of the donor organisation, I tended to claim for myself the power I *imagined* to be inherent to this positioning. As suggested by the paternalistic development discourse of which I was yet a young subject, I believed that my positioning granted me the ability (power to) to control (power over) the informants' time and movements, to set the topics of our discussions, to demand answers and to have certain expectations of those answers. This belief, which found its origins in the discourse of development, produced material effects. For example, I asked the male field staff member to arrange meetings with groups of people identified by my male boss and myself prior to visiting 'the field', the male staff arranged the meetings, and I held interviews with them and collected the 'data'. Read one way, it is possible to see that these material effects were made possible by my occupation of a positionality that carried with it a particular understanding of power: the powerful Japanese ('First World') donor organisation versus the less powerful 'Third World' recipients. Looking at the same sets of practices through a position of my imagined Others, the informants might have agreed to participate, thinking that their involvement was required as a condition of their current funding and on the belief that it would improve the possibility of their receiving future funding from the donor organisation. Informants' silent acceptance of this imposition may be understood as a consequence of historical global structural inequalities. This possibility and many others that I cannot imagine are the product of speculation made necessary by the limits to knowledge production inherent in the positionalities of those present in the research context.

Such unseen and in many ways unknowable irruptions inevitably colour researchers' interactions with our informants. In implicitly or tactically accepting this imaginary of power I saw myself as able to work between what I now recognise as a local patriarchal discourse and a global paternalistic development discourse. I recognise myself as having appropriated the time and movements of the researched for purposes defined on the organisation's and, therefore, on my terms. Although one of the main purposes of the research was to change the project's policies in a way that would improve the daily lives of the female informants, I was inserted into this relationship in a manner that exploited the researched: I as a 'First

World' researcher (working for a development organisation) was to extract 'data' from poor 'Third World' women for my (and/or the organisation's) ends.[3] That is, to point to one alternative path, I did not see nor did I act on the possibility of negotiating with my informants a research agenda that would serve both parties' interests and produce findings that we could collectively appropriate for our partially shared and possibly disparate ends. The discourses through which I was constituted blocked me from seeing let alone acting on such alternative imaginaries.

The story that I have just told carries with it a vision of 'Third World' women as relatively passive. Read another way, it could be thought that the informants were quite active in negotiating both the positionalities present in and the content of our exchanges such that I became a mechanism by which they communicated with the donor for their own purposes. In that case, I would understand them as structuring our engagements such that they produced knowledge through me that they thought would, positing a hypothetical interest, secure continued funding from the donor for activities in their community. In and among more subtle signs that support this, I found that informants tended to speak only well of the donor organisation in relation to me as a researcher from the organisation. Having noticed this tendency, I actively tried to escape the positionality assigned to me within my initial interviews, that of an agent of the donor, by visiting my informants informally in their homes or teashops and by sharing my personal experiences in the hopes of developing a more 'reciprocal' relationship. Despite these attempts, during the interviews with the female recipients in which I wanted to collect 'honest' comments to 'improve' the project, I was forced into and eventually had to inhabit the positionality of a Japanese researcher working for a Japanese donor organisation that my informants had created for me. By way of example, knowing that my organisation did not support electrification but, rather, literacy and health education, the female informants consistently commented that they were afraid of losing their literacy skills. I delivered this message in my report to the donor, who, acting on the knowledge that my informants and I produced, decided to offer them health-related post-literacy readers. In this reading I had to negotiate with the informants for control over the conditions of knowledge production by actively adopting or sometimes being forced to adopt 'strategic positionalities' (Hernández 1995) in relation to the research subjects' equally strategic shifting positionalities as shaped by our social environments. That is, we negotiated the relations of power out of which knowledge emerged by actively shifting our positionalities in relation to each other through selective presentations of facets of our multiplex subjectivities in this particular local/global context. This presentation is consistent with Fiedrich, a Western-educated male researcher, who in interviewing a female participant from the programme through which he studied in Uganda, noted her power to shape her own self-presentations in relation to himself (Chapter 13 in this volume).

Third dimension

The third dimension of power Wolf suggested is power wielded after field-work: the power exercised in writing and representing. I, as a young femi-nist subject of a paternalistic development discourse, was convinced by the idea that writing *about* and *for* (apparently not *with*) less powerful women was a political tool appropriate for challenging and transforming unjust gender relationships in society. Although I acknowledged to some extent that much of the 'data' was produced in collaboration with the researched, I identified myself as the one who had the right to write a report on what I understood to be their behalf, a report that would result in changing policies that would affect their lives for far longer than they would my own. My assumption of authorial privilege was grounded on my acknowledging the positionality of a feminist researcher within the devel-opment organisation. This identification provided me with a position from which I was able to negotiate what was to be written with my Japan-ese male boss, who gave me detailed comments on my writing. I did this while juggling my overlapping and sometimes contradictory ethico-political commitments to four different yet interrelated audiences who were concurrently though differentially present in the range of environ-ments I traversed during the research process. To wit, I juggled commit-ments to what I now recognise as my own representation of my research informants, to my profession, to my understanding of a feminist political project and to myself. My post-fieldwork literacy practices were shaped by the complex intersections of the power that stemmed from my location between context specific relations of power, such as those within the disci-plinary confines of a development organisation, and my commitments to multiple situated audiences.

While the context-specific discourses of development and feminism through which I was partly constituted enabled me to engage in the liter-acy practices I mentioned above, they prevented me from recognising exploitative moments and contradictory effects of the literacy practice. Two feminist ethnographers' critiques of feminist ethnography and the 'new' or 'postmodern' ethnography provide insight into my work. First, Stacey forcefully reminds us of the danger of deploying ethnographic or other qualitative methods that appear to position the feminist/female researchers and their female informants 'in a collaborative, reciprocal quest for understanding' (1991: 114) and that researchers are 'apt to suffer the delusion of alliance' with her female informants (1991: 116).

Second, Enslin contends that in the new ethnography 'Engagement is merely a tool of representation. Political concerns (for challenging Western hegemony or homogenization) appear to enter into this process only at the time of writing, or representation' (1994: 541). Through these two feminist critiques, which operate through engaging questions of global inequality, my original research can be seen as an attempt to fabricate a mutual relationship with the 'Third World' informants in order to extract 'data' from them so that I, the 'First World' researcher, could secure for myself the subjectivity I desired by giving them voice through my writing. In my case, instead of working to equalise power relations as suggested by Gordon (1995), I spoke, was heard and/or authorised the writing. Thus, albeit I rhetorically acknowledged their agency, it can be seen that I reinforced the existing power relations between the 'First World' researcher *qua* agent and the 'Third World' researched *qua* object within local/global contexts by individually appropriating the fruits of our mutual labour, the knowledge produced, for the purposes that I identified without explicitly negotiating with them. In practice, then, I denied the agency that my text celebrated. The discourses through which I was constituted made it impossible for me to see this contradiction.

Critical reflexivity should not stop here. It is part of the ruse of the master narrative of development to instil a narcissistic and guilt-laden reflexivity in more privileged feminist researchers. This type of reflexivity tends to discipline the researchers and asks them to be excruciatingly humble with their informants as well as in their writing. Yet this ethical practice seems to sustain the existence of the master, whose discipline cuts off the possibility of collective praxis between the researchers and their researched, not to mention a possible transnational feminist praxis; hence, this practice can be seen to keep subordinate the 'illiterate' 'Third World' women it seeks to serve. What is at stake here is *exploitation* in a different sense: without negotiating the research processes with the research subjects the researchers, in remaining as 'individuals', foreclose the possibility of partially connecting and engaging in a collective feminist praxis with their subjects across differences and locations.[4]

The dominant development discourses, and even those critical of literacy practices, tend to produce researchers who recognise writing as an important political intervention, and in so doing, those discourses keep researchers' focus on writing rather than on creating a partially shared vision, thus obscuring possibilities of forming a larger community. This exploitative tendency is less common now, thanks to rigorous engagement with ethics and politics in cross-cultural research among feminist researchers (see Wolf 1996), yet disciplinary power within the discourses of Western academia and development still often appear to privilege solitary academic literacy practice. In consequence, the master narrative of development successfully closes off a potentially destabilising collective feminist praxis between and beyond researchers and their informants. In other words, researchers, who recognise their writing as composed within the discipline imposed by the dominant discourses of Western academia and development as their legitimate moment of political advocacy may secure a condition of existence of the master narrative of development and of the academy whose hegemonies often disadvantage those the researchers seek to serve in so far as they do not recognise their informants as legitimate subjects to be engaged in building a collective praxis.

Conclusion: toward a transnational feminist praxis

This reflexive analysis illuminates possibilities of productive ways to read the interactions between researchers and researched, other than those available through the register of the traditionally understood notion of exploitation. Rather, in acknowledging the agency of the people involved and the individual manifestations of the historical, cultural and/or social forces that acted on us during and after my fieldwork, these interactions can be seen as unequal but mutual exchanges formed by constant negotiations of power/knowledges among researchers and our researched through strategically positioning ourselves in pursuit of our own goals and/or commitments. Within this perspective, the knowledges produced are recognised as shaped and continuously reshaped by power differences stemming from different positionalities of the knowers and the knowns within a shifting context, and as shaped by our respective understandings of our positionings within larger cultural and institutional histories. Further, the knowledges are seen as producing contradictory effects. This alternative perspective brings with it a critical lesson: 'Illiterate' 'Third World' women are not seen to be a homogeneous group of 'ignorant mothers who need to be enlightened' or 'victims' or 'potential rational economic agents' but are seen and are to be engaged as active and specific actors who negotiate power/knowledges with their Others for their own purposes and on their own mutually negotiated terms (Sato forthcoming).

This recognition is necessary in imagining alternative strategies to challenge interconnected yet 'scattered hegemonies' that sustain local/global inequalities. To do this, I have found a notion of transnational feminist praxis crucial. This praxis recognises a need to link subjects who are historically and geographically situated with others who partially share perspectives yet are geographically distant by comparing their overlapping yet unequal engagements in similar political struggles without falling into the trap of theorising a hegemonic gender oppression (see Grewal and Kaplan 1994; Alexander and Mohanty 1997). In creating a transnational feminist praxis, I argue that researchers must be multiply accountable[5] (Abu-Lughod 1991): to research subjects; to communities in which they find themselves, such as an organisation for which they work; to the academic discourses if they are academic researchers; to political movements like feminism, Marxism and anti-imperialism; and to themselves, each in different ways. This multiple accountability, therefore, requires other ways to be accountable than research for political advocacy. For example, some suggestions are for researchers to produce analyses more accessible to multiple audiences in multiple forms (Abu-Lughod 1991; Narayan 1997; Nagar 2002), to represent the embodiment of praxis through their writing[6] (Enslin 1994) and to create a space for subjects to reconstitute their often subordinated subject position through action research processes (Gibson-Graham 1994).

By appropriating their privileges researchers are also urged to create 'new institutional spaces that favor, facilitate, and give due recognition to alternative research products and to new forms of collaboration' (Nagar 2002: 183). These multidimensional strategies can help us to pursue the construction of a transnational feminist praxis with our research subjects and others who partially share common perspectives in different locations. In this process, researchers have to engage in feminist praxis on multiple scales and locations by critically positioning ourselves in relation to specific contexts. This involves taking what is available within their situated contexts into consideration in our efforts to openly negotiate if not attempt to equalise power relations not only with the researched but also with our multiple audiences. By definition, feminist researchers can never be neutral. Tactically juggling our multiple commitments, engagement of feminist praxis on multiple scales will keep the researchers and the researched opening possibilities for continuous collective exploration of means to transform the conditions that sustain local/global inequalities.

Acknowledgements

I wish to thank Ann Ferguson and Sangeeta Kamat for their extensive comments on the earlier text. I have benefited from feedback of the graduate students who took the course entitled 'Issues in Feminist Research' in spring 2000 at the University of Massachusetts Amherst in which I presented the preliminary ideas first. I also thank Kirsten Isgro, Maria Stehle and Beverly Weber for their comments. I am extremely grateful to Peter Tamas, who patiently assisted me throughout this work. Of course, all faults remain mine.

Notes

1 Haraway's claim that objectivity is not about 'disengagement but about mutual *and* usually unequal structuring' (Haraway 1988: 595) is suggestive here.
2 I would add other dimensions depending on my research context such as religion, caste, linguistic background, age, citizenship status, etc.
3 See Patai (1991) for example.
4 I elaborated an idea by Madra (1999), discussed in Community Economies Collective (2001). He argues that exploitation should be considered not as theft but as the deprivation of possibilities to create community and communal subjectivities.
5 Abu-Lughod (1991) uses the term 'multiple accountability', by which she means that feminist and 'halfie' (e.g. Palestinian and American) anthropologists have multiple audiences and need to be accountable to each audience in different ways.
6 See Benmayor (1991) and Ford-Smith (1997) as other examples.

References

Abu-Lughod, L. (1991) 'Writing against culture' in R.G. Fox (ed.) *Recapturing Anthropology: Working in the Present*, Santa Fe NM: School of American Research Press

Alcoff, L. (1988) 'Cultural feminism versus post-structuralism: the identity crisis in feminist theory', *Signs: Journal of Women in Culture and Society*, 13: 405–36

Alexander, M.J. and Mohanty, C.T. (1997) 'Introduction: genealogies, legacies, movements' in M.J. Alexander and C.T. Mohanty (eds) *Feminist Genealogies, Colonial Legacies, Democratic Futures*, New York: Routledge

Benmayor, R. (1991) 'Testimony, action research, and empowerment: Puerto Rican women and popular education' in S.B. Gluck and D. Patai (eds) *Women's Words: the Feminist Practice of Oral History*, New York: Routledge

Chopra, P. (2001) 'Betrayal and solidarity in ethnography on literacy: revisiting research homework in a north Indian village' in B.V. Street (ed.) *Literacy and Development: Ethnographic Perspectives*, London and New York: Routledge

Community Economies Collective (2001) 'Imagining and enacting noncapitalist futures', *Socialist Review*, 28: 93–135

Crenshaw, K. (1997) 'Intersectionality and identity politics: learning from violence against women of color' in M.L. Shanley and U. Narayan (eds) *Reconstructing Political Theory: Feminist Perspectives*, University Park PA: Pennsylvania State University Press

Enslin, E. (1994) 'Beyond writing: feminist practice and the limitations of ethnography', *Cultural Anthropology*, 9: 537–68

Ford-Smith, H. (1997) 'Ring ding in a tight corner: Sistren, collective democracy, and the organization of cultural production' in M.J. Alexander and C.T. Mohanty (eds) *Feminist Genealogies, Colonial Legacies, Democratic Futures*, New York: Routledge

Foucault, M. (1980) 'Two lectures' in C. Gordon (ed.) *Power/knowledge: Selected Interviews and other Writings, 1972–1977*, New York: Pantheon Books

Gibson-Graham, J.K. (1994) '"Stuffed if I know!": reflections on postmodern feminist social research', *Gender, Place and Culture*, 1: 205–24

Gordon, D.A. (1995) 'Border work: feminist ethnography and the dissemination of literacy' in R. Behar and D.A. Gordon (eds) *Women Writing Culture*, Berkeley CA: University of California Press

Grewal, I. and Kaplan, C. (1994) 'Introduction: transnational feminist practices and questions of postmodernity' in I. Grewal and C. Kaplan (eds) *Scattered Hegemonies: Postmodernity and Transnational Feminist Practices*, Minneapolis MN: University of Minnesota Press

Haraway, D. (1988) 'Situated knowledges: the science question in feminism as a site of discourse on the privilege of partial perspective', *Feminist Studies*, 14: 575–99

Hernández, G. (1995) 'Multiple subjectivities and strategic positionality: Zora Neale Hurston's experimental ethnographies' in R. Behar and D.A. Gordon (eds) *Women Writing Culture*, Berkeley CA: University of California Press

Lal, J. (1996) 'Situating locations: the politics of self, identity, and "Other" in living and writing the text' in D.L. Wolf (ed.) *Feminist Dilemmas in Fieldwork*, Boulder CO: Westview Press

Mohanty, C.T. (1991) 'Under Western eyes: feminist scholarship and colonial discourses' in C.T. Mohanty, A. Russo and L. Torres (eds) *Third World Women and the Politics of Feminism*, Bloomington IN: Indiana University Press

Nagar, R. (2002) 'Footloose researchers, "traveling" theories, and the politics of transitional feminist praxis', *Gender, Place and Culture*, 19: 179–86

Narayan, K. (1997) 'How native is a "native" anthropologist?' in L. Lamphere, H. Ragoné and P. Zavella (eds) *Situated Lives: Gender and Culture in Everyday Life*, New York: Routledge

Patai, D. (1991) 'US academics and Third World women: is ethical research possible?' in S.B. Gluck and D. Patai (eds) *Women's Words: the Feminist Practice of Oral History*, New York: Routledge

Rankin, K.N. (2001) 'Governing development: neoliberalism, microcredit, and rational economic woman', *Economy and Society*, 30: 18–37

Sato, C. (forthcoming) 'Rethinking adult literacy training: an analysis through a Third World feminist perspective', *Women's Studies Quarterly*, 32

Stacey, J. (1991) 'Can there be a feminist ethnography?' in S.B. Gluck and D. Patai (eds) *Women's Words: the Feminist Practice of Oral History*, New York: Routledge

Wolf, D.L. (1996) 'Situating feminist dilemmas in fieldwork' in D.L. Wolf (ed.) *Feminist Dilemmas in Fieldwork*, Boulder CO: Westview Press

Part II

Identifying the issues

A gendered perspective on literacy policy and programming

This part of the book focuses on the questions foremost in the minds of planners, policy makers and those involved in implementing literacy programmes. The writers analyse issues around language policy, literacy teaching and facilitator training approaches, sectoral linkages, planning and evaluation. The authors in this part draw on their experience as practitioners within a range of institutions and contrasting educational programmes (government, multilateral and bilateral development agencies, international and local non-governmental organisations) across three continents. They share in common a desire to find ways of responding to women's and men's needs through appropriate training and literacy teaching models.

The chapters in this part all engage with ideas about gender roles and changing gender relations, recognising that there is a need to understand and respond to where people are now, yet also to provide the impetus for reflection and to initiate change. For Rogers, Patkar and Saraswathi this means looking more critically at what the term 'functional' literacy implies in the context of individual women and men (both literate and 'illiterate') in two Indian cities. There is a tension between the desire to respond appropriately to 'women' as a group (for example, through women-specific programmes) yet also to recognise diversity. The danger of functional literacy programmes is that they can disregard women's changing and multiple identities through 'fixing' that identity in terms of assumed roles and work activities: 'functions imply roles, and roles imply identities'. As Rogers *et al.* point out, the work-related identities are only a small part of people's whole identity: 'many other aspects of life and human aspirations are commonly left out of functional literacy programmes' (as illustrated by the research conducted by Zubair and Betts in the first part of this book).

Donna Bulman's case study of Sarah, an HIV-positive woman in Canada, presents a similarly strong argument for the recognising multiple identities and responding to diversity in adult learning programmes. Like the individual women in Chopra's chapter, Sarah is intelligent and 'not dependent on others', countering the many stereotypes about people with reading difficulties. Arguing that Sarah's educational needs should not be viewed only in relation to employment, Bulman suggests that a rights-based approach 'would view adult literacy education as a right rather than a second chance for those who were not successful within the formal school system'. Building on the notion that women do not form a homogeneous group and that individual women have changing and multiple identities, these writers all explore the ways in which literacy programmes could become more demand-led and flexible.

Looking at the structures within which adult learning takes place is the focus of Attwood, Castle and Smythe's chapter where they examine the REFLECT literacy circles as a new space for women to challenge power relations more generally and gender relations within the home. Their detailed analysis of the learning process within the REFLECT circles in Lesotho brings out the difficulties faced by staff facilitating discussions on gender relations which aimed to 'renegotiate' gender contracts and challenge traditional practices. This chapter raises issues about the ownership of such participatory approaches – ironically, similar to those critiques of traditional literacy teaching methods. Like Marc Fiedrich's chapter in Part III of this book, Attwood *et al.* suggest that 'literacy is a "by-product" of the REFLECT learning process'. As an educational approach, REFLECT is valued for providing a new more neutral and public space for women to discuss issues. In this respect, the chapter highlights many of the non-literacy and social aspects that have drawn women to other literacy programmes too (including functional literacy). The attention to the literacy class (in this case, the REFLECT learning circles) as a social structure contributes to our understanding about how far changes in people's attitudes and practices (this may be health education as well as gender awareness) may be initiated by educational interventions.

In the Nigerian and Egyptian contexts where she has worked as a trainer, Juliet McCaffery looks in detail at how gender issues were addressed in the implementation of training programmes for literacy facilitators. As well as analysing the programme content and approach, she explores issues around the hidden curriculum, including childcare arrangements and gendered forms of language used. For example, the neutral English term 'literacy facilitator' (meaning man or woman) had been translated into the masculine form only. McCaffery's reflections on the training process raise questions about how to develop programmes that challenge traditional gender norms. In contrast to many polarised discussions of the relationship between 'developer and developed',[1] McCaffery's account brings out the differing, contrasting and contradictory perspectives of the range of actors involved. The complex picture of gender relations presented here – like the other chapters in this part – suggests that programme planners need to take account of ways in which training and teaching approaches are transformed in practice.

The contributions to this part suggest that a more reflexive approach to planning and training should be adopted, in order to respond to people's educational needs. Whether they take a 'gendered' approach to literacy programmes as a whole (i.e. for women and men) or consider how specific programmes for women could be more gender-sensitive, all the writers here advocate an approach that recognises and values the learner's perspective and their existing social practices. Though stressing the need for clear policy objectives, this part of the book gives insight into the ways in which interventions are shaped by the people involved – trainers, planners, facilitators and above all, participants.

Note

1 See, for example, R. Grillo and R.L. Stirrat, *Discourses of Development: Anthropological Perspectives*, Oxford: Berg (1997).

7 Functional literacy, gender and identities

Policy and practice

Alan Rogers, Archana Patkar and L.S. Saraswathi

The term 'functional literacy' has, over the years, acquired symbolic status. It is applied to literacy learning programmes without any clarity as to what the term means. When asked what feature in the programme is 'functional', attention is usually directed to the non-literacy elements – to the add-on skill training, or to 'empowerment' or awareness-raising elements. Its interpretation is in each case idiosyncratic.

Policy and programme makers can choose from a variety of interpretations (Verhoeven 1994). Gray was the first[1] to popularise the term with his definition 'to engage effectively in all those activities in which literacy is normally assumed in his [*sic*] culture or group' (1956: 24), that is, the *normal* social uses of literacy, literacy practices employed in the 'spontaneous and routine pursuits of his [*sic*] daily affairs' (Schutz 1970: 320). This is a flexible definition, for it will change from culture to culture, whether occupational, tribal, linguistic, urban or rural, religious or caste group, as socio-cultural contexts change over time.

UNESCO however took the definition of functional literacy further, applying it to literacy learning programmes in 'developing' societies rather than social uses of literacy. At first it was seen as a second stage of literacy, not initial literacy learning:

> A person is *literate* who can with understanding both read and write a short simple statement in his [*sic*] everyday life.

> A person is *functionally literate* who can engage in all those activities in which literacy is required for effective functioning of his group and community and also for enabling him to continue to use reading, writing and calculation for his own and the community's development.
> (UNESCO 1978, cited in Verhoeven 1994: 410)

But it was not long before UNESCO identified functional literacy with initial literacy learning programmes. At the same time, a definition of functional literacy to mean 'work-related' or 'income-generation' uses of literacy skills entered into common currency. As a consequence of the Persepolis conference in 1965, UNESCO sought to promote production-oriented functional literacy as the basis of all adult literacy learning programmes (Jones 1988). Functional literacy became 'the process and content of learning to read and write [related] to the preparation for work and vocational training as well as a means of increasing the productivity of the individual' (UNESCO, cited without reference in Verhoeven 1994: 6). Thus Farmers' Functional Literacy Programmes were launched, and similar programmes were devised for fisherfolk and other occupational groupings. The aim of these programmes was to 'improve the general skills for efficient functioning' (UNESCO 1988).

The significance of this change does not seem to have been recognised at the time. What it did was to free functional literacy from the relativism that Gray saw in it. Gray's approach tied literacy (and therefore literacy learning) to a specific context: what is 'normally assumed *in his* [*or her*] *culture or group*' (our emphasis). By moving functional literacy into a universalised context of 'work', UNESCO discharged literacy learning from any need to research the unique socio-cultural context of the particular group of literacy learners and each individual learner. Generalised sets of competences came to be included whenever functional literacy was glossed: for example, functional literacy in one definition meant:

> being able as a member of a particular society to cope with the demands of everyday life that involve written language. Such demands include being able to read a popular newspaper, write a job application, follow the instructions that explain how to use a household gadget or complete an official form.
>
> (Wells 1991: 51–2, cited in Hammond and Freebody 1994: 438)

Gray's definition is wider than UNESCO's in that it includes all uses of literacy, religious and social as well as economic, but at the same time it is narrower in that it is confined to *existing*, not new, uses of literacy. UNESCO functional literacy is limited to work-related literacy activities, but it extends 'beyond the current functions' of literacy within any particular culture (Barton 1994a: 194). Second, both these approaches and the subsequent models of literacy learning built on them are based on the uses of literacy skills. Their ideology is that literacy is *for* something (income generation, health, political participation, etc.), and that that something cannot be achieved without literacy – a view which some have challenged (Rogers 2001). Equally, both assume that to possess skills is to use them. This is a product of the Enlightenment project of modern Western society, the rationalist belief that 'to know is to do', that 'to be able' is the same as actually doing. We are more aware today that such a belief does not make sense of reality: smoking is one example of this, for knowing that smoking will kill one does not always (or even often) lead to action to stop smoking. And third, whereas Gray's approach might have led to literacy 'breaking out of the education silo', as the influential paper *Literacy in Africa* (UNESCO 2002a) puts it, UNESCO put it firmly back into the educational mode, with its 'learn first and then practise' approach. Today, functional literacy tends to mean a training programme, not a life-long functioning programme.

Functional literacy for work

UNESCO, with its enormous international prestige and social (if not financial) capital, won the day. In practice, 'functional literacy' became a third thing – a series of literacy learning programmes *plus*. The *plus* element usually consisted (and consists) of skills for income generation in the belief that development means increased productivity and ultimately consumption by workers in developing countries (Street 1984: 183). The range of such skills taught was very limited – mainly small-scale handicraft production in the informal economic sector without any pre-production planning or post-production activities, so that those engaged in such programmes were frequently exploited by those who commissioned their production or sold their products. And almost without exception, the skills taught in functional literacy learning programmes were non-literate skills – they were very rarely taught to use literacy for earning (Rogers 1994; see Oxenham *et al.* 2002).

Functional literacy programmes today are still based on the provision of additional training for production rather than for employment. Oxenham reports that Mali's functional literacy programme is designed 'to support credit, marketing and agricultural production' (Oxenham *et al.* 2000: 32–3). Uganda's Functional Adult Literacy (FAL) programme is designed 'to build the capacity of FAL groups to practise modern farming techniques and also engage in income-generating activities by equipping them with practical entrepreneurial and agricultural skills so as to increase household incomes and eradicate poverty ...'. The programmes include provision 'for special interest groups e.g. pastoralists and fishing communities', but 'most of the FAL learners are engaged in agricultural projects for the functional part of the literacy programme ...' (FAL 2001: 16, 21; Guidelines 2002: 2, 75).

The problem with such programmes is that, despite the definition, they are not based on real research into the literacy practices which are normal in the specific economic activity they advocate. Everything is generalised rather than specific. Farming texts (frequently written by journalists rather than farmers) are the same irrespective of the kind of agriculture engaged in or the soil and climate of the region. There is little real research done into the used literacy practices, even when programmes deal with employment opportunities.

We can illustrate this with a specific example. A functional literacy programme in a southern African country aimed at providing work in the tourist industry (especially hotels) consisted of training the participants how to dress, how to lay the table and how to wait on guests. Apart from a simplified menu, no text from any hotel was used in the training programme. But as Hunter reveals in a study of one such a situation, hotels have their own forms of literacy which any worker in that sector will need to master effectively.

> At the Urban Hotel, Karen, the night banquet manager, was preparing the orders for the conference room service the following day. She was transferring relevant details from the conference centre BEOs (Banquet Event Orders) to the hotel room set-up and kitchen transfer work sheets. She wrote on prepared forms in the usual hotel jargon: 'U/S' for U-shaped table arrangements, 'Rds × 3' for three round tables, '52 cookie monster' for an assortment of large cookies for fifty-two guests. When she first arrived on the job, with a recent degree in hospitality services, she carefully wrote out the orders 'in full', in simple, clear English prose so that the workers would understand. To her surprise, it wasn't well received. She ... 'had to be told' by the workers that they couldn't follow that kind of writing. I asked about literacy issues among the workers, and she said that the housemen could speak well enough, but their reading and writing were not as good. They needed the shorthand language of the hotel to do their jobs efficiently. So she learned to use their code.
>
> Karen presented this story as indicative of their limited language and literacy, that they could only read the hotel jargon and symbols ... but [they] didn't understand much more. The answer might be to improve their decoding and encoding of language ... But ... by telling the new banquet manager to use the hotel code, the housemen demonstrated their own knowledge and skill in the cultural literacy of the hotel, and what's more, they positioned themselves to teach her.... By teaching Karen what they needed as instructions, they could be seen as challenging the hotel hierarchy. In that sense, they might have been taking a critical stance on the power relationships in the workplace. On the other hand, they also could be seen as engaging in a critical evaluation about the most efficient means of communicating instructions. For at the least, reading an abbreviated code like the examples above takes less time than reading long sentences;

plus the codes have standardised, shared meanings for all the workers in the department. They are an efficient communication system.

(Hunter forthcoming)

The hotel workers here were functionally literate: it was the university-trained manager who was not functionally literate. Functional literacy is not a set of general skills but quite specific to different contexts. We are faced here (as elsewhere) with the fact that literacy is multiple; as Gray recognised, there are many different functional literacies.

Widening functional literacy to other aspects of life

Functional literacy (especially the UNESCO interpretation) has been the subject of much criticism (e.g. LeVine 1985; Street 1984: 183–4; Lankshear 1985; Barton 1994b: 192–5; LeVine 1994: 123–4). For one thing, such programmes are based on what may be called a 'single injection' model (Freire would call it 'banking education'): a single literacy and skill training programme is designed to train the learners once and for all so that they can become 'functionally literate' and engage in income-generation programmes for the rest of their lives. Continuing or lifelong functional literacy would be seen as a contradiction in terms. Again, functional literacy programmes omit religious and home literacies, leisure and interest literacies, consumer literacies, self-gratification. There is about functional literacy a seriousness; it must be *for* development (whatever that may mean). It is a 'worthy' construct.

Several other subjects have thus been added to the economic focus of functional literacy learning programmes, as 'development' has changed towards a basic human needs approach – learning for health, or for the environment, for communal harmony or civic engagement (Stromquist 1997). Such aspects are often described as 'literacy for empowerment'. One manifestation of this is the 'literacy for sustainable livelihoods' which however takes a holistic approach to the literacy learner and avoids the negative attitude towards the capabilities of the participants (DfID 2002 and reports cited there; the rhetoric of 'livelihoods' is however increasingly being used to hide the traditional top-down approaches to literacy learning). But there is still a normative element in this wider definition of functional literacy as 'the use of written language in the full range of functions that can be distinguished in modern society' (Hammond and Freebody 1994: 440; Verhoeven 1994: 26). 'Modern society' is taken for granted, a universal reality which can be recognised by any normal human being in every culture. People who live in modern society 'should' be literate in the forms which the educated elites take for granted. It is this which has led to the contemporary stress on computer literacy and the use of

ICT for literacy learning and literacy use (Wagner 2002; LeVine 1994) – for computer use is now thought to be 'normal' in all modern societies.

And just as functional literacy has been widened to include many different developmental subjects, so too has its target group been elaborated and differentiated. The Uganda FAL programme is aimed at 'men, women, youth, persons with disabilities, and the elderly'. Increasingly, different functional literacy learning programmes are being developed for different groups. Such groups however are not analysed further – all youth, disabled and elderly are assumed to have a common identity. It is in this context that special functional literacy programmes have in some cases been developed for women, similarly undifferentiated.

Four paradigms of teaching functional literacy:

- *Gray*, teaching the normal everyday literacy practices of the local community.
- *UNESCO 1*, teaching usable literacy practices *after* initial basic literacy.
- *UNESCO 2*, teaching literacy related to and needed for production.
- *FL in practice*, teaching basic literacy and income generation skills separately and alongside each other; the economic skills do not use the literacy being learned.

Functional literacy and gender

Functional literacy programmes are founded in part on statistics and in part on assumptions.

The uses and limits of statistics. Because functional literacy is seen to be closely linked with development, its construction is deeply influenced by development statistics (see for example UNESCO 2002b). Such statistics are deemed to be objective, apolitical – although of course they are not; the statistics chosen are collected and used for political purposes. Literacy statistics are based on the division of the world into two exclusive categories, 'literate' and 'illiterate'. These are then further disaggregated into categories such as urban–rural, male–female, and age groups. The picture drawn by these statistics is one in which men, the young and urban dwellers are seen to have developed acceptable literacy skills more than women or rural dwellers or the elderly – which Street suggests may in part be the result of Western culture which favoured men and towns (Street 1992).

Statistics however are very uncertain foundations on which to build literacy learning programmes. We are all aware that countries vary (some of the Caribbean countries for instance show higher literacy statistics for women than for men). Equally, the sources of these statistics are very shaky indeed, based as they are on very different kinds of premise, some self-referential, others on years of schooling, yet others on an administered test. Further, statistics, however carefully collected, often get their facts wrong.[2]

Despite this, huge conclusions are drawn from statistics. For example, the frequently cited 'fact' that there are some 860 million illiterates in the world fails to ask in which literacy this assessment has been made, and how many of these persons have acquired and use other literacies and how many engage in literacy practices through secondary literacy (mediators and scribes, etc; see Mace 2002). Again, statistics show that most of the so-called 'illiterates' are in rural areas, which helps to account for the fact that most functional literacy skill training programmes are in rurally oriented handicrafts for local markets. It is the often repeated statement that 'the vast majority of illiterates in the world are female' (Westen 1994: 258) that accounts for the gender dimension of functional literacy policies.

The assumptions on which functional literacy programmes are based. Functional literacy programmes however are built not on statistics alone but on a range of assumptions as well. For example, statistics suggest that there are more elderly persons who are 'illiterate', but this is not used as grounds for launching major functional literacy programmes among the older population. Functional literacy is aimed especially at those between the ages of fifteen and thirty-five, on the assumption that they will use their new literacy skills to greater advantage than older age groups.

It is this mixture of statistics and assumptions which forms the foundation of functional literacy programmes for women. Statistics show that there are more women non-literate in the dominant literacy than men; hence more programmes are needed for women than men if their human right to literacy is to be achieved. On the other hand, there are instrumental assumptions such as the view that women have more influence over their family choices, health, schooling practices, etc., which suggest that investments in women's functional literacy are more beneficial in the long run than in men's programmes.

But it is, above all, assumptions about the gendered nature of economic activities which have coloured functional literacy learning programmes. Women, it is believed, engage in certain kinds of occupations; therefore the learning programmes for women need to concentrate on those kinds of work and ignore other kinds.

Gendered functional literacy programmes

Although there are some functional literacy programmes, such as the Uganda programme, which are not gendered (the same contents and teaching–learning materials are provided for both men and women), a considerable number of functional literacy programmes were (and continue to be) designed on the basis of such gendered 'conclusions'. Thus, despite women's role in farming in many communities, the teaching–learning materials for men frequently include discussions of field crops, while women are encouraged to grow vegetables in small gardens and to learn non-agricultural subjects such as cooking and health. The skills taught are also often (though not always) similarly gendered. Thus in some national functional literacy programmes, women are taught tailoring and dressmaking while men are being taught carpentry, decoration, plumbing and electrical skills. In Bombay women learn to make jam, bags and ornaments; in Egypt they are being taught sewing, knitting, macramé, food processing and home economics (Rogers 1994). Some of these programmes are designed for individual use, others for women's self-help groups.

In almost all the gendered functional literacy learning programmes, women are constructed in a homogeneous way. Women are seen as potential producers of a limited range of handicraft products. This kind of functional literacy ignores the important community roles which many women have. Above all, the ideology behind it is that the literacy learner must change to fit into modern society; there is virtually no discussion of how society as a whole must change (Dighe 1995). The strong and limited stereotyping of occupations (men in the formal sector, women in the informal) is rarely challenged. Issues such as the division of labour, equal pay for equal work, women's rights, are rarely if ever discussed. Women's agricultural programmes, for example, are almost always confined to production and hardly ever discuss marketing, which is seen by many policy makers as men's work (despite the fact that most marketing in Africa and much of Asia is done by women). The aim in most functional literacy programmes is to increase women's 'efficiency' in their existing roles rather than to transform society fundamentally and to change women's roles overall. For, above all, functional literacy learning is a tool of the elites.

Such literacy learning programmes for women then are based on unsound statistics and on a set of unfounded assumptions. They assume that women are women are women, that the identity of women is inevitable, unchanging and unchangeable, and they ignore the 'multiple and socially varied constructions of gender' (Street 1992). They are based on a belief that experts can identify women's (genericised) needs; that a uniform programme for 'women' will be effective; that all women want more income and that they will get it through work; that they will obtain work through literacy; and that the barriers to (all) women participating in adult literacy learning programmes is the difficulty of combining work with traditional women's roles as wives and mothers.

Gender, identities and the life worlds

It is not at all clear how far the participants – and even more relevantly those who do not participate – feel about such women-specific functional literacy programmes. For it is paradoxical that programmes designed specifically to overcome gender blindness and highlight women's special needs can be seen as adding to the general stigma of women. Such attitudes have been found among programmes aimed specifically at the poorest of the poor (see Brock and McGee 2003).

But functions imply roles, and roles imply identities. Thus functional adult literacy, above all other forms of adult literacy learning programmes, engages with the identities of the participants – who (men and) women feel they are, how far they see themselves first and foremost as (man and/or) woman, what kind of identities they are creating for themselves, and how far these identities correspond with the identities created by the programme providers. Work-related activities form a large part of those identities, but they are not the whole identity, even of the very poor. Many other aspects of life and human aspirations are commonly left out of functional literacy learning programmes.

Nevertheless, many of the assumptions of the functional literacy providers appear to have been internalised by a number of the participants; and it is from participants that data on women's motivations has been collected, very rarely from non-participants. It is not always recognised that women's demands might reflect rather than challenge the gender construct of the society they live in, especially as several functional literacy programmes for women tend to be dominated by relatively well-off women who have more time available for classes. But there are others who do not see themselves as (genericised) women in deficit, confined to certain work practices and other roles. And it is not at all clear that it is the role of functional literacy to continue to circumscribe women in this way.

The diversity of women and their identities, roles and aspirations, then, is ignored in most functional literacy programmes, despite statements that not all non-literate women are poor or that 'not all low-income women have the same needs and interests' (Westen 1994: 266). In particular, the assumptions behind functional literacy ignore issues of power. Sen's view of development (Sen 1999) as capabilities, as choices, freedoms (in the plural) has outdated this view of functional literacy, although the rhetoric and practice continue.

So what does 'to function in society' mean today? I find the concepts of Bourdieu helpful here. Functionality can be seen as to live and act in a *habitus*, a world of roles, power and confidence; it is to use identities which are multiple and flexible. Functionality may be described in terms of the interaction between *habitus* and identities – and literacy plays a part in the creation of this *habitus* and these identities.

Two features of Bourdieu's discussion may be important here. First, his concept that some people 'fall into practice that is theirs rather than freely choosing it or being impelled into it by mechanical constraints' (Bourdieu 1990: 132) is a challenge to traditional functional literacy assumptions about women's oppression, intentionality and motivations. And second, his view that the legitimacy of social and human capital (such as the possession of literacy skills) may be provided by the more imme- diate social group rather than the dominant group. In other words, some people (men as well as women) come to regard literacy more in terms of their own identity in their own *habitus* than in terms of universalist defini- tions of being men or women, illiterate or literate, even young or old. Attempts to identify women's felt needs must take into account the imme- diate context of each of the participants and the identities they are build- ing for themselves with the functions that go with those identities, rather than over-generalise on the basis of gender or other feature.

Case studies of literacy and identities

The following case studies from separate areas of India taken by two dif- ferent field researchers illustrate the poverty of the assumptions of func- tional literacy. The case studies were chosen at random and may not be typical, but they are 'telling' case studies; the remarkable similarities would seem to be entirely coincidental. Both look at men and women in their family settings rather than cutting women off from their context. We do not wish to draw huge generalisations from these case studies, but simply to ask, what does functional literacy mean to these four adults? And is it gendered?

Case study 1

Krishna and Sunita, living in Chennai (Madras), are husband and wife aged forty-three and forty-two. She has been taught by her daughter to sign her name, but he cannot. He said he tried to learn his name so that he could sign when he received his wages but he found it difficult as his name is too long and there are too many letters to remember and write down (in Tamil).[3] The family consists of three daughters and one son; they were pressured by 'the family elders', especially both grandmothers, into trying for a son, for, as Sunita said,

> in our community our share of the property will not be given to my
> daughters. Only a son will get it. If I do not have a son, our property

share will go to the sons of my husband's brother. Once we had the male child, we went in for the family planning operation. Both of us didn't want to have more children – we were clear about that.

When asked, they both said casually that she had had the operation.

Sunita came from a farming family which had recently moved into the city (Chennai). Her father was a nightwatchman for a local school, and her mother worked as a domestic helper in several households. Sunita had one sister and two brothers. The boys were sent to school but the girls were not.

At about seventeen, she married the brother of her cousin's wife, a farmer from another village in Tamil Nadu, and she went to live in that village. Her husband was trying to make a living along with other family members from a small plot of land. When their first child was due, Sunita went back to her mother in the city for the birth and eventually this daughter was sent to the grandmother to be brought up in the city, going to a school there. Back in the village, Sunita and Krishna had two further daughters and a son who were all started in the village school; but then because of family tensions, the whole family moved into the city where Sunita's mother was already looking after her eldest daughter. The family still has links with the village because of the land and their relations, and visit it regularly.

From the age of eight Sunita had worked as a domestic servant along with her mother, so on her return to Chennai she took up that work again. Krishna obtained casual work in the construction industry but his work is irregular. She and one of her daughters who helps her are the main support for the family.

She is very happy with her domestic work: 'I am used to doing this work for several years. I feel strongly that whatever job we do, we should respect our work. It may be seen as a menial job by some. But for me no work is menial.' Despite the fact that her two younger daughters have been educated at school, they have each joined her – 'even they do not see this job as menial ... I earn as much or even more than what an educated person earns ... as much as Rs 5,000 per month. When she [her second daughter] left after her marriage, I had to give up work in some houses. Now I earn a little less.' She fixes her monthly wages with each household and revises them at intervals in tune with the rise in prices of essentials as well as in terms of the amount of work given to her in the households. She learned this from experience. She deals with her pay firmly and feels justified when she asks for a rise – she quits her job in households unwilling to meet her demand. She does not complain but finds another house; she is confident of finding work. According to her, she is regular in her work; when she takes a day off once in a while, the households in which she works do not cut her pay. As soon as she gets into a house she starts working, and as soon as she completes her work she leaves – she hardly has time to spend on unnecessary talk.

The literacies in her work are limited. But she knows what they are. Because she is non-literate, she says, she does not agree to do jobs such as shopping, as it requires writing lists of the items, buying them, getting the bill accurately, getting and checking the receipt, giving accounts to the household concerned. She has learned to count rupee notes and recognise the numerals, and can decipher the calendar. She calculates mentally and can take care of her own accounts. She takes wage advances for emergencies from the households in which she works and pays back in instalments. She keeps track of what has been paid and what remains to be paid. When the payment is complete, she makes sure that the household understands that. She says with confidence that she does not make mistakes. She thinks that the households which give her advances keep an account in writing – but they have had no complaints about her accounting. In the two offices where she works they require her to sign her name to get her monthly pay, so she got her daughter to teach her (as she said, laughing) to 'sign my name in very big letters'.

Krishna says that he does not need literacy skills for his work, which consists of digging trenches, carrying bricks and sand, preparing cement, centring work for terraces, whitewashing and painting. He does not feel very secure in his current work:

> a few years ago, a lot of construction work was going on and I was getting work every day. But at present, there is a kind of lull – I hardly get work two days a week. I find my job by just sitting in the bus stand near my house; some involved in construction come in search of labourers and offer the job for the day. I get a wage of Rs 100 per day. It is difficult to work with contractors as they hold at least one week's wages as security; we lose that money when we quit.

Through talking to shopkeepers or on the construction sites, he has learned about the market availability of different brands of cement, paint, varnishes and colour washes, and can orally list them all. During his farming days he learned to read rupee notes and count money accurately and make calculations of his day-to-day earnings and spending. Asked whether he was a member of the Construction Workers' Union, he said 'No,' because he finds that the membership card is not given out although membership fees are collected, and 'nothing much is done for the workers'.

Their family work is gendered. Most of the activities within the house are carried out by the women, and their outside shopping is limited to what they require for their work in the home. Krishna and his son do the work that requires dealing with outsiders – with the fuel gas supply, the public distribution system for rice and kerosene, etc., the public health system, the owner–tenant relationship. They obtain information from television and radio or through mediation: as the quantity of rations supplied to the family is fixed and the price variations are announced to the public, they can calculate mentally how much they need to pay and they take a receipt. Whenever he goes to the doctor, he gets the doctor to explain which medicine is to be taken and when, and again he checks with the pharmacist if he has any doubts. Whenever he needs to fill in forms, for example for gas registration or for a ration card, he takes the help of his daughters. The women's literacies are limited to their household work (recipes, cleaning and washing materials, making lists for shopping and getting receipts, checking and making payments). The only such activity Krishna and Sunita do together is pawning jewellery to meet urgent financial needs of the family. She knows the weight of the jewels, checks the price of gold at the time of pawning, is aware of the practice of the pawnshop and the interest rate, and calculates mentally what is due. They check the receipt given by the shop with one of their daughters.

Both are happy with each other as a partner. Sunita is ever smiling and cheerful; she seems to be a very happy person in spite of her heavy work life and financial problems. She feels she is very lucky in getting Krishna as her husband. 'He understands me and I understand him. We trust ourselves and each other. I know what he will do and he knows what I will or will not do.' Krishna appreciates Sunita for her hard work and regular contribution to the family.

Both of them seem to think that learning literacy skills is important, and say that that is the reason they wanted their children to go to school. All their children have been to school. The eldest daughter was brought up in the city by her grandmother and studied up to BCom level, failing the final examination. But as the parents said, educated unemployment is rife in Chennai. To help her find work, they used an employment exchange without result, and eventually found her a job as an accountant with a food processing works. They arranged a marriage for her, but three days before the marriage she went to a registrar's office and married a man 'outside our community'. The crisis this caused was solved by marrying their second daughter to the boy concerned on the day previously arranged. 'She was totally unprepared. She agreed to help her parents. She is happy now with her marriage.' She had been educated up to Standard 10 and is now living in a village with one son.

The third daughter began to help her mother with domestic work when the second daughter left home. She too had studied up to Standard 10 but failed the final examination. The son however dropped out of school – he was not interested in studies. Sunita and Krishna and the daughters tried to help him to remain in school, for 'he is good at understanding whatever is taught. He doesn't like writing examinations.' Sunita suggested he go to a residential school but he threatened to run away, and as they do not want to lose their only son, they allowed him to drop out. She has put him into a jewellery shop running errands and he is happy doing that job.

The couple appear to 'engage effectively in all those activities in which literacy is normally assumed in [their] culture or group' through mediation. The social networks they have built up, especially Sunita's, seem to be very powerful for this purpose and they exploit them to the full. The school literacy activities included getting an affidavit about her children's age for entry to school ('signed by a judge with the help of a lawyer in whose house I was working as a domestic help'), getting receipts for school fees, reading school reports. 'My husband took them [the children] to the bookshop to buy [text]books. . . . I couldn't help my children with their homework. But I did keep telling them to study – to read aloud so that I could hear. When the teacher sent word to meet one or other of the parents, I used to go and meet the teacher.'

The marriage literacies they engaged in differed according to the practice adopted. Weddings involve horoscopes, invitations, shopping, drawing up a 'gift book' and loans: these records are carefully kept in the house even if they cannot be 'read'. The traditional in-community marriage, however, 'is not registered, as it is possible to have the family/community elders' intervention in case of any problems'. But in relation to the marriage of their eldest daughter which took place at the registrar's office, Sunita says very firmly that 'registering the marriage is essential as they need the marriage certificate when the girl faces any problems to file any case with the police or in the court of law. We can no more ask the family elders for settlement of disputes.'

Births involve religious rites, the use of a hospital (in the city) and obtaining a birth certificate, also carefully kept. Deaths again create literacy tasks: a younger brother was run over by a train, which involved a police station, hospital and cremation grounds. All this work and the religious rites were undertaken by the male members of the family, seeking help from literate persons in all the various places to write the necessary details as required. Festivals bring with them songs but most of these are kept on audio-cassettes; choosing which cassettes to play is usually determined by colour and shape rather than reading the titles. Films in cinema or on television are a passion but require little literacy skills except in subtitling, and they get a daughter to read these for them.

This couple express few regrets about their lack of literacy skills. Sunita says she would like to be able to read and understand the bills and receipts, particularly those from the pawnshop receipts which they get when they pawn her jewellery to meet urgent family needs; and she would like to read and understand the different bus routes and numbers as she travels back and forth from Chennai to her village and also within the city. In addition, she would like to read letters, marriage invitations, etc., for herself, for she feels she would wish to reply to every letter received. But she does not feel these as pressing needs.

Krishna however is more regretful. When in the village he belonged to a political party and aspired to rise in the party cadre. He believes he would have risen 'if only I had some education'; perhaps he would even have met the former Chief Minister. He is interested in reading and writing petitions to officials on issues such as water and electricity supply to their house and area, and the proper distribution of rations, but he is dependent on others to write even small petitions or applications. 'Those who write take a fee of Rs 10–15.' But neither of them had ever considered attending an adult literacy class, despite the Total Literacy Campaign of recent years. Both vote regularly – they 'look for the symbol of two leaves' – they say they 'never try to look at other symbols given on the ballot paper; we cannot read the names'.

Which raises the question: what kind of functional literacy would be appropriate for these two non-literate adults? How far should it be gendered, one programme for Sunita and a different programme for Krishna? So many of the functional literacy assumptions seem to be challenged by this case study – that boys are more educated than girls; that education leads to jobs; that the woman is unable to obtain a sustainable livelihood without extra training; that production is 'better' than domestic work. A programme of learning aimed at wives and mothers would no longer appeal to Sunita, and she shows no sign of wanting another kind of job, entering the risky business of production; she is supporting what remains of her family. She is happy with her work and her husband. In earlier years, she would like to have had more literacy skills to help her children when they were young, but not now; that time has passed. Krishna again would find it hard to change his job at his time of life, but he might attend a learning programme aimed at increased political involvement.

Certainly the traditional functional literacy programme appealed to neither of them. Functional literacy for them might be more attractive if centred round their leisure activities of film and festivals, for these are activities which are 'normal' in their context. They have 'fallen' into their identities within the *habitus* of more elite households, extended family relations (including village dwellers far away) and local community. And these identities are fairly well established, she as proud and loyal domestic helper, supportive wife and mother, he as husband and casual labourer and political activist – but literacy plays little part of the creation of those identities.

Case study 2

Chandra and Ratna are a couple living now in Mumbai, aged between approximately thirty and thirty-two. She is literate to some extent, having learned the skill through ten years of schooling in Kerala. He is non-literate, having attended primary school for one year only in Kerala. They have two daughters.

Ratna comes from a farming family consisting of five daughters and one son. All six children went to school for eight to ten years, as schooling is relatively cheap in Kerala. The family's resources were however meagre, as they were entirely dependent on a dry piece of land and the unreliable annual monsoons. But Ratna wanted to leave the village, not so much for economic reasons as for reasons of fashion:

> In the village we girls would be given two dresses a year, often hand-me-downs. I and my sisters longed for the fine clothes, sandals and accessories that our neighbours and friends who worked in Bombay wore when they came back to visit. Such luxuries were impossible to come by in our village in Kerala.

She persuaded her father to send her first to Gujarat for one year 'with a promise not to do anything that would disgrace the family name'. When she came back after a year and asked to go to Mumbai, her father agreed.

Through friends from Kerala then based in Mumbai, she obtained accommodation and work in the fisheries. She started in the shelling and packing department, and her nimble fingers and ability to write the label of contents on each box in Hindi quickly earned her the title of supervisor. Although the hours were long (most employees worked for twelve hours but were paid for eight hours) and although there was little freedom (employees were not allowed to leave the premises once they had entered it for the day), she was happy with her work, the respect she enjoyed, and the wages of Rs 2,000–3,000. After eight years, her brother joined her and then later two of her sisters.

Chandra too came from Kerala. An orphan and an epileptic, he was brought to Mumbai by a missionary nurse who looked after him until he was sixteen. He started work as a general helper at a tailoring company and quickly learned to become skilled at stitching seams of shirts, earning some Rs 3,000 per month (women are paid Rs 1,500 for the same work). Because of his epilepsy, however, he needs to find new jobs regularly.

Ratna and Chandra met when Chandra visited the fishery, and they married. After Ratna had her first daughter, she found she needed to give up the long hours at the fishery and instead is now engaged in domestic work for a number of families. She and her family have moved in with Chandra's married sister in Mumbai, but relations with that family are strained and her sister-in-law 'has tried to throw us out several times'. She feels that lack of mobility, especially after dark, 'restricts women considerably, even if they are clever and literate'. She feels that she is now confined to domestic work but has no choice, as she has to support the household with whatever work she can get. She feels that she does not use her literacy skills in a formal way but that they have helped her to aspire and dream for her daughters.

The family feel strangers in Mumbai. Their family language is Malayalam; their two daughters aged nine and four speak Malayalam and English. Since the main languages in Kerala are Malayalam and English, and since English is felt to be an asset in Mumbai's urban job market, Ratna was not keen on the girls learning Marathi, the local and school language in Maharashtra. Both the children therefore have been sent to a private English-medium school for which she pays very high fees despite the fact that she could educate them for free in a state-run school;[4] the couple are constantly seeking loans for fees and uniforms. Ratna is not literate in English, and therefore she cannot help her children with their school work very much. If she needs to read any correspondence or instructions in English, she asks the neighbours and also her daughters. She is very proud of their achievements already. But they are considering sending the girls back to relations in Kerala where schooling is cheaper and will be in the two languages they value. Ratna still has a ration card (entitlement to public distribution) in Kerala, and they have retained strong links with their village where she and her husband will inherit her parents' land one day. Despite having been in Mumbai for more than ten years, which gives them entitlement in that city, they still have not obtained confirmation of this, and a legal case has been registered.

Ratna is very happy with Chandra. She feels that she has 'married a good man overall' – although there have been times when

> I feel like leaving him because his family hates me, but I feel bad because he really cares for me and cannot help his epileptic fits which are brought on by stress. Although he has not studied much, he is very clever and more versatile than me and quick to know new things. He knows everything and because he is very mobile, quite aware of everything. Because he grew up as an orphan, he has strong survival skill.

His illiteracy and her literacy count for little in the identities they are building for each other. And this couple share their domestic activities together:

overall in our home, whoever gets time does the work – whether it is helping the children put on their uniforms, share in the housework, cooking, filling water or help with school-related or medical duties, caring for the children when they are sick. Our neighbours do not like us because we are different – in all their houses the women do all the work and the men sit around drinking, chatting or playing cards.

The work in the fisheries was gendered. Ratna described the employee profile at the fisheries as predominantly female, young and without children. Men were employed only in positions which called for physical strength (packers and loaders). Women were preferred for their diligence and skilled fingers and because they were prepared to work for lower wages. However, for fewer hours, and with no reading or writing skills, the young men earned almost double what the women took home. The domestic work which Ratna was now doing – cleaning floors, washing clothes and kitchen utensils – does not call for the exercise of her literacy skills.

Both Ratna and Chandra have clearly learned quickly in the course of their livelihood activities. Chandra acquired tailoring skills but felt that literacy skills were not necessary to advance his work. Ratna had learned to write labels in Hindi during her work in the fishery. She said that she did not particularly feel in need of enhanced literacy skills, and sees herself as being completely functionally literate even in Hindi, which she only learnt after starting domestic work about six years ago; she did not wish to learn Marathi, the language around her. The only regret she had was at not being able to help her girls with their school work, but that was related to lack of competence in English, as Ratna was clear that she had no problem whatsoever in Malayalam. She also said that she had a very able neighbour (an out-of-work lawyer who doubled as a neighbourhood tutor) who made sure that the girls could cope with the homework and examinations.

So again the question here is, what kind of functional literacy learning programme would be appropriate for these people? Chandra might benefit from literacy related to his livelihood of tailoring, but his economic instability is caused by a medical problem more than illiteracy. They would value school literacy but the issue is what language would most help the children; and in any case it would be for only a short time. It is clear that their urban surroundings and the livelihood opportunities they have directly accessed or know of in Mumbai have shaped their views of desirable and essential skills for their children. Ratna already has literacy skills in more than one language but not in the core language of the city, and she is therefore unable to use her skills widely. Her work makes few demands on her in this respect. She is clear that she is 'educated'. She also feels that learning any other language for survival (for example Hindi) is not very difficult and can easily be acquired when needed, but English is another matter. She strongly feels that good English and a college education may help her daughters to obtain an office job – although that will not necessarily mean that they will have an easier life. Ratna today is unable to articulate a clear demand for literacy of any kind. She does not see added value for herself or her husband but she sees a formal education for her children as the route to a better future.

Some issues arising

The case studies show that the picture drawn by the functional literacy policy makers is far too simple. Life is much more complicated and in particular more immediate. Indeed, we might even wonder whether sometimes the gendered aspect of many recent studies may be exaggerated in much the same way as functional literacy assumptions are untrustworthy. Certainly gender constructs are very important: the case studies confirm that 'women and girls [in India] have traditionally had literacy-independent social roles' (Daswani 1994: 287), and the fishery industry of Ratna was clearly abusive of women employees. But it would seem that, to some of those closely involved, the gender constructs are not the most important issue in their lives. The case studies suggest that in certain circumstances geography, culture and immediate environment (including upbringing, inherited and circumstantial life-shaping factors) and power relations other than gender may be felt to be more urgent.

In terms of motivation, the person who is most unhappy and ready to take advantage of further training is the one person of the four who is excluded from functional literacy programmes because she is already deemed to be 'literate'. And in each case, their situation is constantly changing. 'Literacy for schooling' would be no use for Krishna and Sunita, whereas it would be of immediate help to Ratna and Chandra with their two younger children, although in a few years it will no longer be of any interest. Demand is immediate and temporary, not permanent. The *habitus*, that life world of conjoint assumptions and interrelationships, is constantly being built and rebuilt along with others in 'communities of practice' (Wenger 1998); and some people like Ratna 'fall in' with it rather than deliberately set out to change it. And identities are multiple and constantly being reshaped by themselves and by others – a daughter in the bright lights of the city becomes a fishery supervisor becomes a wife and mother becomes a domestic helper; a tailor is a person with epilepsy; a construction worker is a party activist. Even the one person of the four who is most conscious of her literacy skills in the construction of her own identity does not regard the literacy or lack of literacy of others as important in the construction of their identities. Life moves on – and a common fixed programme of functional literacy learning cannot meet the changing needs of adults.

The issue that functional literacy poses for us then is how to devise formats of learning programmes which can meet the *immediate, changing and wide-ranging* needs of men and women, especially in the different contexts of rural and urban environments which many people move between with remarkable facility and frequency? Clearly a 'one size fits all' learning programme will not be effective to meet these needs.

Notes

1 The term was used by the US army during the Second World War: functional literacy in that context was 'the capacity to understand written instructions necessary for conducting basic military functions and tasks' (Castell *et al.* 1986: 7).
2 A striking instance of this is revealed in a study of schooling in India. Sarangapani 2003: 38: census statistics showed that livestock management in her study area was almost exclusively engaged in by men, whereas fieldwork revealed it was done almost exclusively by women.
3 The names have been changed but not the locations.
4 Education is free for girls up to class 11 in Maharashtra state if they study in state-run schools.

References

Barton, D. (1994a) *Literacy: the Ecology of Written Language*, Oxford: Blackwell
—— (1994b) 'The social impact of literacy' in L. Verhoeven (ed.) *Functional Literacy: Theoretical Issues and Educational Implications*, Amsterdam: Benjamins, pp. 185–97
Bourdieu, P. (1990) *In Other Words: Essays Towards a Reflective Sociology*, Stanford CA: Stanford University Press
Brock, K. and McGee, R. (2002) *Knowing Poverty: Critical Reflections on Participatory Research and Policy*, London: Earthscan
Castell, S., Luke, A. and Egan, K. (eds) (1986) *Literacy, Society and Schooling: a Reader*, Cambridge: Cambridge University Press
Daswani, C.J. (1994) 'Literacy and development in south-east Asia' in L. Verhoeven (ed.) *Functional Literacy: Theoretical Issues and Educational Implications*, Amsterdam: Benjamins, pp. 279–90
DfID (2002) *Improving Livelihoods for the Poor: the Role of Literacy*, Background Briefing, London: DfID
Dighe, A. (1995) 'Deconstructing literacy primers' in *Economic and Political Weekly* (New Delhi), 30 (26): 1559–61
FAL (2001) *Functional Adult Literacy Programme Strategic Investment Plan 2001–2*, Kampala: paper issued by the Ministry of Gender, Labour and Social Development

Gray, W.S. (1956) *The Teaching of Reading and Writing*, Chicago: Scott Foresman

Guidelines (2002) *Guidelines for the Functional Adult Literacy Programme*, Kampala: Ministry of Gender, Labour and Social Development

Hammond, J. and Freebody, P. (1994) 'The question of functionality in literacy: a systemic approach' in L. Verhoeven (ed.) *Functional Literacy: Theoretical Issues and Educational Implications*, Amsterdam: Benjamins, pp. 425–43

Holland, C., Hunter, J. and Kell, C. (2002) 'Literacy in three dimensions: dilemmas of measurement', unpublished paper presented at the twenty-fifth ACAL Annual Conference on Literacy and Numeracy, Sydney, Australia, November

Hunter, J. (2002) Case Study, cited in C. Holland, J. Hunter and C. Kell (eds) 'Literacy in three dimensions: dilemmas of measurement', unpublished paper presented at the twenty-fifth ACAL Annual Conference on Literacy and Numeracy, Sydney, Australia, November

Jones, P.W. (1988) *International Policies for Third World Education: UNESCO, Literacy and Development*, London: Routledge

Lankshear, C. (1985) 'Functional for whom? Two models of functional literacy' in *Conference Proceedings*, Australian Council of Adult Literacy, Sydney

Leseman, P. (1994) 'Socio-cultural determinants of literacy development' in L. Verhoeven (ed.) *Functional Literacy: Theoretical Issues and Educational Implications*, Amsterdam: Benjamins, pp. 163–84

LeVine, K. (1985) *The Social Context of Literacy*, London: Routledge

—— (1994) 'Functional literacy in a changing world' in L. Verhoeven (ed.) *Functional Literacy: Theoretical Issues and Educational Implications*, Amsterdam: Benjamins, pp. 113–31

Mace, J. (2002) *The Give and Take of Writing*, Leicester: NIACE

Moser, C. (1993) *Gender Planning and Development: Theory, Practice and Training*, London: Routledge

Ooijens, J. (1994) 'Literacy for work programs' in L. Verhoeven (ed.) *Functional Literacy: Theoretical Issues and Educational Implications*, Amsterdam: Benjamins, pp. 445–71

Oxenham, J., Diallo, A.H., Katahoire, A.R., Petkova-Mwangi, A. and Sall, O. (2002) *Skills and Literacy Training for Better Livelihoods*, Washington DC: World Bank

Rogers, A. (1994) *Women, Literacy, Income Generation*, Reading: Education for Development

—— (2001) 'Afterword' in B. Street (ed.) *Literacy and Development: Ethnographic Perspectives*, London: Routledge

Saldanha, D. (forthcoming) 'Literacy–communication, urbanisation–development: uneven development in India' in A. Rogers (ed.) *Urban Literacy: Communication, Identities and Learning in Development Contexts*, Hamburg: UNESCO Institute of Education

Sarangapani, P. (2003) *Constructing School Knowledge; an Ethnography of Learning in an Indian Village*, New Delhi: Sage

Schutz, A. (1970) *On Phenomenology and Social Relations: Selected Writings*, Chicago: University of Chicago Press

Sen, A. (1999) *Literacy as Freedom*, Oxford: Oxford University Press

Street, B.V. (1984) *Literacy in Theory and Practice*, Cambridge: Cambridge University Press

—— (1992) 'Literacy practices and the construction of gender' in T. Ingold (ed.) *Companion Encyclopedia of Anthropology*, London: Routledge

Stromquist, N. (1997) *Literacy for Citizenship: Gender and Grassroots Dynamics in Brazil*, Albany: SUNY Press

UNESCO (1988) *Compendium of Statistics on Illiteracy*, Paris: UNESCO

UNESCO (2002a) 'Literacy in Africa', paper for Ministers of Education meeting, Paris: UNESCO

UNESCO (2002b) *Education for All: Is the World on Track?* EFA Global Monitoring Report 2002, Paris: UNESCO

Verhoeven, L. (ed.) (1994) *Functional Literacy: Theoretical Issues and Educational Implications*, Amsterdam: Benjamins

Wagner, D.A. (2002) 'The digital divide and literacy: focusing on the most poor' in D. Istance, H.G. Schuetze and T. Schuller (eds) *International Perspectives on Lifelong Learning: from Recurrent Education to the Knowledge Society*, Buckingham: Open University Press

Wells, G. (1991) 'Apprenticeship in literacy' in C. Walsh (ed.) *Literacy as Praxis*, Norwood NJ: Ablex Publishing

Wenger, E. (1998) *Communities of Practice: Learning, Meaning and Identities*, Cambridge: Cambridge University Press

Westen, M. van den (1994) 'Literacy education and gender: the case of Honduras' in L. Verhoeven (ed.) *Functional Literacy: Theoretical Issues and Educational Implications*, Amsterdam: Benjamins, pp. 257–77

8 'Women are lions in dresses'[1]

Negotiating gender relations in REFLECT learning circles in Lesotho

Gillian Attwood, Jane Castle and Suzanne Smythe

It is a popular belief that women embody a force and hope for change in Africa, and in the world more widely. In a message on International Women's Day, Dr Kofi Annan, the Secretary General of the United Nations, suggested that it is women who hold the key to a better world:

> When women are fully involved, the benefits can be seen immediately: families are healthier and better fed; their income, savings and reinvestment go up. And what is true of families is also true of communities and, in the long run, of whole countries.
>
> (Annan, March 2003)

In order to achieve the Millennium Development Goals and a 'better world', Dr Annan emphasised the importance of promoting literacy among women and girls:

> [Achieving these goals] means promoting the education of girls, who form the majority of the children who are not in school. It means bringing literacy to the half billion adult women who cannot read or write – and who make up two thirds of the world's adult illiterates.

Calls to educate women for the benefit of the nation are not new. It was Malcolm X who first coined the now famous slogan 'To educate a man is to educate an individual but to educate a woman is to educate a nation', a maxim that has since been echoed around the globe. In a 1999 address to the International Conference on Population Development in The Hague, Hilary Clinton asserted that we should 'understand that when we educate a woman, we educate a family and when we educate a family, we educate an entire society'.[2]

Working within a Gender and Development (GAD) theoretical framework, this chapter critically examines and contests the assumptions underlying the logic of the call to educate women and girls as an investment in wider human and economic development. We argue that achieving equal access to education and improving literacy levels among women is not sufficient. We look at the ways in which gender relations between women and men constitute particular constellations of power that frame the terms on which education, development and change are negotiated. And we examine what can be done to reconfigure these relations. Drawing from the experiences of a REFLECT project in Lesotho, we make a case for using REFLECT circles as fora, not only for promoting literacy, but for challenging power relations more generally, and gender relations more specifically.

Theoretical framework

The widespread view that women are best positioned, by virtue of being mothers and caregivers, to impact positively on society is a concept which underlies the 'Women in Development' (WID) paradigm. 'Women-targeted' programmes within this paradigm are premised on the belief that explicit support of women is an effective way to reshape the attitudes and values of society. If women are supported with the means to generate income and become literate, they will in turn pass on these values to their children, who will gradually adopt more 'modern' behaviours and positive attitudes, contributing to change in social, economic and political institutions. These assumptions are strongly influenced by the logic of modernisation theory whereby development is measured in terms of economic growth and a transition to modern society that is characterised by high levels of literacy and a market economy supported by foreign aid, appropriate governmental measures and external investment.

A problem with the women-targeted approach to development is its inherent patriarchal bias. Women are entrenched in positions of nurturer, caregiver and teacher; they are idealised as saviours and granted primary responsibility for reshaping the attitudes of their children and changing the world. Men are positioned as 'the problem', rather than as part of the solution. Their influence and role in shaping attitudes and taking positive action are discounted. However, numerous studies have challenged such a reductionist view of the social influence of men. A study by a South African gender researcher, Nolulamo Gwagwa (1998), shows how sons adopt their fathers as role models. In her study, Gwagwa illustrates how sons learn from their fathers to retain the majority of their income for alcohol, tobacco and girlfriends, while daughters on the other hand adopt their mothers' behaviours, and pool income for household use.

A more recent approach that pays closer attention to the role and contribution of men within the broader socialisation process is the Gender and Development model. Within this conceptual framework, 'gender' is understood to be a socially acquired (rather than a biologically defined) identity based on what it means to be male or female in a particular situation. The basic assumption is that men and women have different experiences based on their respective genders, although a gendered identity might differ according to an individual's class, race, age, religion, sexuality or disability (Kothari 2002). Gender is thus understood as a social and cultural arrangement with forms of social differentiation (such as class, race, caste, etc.) as contributing and intersecting factors within the gender equation.

Within Gender and Development, there is a focus on the continual construction and reconstruction of relationships between men and women with inequalities and power relations expressed in different ways according to the particular constellation of socio-cultural forces at play. For example, white middle-class men and women inherit power in different ways from black working-class men and women. Access to economic and political power differs, as does access to information and other resources such as childcare, medical care and legal assistance. These differences influence people's experience of everyday social reality in profoundly different ways.

The notion of a 'gender contract' (Hirdman 1991) as a particular form of social contract between men and women is useful in terms of understanding how the relations between men and women are socially constructed and negotiated. According to Kimane *et al.* (1998: 124), a gender contract is 'the understood but invisible agreements which regulate relations between men and women at the various levels of society. Collectively, these agreements create a gender system.' The gender system positions men and women in particular ways that contribute to the maintenance of existing social relations, often in favour of men. For example, in Lesotho the dominant breadwinner–homemaker gender contract positions men in the workplace and women within the domain of the home. Work becomes defined predominantly as 'male labour in the workplace', and men are naturalised within this domain. Their role is to earn money and contribute to the well-being of the household. Women take on the reproductive role of child rearing, managing the home and doing household chores, such as cooking, washing and fetching wood. However, within a patriarchal discourse, these types of work are not perceived to be 'real' work. Women who collude with definitions of 'real' work as 'paid work outside the home' are more likely to feel a diminished sense of self-worth and accept subordinate positions within the home. The 'separate spheres' gender contract helps to maintain men's control of women by keeping women subjugated and financially dependent on men.

However, the gender contract is not a closed system. Rather, it changes over time, and with other changes in society. For example, studies have shown that, with the growing unemployment rate, women in southern Africa are increasingly actively looking for work, both formal and informal, in order to supplement the household income that used to be supplied by employed men (Gwagwa 1998: 42). In such cases, women may take over as the breadwinners, with different implications for the gender contract, depending on how the parties concerned acknowledge and adjust to the new arrangements. Mapetla and Schlyter (1998: 2) explain that deviations from contracts are constantly negotiated, 'Negotiations are continuously ongoing, at all levels of society such as in parliaments, at the work places, in the homes and bedrooms.'

Using the notion of a 'patriarchal bargain' Kandiyoti (1997) presents a comparable argument. She argues that women strategise within the constraints of a particular set of social rules and scripts that regulate gender relations. On the surface, both genders accommodate and acquiesce to these rules, yet they are nonetheless contested, redefined and renegotiated (1997: 97). This process of bargaining influences particular forms of resistance in a context and can create space for new areas of struggle:

> These patriarchal bargains ... influence both the potential for and specific forms of women's active or passive resistance in the face of their oppression and are susceptible to historical transformations that open up new areas of struggle and renegotiation of the relations between genders.
>
> (Kandiyoti 1997: 86)

The notion of power underlying the 'gender contract' and the 'patriarchal bargain' is of power as a dynamic and variable factor that can be expressed and exercised in a variety of ways from a variety of positions. Such a notion of power resonates with a Foucauldian perspective on power: 'Power is not something that is acquired, seized or shared, something that one holds on to or allows to slip away; power is exercised from innumerable points' (Foucault 1978: 94).

Even from a position of so-called 'weakness', as the vulnerable homemaker without control over the household income, women exercise power by inventing different strategies to gain access to resources. Gwagwa (1998: 51) illustrates how women in her study employed a variety of other (sometimes devious) tactics to gain access to men's income:

> Elizabeth (42) is involved with a married man. He built her a house, although he stays with his contractual household. When she gets a chance, she steals ... money from him. He is a taxi owner so he

normally travels with cash. Besides all this, Elizabeth clearly says that she expects and will try and get more from this man.

Gwagwa (ibid.) gives another example of a woman who seemingly co-operated with her fiancé's requirement that she disclose her income. However, she confesses to doing so only because she was earning so little and saw the disclosure as a strategy to get more money from him.

The Sesotho proverb 'Basali ke tau li mesana', translated as 'Women are lions in dresses',[3] reveals these hidden power dynamics. This proverb acknowledges the ways in which women outwardly appear to conform to the expectations of the gender contract (symbolised by the wearing of dresses), but inwardly exercise the power of 'a lion', a form of power not manifestly scripted within the gender contract. The power which women have is downplayed as they assume traditionally submissive gender roles.

Acknowledging this particular power dynamic challenges the conventional notion of women as powerless beings who should be given opportunities (often by an outside agent such as an aid organisation or a male) to acquire power. Within such a conventional understanding, women are seen as perpetual victims of gender contracts that position them as losers and men as winners. Sparse acknowledgement is granted to the ways in which women negotiate and exercise power within existing gender contracts. The ways in which such contracts are disrupted are not recognised. According to Kimane and Ntimo-Makara (1998: 124), it is at the point at which gender contracts are disturbed that possibilities for opening up and questioning those contracts become available: 'Over time and depending on the rate at which changes occur in society, these contracts also change. When that happens, the gender contracts get disturbed thereby opening up to questioning.'

The remainder of this chapter describes how communities in Lesotho used REFLECT circles, not only to learn literacy, but also to develop a heightened awareness of gender which enabled circle participants to question and begin to renegotiate gender contracts in their lives. We begin by providing some background information about gender relations in Lesotho, and the REFLECT approach used in the case study.

Gender relations in Lesotho

Lesotho is a small southern African country, completely landlocked by South Africa. After gaining independence from the United Kingdom in 1966, Lesotho underwent a long period of military rule, finally establishing itself as a parliamentary constitutional monarchy in 1993. According to the constitution, the head of state should always be a king. Only in exceptional circumstances (such as when the King is temporarily out of the country) can a Queen or Queen Mother act as the head of state. A woman cannot qualify to be a monarch in her own right (Letuka *et al.* 1997: 23).

Men in Lesotho are legally and culturally the head of the household. They are (officially) responsible for providing for their families, and as such they have overall control over the use of resources, including land, property, livestock and income (ibid.). Traditionally, men dominate the public arenas, while women are restricted to the private domain of the home where they take on domestic and reproductive responsibilities. Women do not commonly participate in the traditional public decision-making meetings, although they make most of the day-to-day decisions in the household. As with the monarchy, positions of 'chief' and 'headman' are inherited through the male line. A woman may only take the office of chief if the male who should succeed is dead, absent or otherwise incapacitated.

Despite the legal and cultural barriers faced by women in Lesotho, some advances were made in the 1990s. For instance, Village Development Councils (VDCs) have been established, and there are apparently more women than men on these community-based democratic leadership structures (ibid.).[4] At a national level, there are now twenty-six women members of the 153 strong National Constituent Assembly.[5]

REFLECT

REFLECT is an acronym for *Re*generated *F*reirean *L*iteracy through *E*mpowering *C*ommunity *T*echniques. REFLECT brings literacy and development together, drawing on two major theoretical strands: the work of the Brazilian educator, Paulo Freire, as well as the participatory development methodology, known as Participatory Rural Appraisal (PRA) (Archer and Cottingham 1996; Fiedrich 1996). PRA is most often used in rural contexts as a means to empower people by using local knowledge as a starting point for development action (Fiedrich 1996: 1). Literacy is seen as intrinsic to a broader educational and development process which emphasises empowerment and the connections between literacy and power (Phnuyal *et al.* 1998). However, REFLECT is quite clear that literacy in itself does not empower, and that the process of broader learning is fundamental to empowerment. The REFLECT process thus encourages participants to think beyond literacy, while at the same time paying close attention to how meaningful use of literacy enables access to other basic rights and avenues of power (Archer 2002).

REFLECT participants meet together as a group regularly, usually twice a week. A facilitator guides the participants through a structured participatory learning process focusing on the issues that the circle members themselves have identified as relevant. There is no predetermined curriculum or printed primer. Using the PRA approach, participants develop their own learning materials as they construct maps, calendars, matrices and other diagrams on the ground, using locally available materials such as seeds, stones, sticks, etc. (Plate 8.1 shows circle participants constructing a map to illustrate deforestation in the area.) This active construction process enables participants to understand more about an issue as they draw on what they know to build their representation of local reality. Literacy is integrated into the process of constructing and recording the graphics as participants label and record their graphics on paper. These recorded graphics become a permanent record of local knowledge that has been systematised in the process of analysing local issues. Participants are encouraged to take ownership of the issues that arise, and respond by taking appropriate action in their communities.

Within REFLECT, gender is understood as an integral part of both understanding and transforming the ways in which oppression operates and power is distributed. REFLECT encourages women and men to look for solutions that will lead to a critical analysis of their environment and transformative action within that environment:

Plate 8.1 Map construction (source: Gillian Attwood).

A gender approach in REFLECT is not just about making women equal to men but transforming the whole structure of society and social relations. . . . Only by analysing and understanding the complex reality of gender oppression and its relationship to other types of oppression can action be taken to transform it.

(Metcalf and Gomez 1998: 99)

The gender perspective promoted by the REFLECT approach is thus compatible with the notion of a gender contract. REFLECT participants are encouraged to analyse and understand the social contracts that shape their lives. They are encouraged to explore how they are implicitly and explicitly implicated in maintaining existing power relations inherent in social contracts.

REFLECT circles in Lesotho

A total of twelve REFLECT circles have been set up in Malealea, a remote area in south-western Lesotho[6] where inhabitants are primarily subsistence farmers. What sets this valley apart from similar areas in Lesotho is the existence of a tourist lodge offering tourists accommodation and a range of activities, including pony trekking and hiking. The lodge has created a variety of employment and development opportunities for local inhabitants.

The REFLECT circles established in Malealea have responded to tourism in different ways. The first REFLECT circle to be established was set up as a craft co-operative, with circle participants generating income by producing and selling craft to tourists. Learning in this circle (termed the 'Co-op circle') focused primarily on income generation opportunities linked with tourism. Participants used REFLECT to structure learning related to managing, operating and organising their craft business. The other eleven REFLECT circles (termed 'village circles') were established in villages farther away from the Malealea Lodge. They were thus less directly concerned with tourism, placing greater emphasis on development issues. The circles were used as spaces to learn more about improving practices related to the management of natural resources, health and sanitation. At certain times tourists wanting to learn more about development activities in the community visited these village circles, but unlike the Co-operative learning circle, the focus of the village circles was less explicitly related to income generation through tourism, especially during the first few years of their existence.

Members of the REFLECT circles ranged in age from sixteen to seventy years, with the majority of members in the thirty to sixty-five age group. Some of the village circles were composed predominantly of shepherds, while others, including the Co-op circle, were a mixture of housewives, farmers, retrenched miners and self-employed people. In five of the twelve circles, the chiefs of the villages joined as participants. In total, 65 per cent of all circle members were women, 35 per cent men. None of the participants or facilitators was significantly better-off than another, all participants being from the same socio-economic background (i.e. peasant farmers).

REFLECT circles were facilitated by local facilitators trained in the REFLECT approach. Only six of these twenty facilitators were men. The predominance of women – facilitators and participants – reflects the skewed gender demographics of the area. (A high proportion of men work as migrant labourers in cities or mines in South Africa, with women staying at home to run the family household.) Some researchers may also explain the predominance of women with the argument that women in Lesotho are generally more adaptable to change and more responsive to issues of development than men, as a result of staying home to look after their families while the men are away (Letuka *et al.* 1997: 29).

Establishing a gendered perspective

Certain mandatory ground rules were established at the inception of all REFLECT circles. These rules guaranteed all participants, men and women, an equal opportunity to participate in discussion and decision making. The establishment of this principle was especially important in a patriarchal context where male participants, already accustomed to public forum participation, entered the circles with more self-assurance and culturally legitimate authority than the female participants. The equal valuing of men and women's knowledge had to be slowly and consciously nurtured in a context where men's knowledge was unconsciously assumed to have more value. The establishment of ground rules highlighting these issues at an early stage in the learning process formed an essential foundation for a gendered perspective and further gender work.

'Further gender work' took different forms over the course of the project. At times, participants looked at gender as part of broader discussions related to more general development issues. For example, participants discussed how deforestation impacted most directly on women as the principal fuel collectors. Women talked about how they were forced to walk longer and longer distances in search of suitable wood for fuel, a time-consuming activity that took them away from other chores. Similarly, when water sources dried up or became polluted, participants discussed how women, rather than men, shouldered the burden of having to cover greater distances to find alternative water sources. Gender concerns were also raised in relation to health and sanitation issues, with participants observing how women, as the primary caregivers, were more directly affected by illness in the family than men.

At other times in the REFLECT project, gender formed a particular learning focus, with participants using a variety of PRA tools to look specifically at the ways in which men and women's lives were structured in relation to gender. For example, participants constructed a daily and a seasonal gender workload calendar to examine how the kinds of work traditionally assigned to men and women influenced their life experience on a daily and yearly basis. The daily workload calendar illustrated how women generally rose earlier and went to bed later than men in order to complete their chores of fetching water, preparing meals, washing clothes, etc. This calendar also showed that women spent more time during the day engaged in chores than men did, although men's chores, for example digging graves, tended to be more demanding in the intensity of labour required. The seasonal gender workload calendar (see Plate 8.2) showed how gender work patterns differed over the course of a year, as opposed to a day. For example, ploughing and planting, done mostly by men, was at its height from September to November. Women on the other hand carried a heavier work load from December to March when crops had to be weeded and again from April to August when crops were ready for harvesting. Women also had more perennial responsibilities, such as childcare, household work and the collection of water and firewood, than men did.

Initially, participants constructed the PRA tools described above in separate gender groups. Once each group had completed the tool, men and women came together to question and discuss their respective perceptions of work loads and what it meant to be a 'man' and a 'woman'. The opportunity for both genders to discuss gendered practices in a space not circumscribed by the usual rules of patriarchy allowed participants to begin to look at cultural attitudes and practices from a different perspective.

Seeing a gendered perspective

Over the course of time, participants developed a heightened awareness of gender and a deeper sense of the ways in which this construct structured their lives. In the words of one of the participants:

> This discussion [about gender] has helped us to appreciate each other, and our work. Even if we are not always able to take on each other's tasks, at least we have a better understanding of what they involve. For example, I didn't know how many different things women do at the same time – cooking, drawing water, looking after the children . . .

Plate 8.2 Constructing a gender calendar (source: Gillian Attwood).

However, such understandings were not easily assumed. A maze of conceptual and emotional obstacles had to be negotiated before an awareness of gender could find root.

One such obstacle was the defensiveness which both men and women seemed to feel when their respective groups came together to discuss the trends or patterns identified within their groups. This was particularly evident in comparative situations, for example when women and men compared work loads. Debate between the two groups easily degenerated into unproductive arguments about the biological superiority of one or the other group. In more than one instance, discussion reached a stalemate, with participants pitted inflexibly against each other. This was especially noticeable when circle facilitators themselves did not fully understand the socially constructed nature of 'gender' as a concept.[7] In such cases, facilitators struggled to reorientate discussion in a way that challenged rather than reinforced gender divisions among participants.

However, more skilled facilitators were able to refocus the attention of a group away from biological gender rivalry, towards an analysis of gender divisions and gender conflict. For example, in some circles facilitators encouraged participants to talk about how life 'as it used to be' had changed. Participants discussed how men were returning to their villages in increasing numbers because of large-scale retrenchments in the South African gold mines. They talked about the difficulties of unemployment, for both the men and their families. One man explained how being retrenched had affected him emotionally as well as financially. Because he was no longer bringing in money to support his family, he felt he had lost his meaningful role as the head of the household. What was he now? He spent most of his time drinking, a pastime which also helped him to forget his problems. Men and women talked about heightened family tensions as women were forced to take on the burden of supporting their families under different conditions. Such discussions were both constructive, and moving. Defensiveness dissolved as participants began to see the commonality of their struggles, and understand the social, rather than personal or biological, origins of their problems. In these instances, participants were more willing to look beyond blame to ways of resolving issues. They discussed how sharing work loads, rather than dividing them, could lighten the burdens they faced. Time availability and capacity, rather than gender, became the determining criteria in negotiating alternative workloads. In a follow-up interview, one participant described the kinds of changes that he and his wife had negotiated:

> I go and draw water now, instead of always expecting my wife to do this. Sometimes when she is away or busy, I go to the pump. And she will tether the animals if I am not around. . . . I used to think it was just natural for women and men to do certain kinds of work, men in the kraal and women in the house, but now I see it can make sense to share these tasks.

However, the cultural stereotypes concerning men and women's work were not always so easily overcome. In fact, 'culture' proved to be a major obstacle in the way of shifting gender relations. It was difficult for participants to imagine changing particular gender relations and roles inscribed within Basotho culture. For example, it is seen as a man's duty to both provide for and discipline his family (including the right to beat an insubordinate wife or child). Men who do not act according to these cultural expectations are not considered 'real' men. Similarly, women who do not bear and raise children in obedience to their husbands are not 'real' women. Many participants saw such cultural notions and practices as static, as 'the Basotho way'. They expressed disbelief that such deep cultural beliefs and practices could (or should) be challenged or negotiated, especially in 'real life' outside the learning circle. Women in particular laughed with incredulity at the idea that men would consider negotiating their authority.

However, there were instances, such as the one described above, where participants were prepared to attempt alternative ways of acting. In another instance, one of the women in the Co-operative learning circle took the discussion about gender and workload division home to her husband. They discussed their respective work loads, and she explained her difficulty in coping with the double work shift, at the Co-op and at home. She asked him whether he could help with the housework, but his immediate response was to dismiss her and laugh at her suggestion that he should take on some of this work. He said that as a man, he could not do women's work. However, the next day she arrived home to find he had done all the laundry, which was drying on the line outside. She was delighted and reported that it had made a real difference to 'the feeling' in the home.[8]

This story was taken back to the Co-operative, and served as an actual example of the possibilities of change, and the potential benefits for the family as a whole. From the Co-operative this story spread to the village learning circles and was used to encourage these facilitators and participants who felt resigned to the inevitability of cultural tradition.

Negotiating a gendered perspective

The explicit focus on gender in the learning circles encouraged debate about the possibility of negotiating gender contracts. Both male and female participants started admitting to the different ways in which they contravened and negotiated traditional gender roles. One facilitator described how she would perform 'male chores', such as feeding the horses, as a way of legitimately being able to ask her husband to assist with household chores in return. Another facilitator explained how her husband would help with the chores, but only within the confines of the home where others could not see this transgression of gender roles:

> My husband will cook and help in the house when I am working in the Co-operative or facilitating my circle. But he won't go outside to draw water because he says the other women will laugh at him and say he has eaten *pehla* [a traditional medicine believed to make men submissive to women].

Participants talked about the benefits of sharing work loads. One man explained how he and his wife were able to get more done when they shared work loads. These discussions not only made the point that gender roles were socially, rather than biologically, constructed but also pointed to the fact that gender contracts can be negotiated and are not always what they appear to be from the outside. Women were not always as submissive and passive as was supposed. It was in this context that the proverb 'Women are lions in dresses' was raised to illustrate the power women have, in spite of the social restrictions they face.

Participants debated who *should* make decisions in different contexts. They began to see alternatives and ask questions about previously accepted social norms regarding gender relations and work loads. They began to see possibilities of negotiating other options. In the words of one of the participants (a newly married woman with a young child):

> Before [coming to the circle] I was afraid to ask these kinds of questions. These discussions have helped me to gain courage and confidence. Before I thought that if I asked such questions I would be running away from my responsibilities as a woman. I thought that I should not bother my husband.

REFLECT learning circles – fora for going beyond literacy

We have argued so far that the REFLECT learning circles offered participants a means to reach beyond literacy to an exploration of gender relations. Participants used the REFLECT meetings to learn more, not only about literacy, but also about each other, and how relations between them were structured. The circles provided a forum for establishing, exploring and negotiating such relations in a number of different ways, at both an individual and a collective level.

First, the ground rules of the mixed-gender learning circles encouraged all members to participate equally and thus supposed a different kind of gender contract from the traditional gender contracts that existed outside the circles. A safe(r) space was created for women to express their opinions in front of men. Both women and men were urged to discuss and question the relationship between the genders, and in all circles, to a greater or lesser extent, participants were able to debate gender and its implications as they explored the ways in which labour was divided. Participants themselves remarked on how space within the circle was different from the space at home. Several of the participants said that they would have loved their husbands or partners to come to the circle and hear the discussion, but expressed reservations about raising the issues themselves at home for fear of abusive repercussions. One participant said that if she had to go home and tell her husband what they had been discussing in the circle, she would not be allowed to return. From this perspective, the REFLECT learning circles offered a protected space for challenging traditional gender contracts and raising awareness of gender oppression, even if only at a conceptual level, for a limited period of time.

Second, the circles provided a constructive and supportive space for women and men to share their respective perceptions of their gender experiences. That there were differences in perceptions became evident in the competitive attitudes manifested when men and women compared their work loads. Such perceptions could be made visible, debated and challenged, and in this way, possibilities of renegotiating or disrupting those relations were opened up.

Third, while the circles created a space for participants to think about gender in their own lives, it also provided a way for the group to take action at a community level. Several circles decided to stage community dramas that dealt with gender issues in a variety of ways. These dramas were performed in public spaces, such as at village meetings, in order to raise wider awareness of gender concerns among both men and women in the community. This kind of action enabled the group to go some way towards merging the space between the public and private spheres, offering both men and women in the wider community an opportunity to think about the possibilities of renegotiating gender contracts. Of particular value in this exercise was the way in which the male circle members, through their participation in the drama, were able to offer other men in the community some alternative models of gender relations and what it means to be 'a man'. Plate 8.3 shows one of the male participants role-playing an active father who takes responsibility for childcare in the home.

The limits of REFLECT learning circles

While the REFLECT learning circles certainly offered possibilities for participants to extend their learning beyond functional literacy towards negotiation of social relations and an engagement with wider empowerment, it is important to recognise the limitations of the circles as spaces for change, and to raise certain questions regarding the process of transformation.

One question relates to the ownership of the learning agenda in circles.

Plate 8.3 Role-playing gender drama (source: Gillian Attwood).

The participatory premise of the methodology assumes that participants themselves identify the issues to be taken up within the REFLECT circles. However, in many patriarchal contexts, gender is not a part of the local agenda (Metcalf and Gomez 1998). There is no word for 'gender' in Sesotho, the local language. Without external intervention from the researchers, it is doubtful that gender would have featured on the list of priorities identified by circle participants in Malealea. The balance between externally introducing an issue and determining its outcome is a fine one. Circle members quickly pick up on what kind of conclusions they are 'supposed to' arrive at, thus casting doubt on the apparently participatory and emancipatory nature of the learning process. Did participants reach certain conclusions because they really believed in the need for change, or because they felt it was required of them?

Linked with this first question is a second question concerning the level of understanding and skill that facilitators require to be able to grapple with the complexity of gender and power relations in a community. Gender is not an easy topic to discuss, particularly when welded to arguments about culture and tradition. It requires a sophisticated understanding of social issues to unravel the relationship between power, gender and culture. Facilitators themselves have often internalised positions of superiority or inferiority and may have no exposure to alternative ways of negotiating gender contracts. Is it realistic to expect facilitators to drive a complex process of social change under such circumstances?

This is a particularly critical question for women, whose knowledge and worth are often questioned within a patriarchal context. Facilitators and participants (who are predominantly women) may face resistance, in the form of physical and verbal abuse, from those reluctant to entertain ideas that threaten the *status quo*. One participant stated openly that if she went home and asked her husband to take on work in the home he would see it as insubordination and would beat her. There is a need for facilitators and participants to be aware of the possible consequences of renegotiating social relationships, particularly within the private sphere where women may be more vulnerable. If facilitators or participants buy into predetermined solutions, they may find themselves excluded or disempowered in other ways (physically, financially, socially), rather than empowered. It is important to acknowledge how, particularly within the private sphere, change may be a gradual process, negotiated on different terms in different ways depending on the context. In the words of one of the participants:

> Circumstances are not the same. Sometimes we can discuss things at home, and sometimes we can't do anything to change the way things are. Sometimes our husbands don't want to change. They go off to the shebeen [bar] and leave us wives working at home.

And finally, while recognising how the particular power dynamics of a context impact on the process of change, it is equally important to recognise that change cannot take place at the individual and community level alone. Commitment to change must also come from 'the top'. If at government level there is not the political will to change discriminatory laws and policies and implement the structures that will enable women to participate fully and equally with men, there is little hope of making headway on any other level.

> [D]evelopment objectives must question structures and superstructures at the same time. Without change in the prevailing superstructure of values, plans and strategies for change in structures will do nothing to improve women's [and men's] lives.
>
> (Bhola 1994: 3)

Conclusion

It is fitting to conclude this chapter by revisiting some of the assumptions that launched it, in particular the belief that promoting literacy among women and girls will result in wider human and economic development. The example of Lesotho makes a case against such an assumption. Women in Lesotho make up the majority of the literate population,[9] yet ironically, in spite of their better education levels, unemployment among women is higher than among men. Where women *are* employed, they continue to earn less than men, and occupy the lower echelons of the job market. And, in spite of being more literate than their husbands, married women in Lesotho still have minority status (Letuka *et al.* 1997: 47). They need the consent of their husbands to get contraceptives from a clinic, or take out a contract on a cell phone. At all levels, men still hold the decision-making positions that matter. Apparently, literacy has *not* empowered women to take their rightful place in the development of either their own households, or of their country. The power of the lion remains restricted by the cut of the dress, designed, it seems, by patriarchy.

This chapter has argued that REFLECT offers a way to loosen the buttons of that dress, to promote a perspective whereby men and women can examine gender and begin to unpack the power dynamics underlying oppressive practices at the family and community level. And therein lies a crucial value of these groups. At least in Malealea, they have provided a vehicle for men and women to begin to reflect on and negotiate the construction and reconstruction of gender relations within the family and even the community. The Malealea case illustrates that these circles can provide a way of engaging men and women co-operatively in debating and slowly reshaping socially defined assumptions, values and attitudes regarding gender in society, surely one of the central challenges facing development. Literacy has certainly come into play, but as a by-product of the learning process rather than as a central learning focus. Seemingly, at least in terms of development and empowerment objectives, dialogue and negotiation constitute a more important function of the REFLECT circles than the promotion of literacy.

Notes

1 A direct translation from the Basotho proverb, 'Basali ke tau li mesana'.
2 http://clinton5.nara.gov/WH/EOP/First_Lady/html/generalspeeches/1999/19990209.html.
3 This proverb, roughly translated as women are 'wolves in sheep's clothing', was identified by a REFLECT circle facilitator during discussions on gender.
4 However, Letuka *et al.* (1997) also point out that while women may predominate

in numerical terms, men who participate on Village Development Committees still hold the positions of power and control.

5 www.ipu.org/wmn-e/classif.htm.

6 These REFLECT circles were established as part of an earlier adult education research project initiated in 2001 under the auspices of the Cyril O. Houle Scholars in Adult and Continuing Education Program. Its objective was to explore how a rural sub-Saharan African community would engage with the REFLECT approach. (Despite the promise of this approach, no REFLECT circles had been established previously in Lesotho. Literacy programmes in Lesotho tended to adopt a more functional approach.) The results of this research are published by the University of Georgia's Department of Adult Education in *Global Research Perspectives* 3 (May 2003). Later funding for the project came from the Canadian Co-operative Association.

7 The fact that there is no Sesotho word for 'gender' also didn't help facilitators or participants to grasp the concept more easily.

8 However, it was not to last. In a follow-up interview a few months later, the woman reported that her husband had abandoned his willingness to help, saying that such things were for people living in cities, not men in rural areas. They followed the 'old ways'.

9 Eighty per cent of women in Lesotho are literate, as opposed to 60 per cent of men (UNDP *Human Development Report,* 1997).

References

Annan, K. (2003) 'UN Press Release: Message on International Women's Day', www.escwa.org.lb/information/press/un/2003/mar

Archer, D. (2002) *REFLECT: Beyond Literacy to Communication,* London: ActionAid

Archer, D. and Cottingham, S. (1996) *REFLECT Mother Manual,* London: ActionAid

Bhola, H.S. (1994) 'Women's literacy: a curriculum of assertion, resistance, and accommodation?' *Convergence,* 27 (2–3): 41–51

Fiedrich, M. (1996) *Literacy in Circles?* Working Paper 2, London: ActionAid

Foucault, M. (1978) *The History of Sexuality I, An Introduction,* trans. R. Hurley, New York: Random House

Gwagwa, N.N. (1998) '"Money as a source of tension": an analysis of low income households in Durban' in A. Larsson, M. Mapetla and A. Schlyter (eds) *Changing Gender Relations in Southern Africa: Issues of Urban Life,* Roma, Lesotho: Institute of Southern African Studies

Hirdman, Y. (1991) 'The gender system' in T. Andreason and A. Borschorst (eds) *Moving On: New Perspective on Women's Movement,* Aarhus: Aarhus University Press

Kandiyoti, D. (1997) 'Bargaining with patriarchy' in N. Visvanathan, L. Duggan, L. Nisonoff and N. Wiegersma (eds) *The Women, Gender and Development Reader,* London: Zed Books

Kimane, I. and Ntimo-Makara, M. (1998) 'The gender dimension of urban migration in Lesotho' in A. Larsson, M. Mapetla and A. Schlyter (eds) *Changing Gender Relations in Southern Africa: Issues of Urban Life,* Rome and Lesotho: Institute of Southern African Studies

Kothari, U. (2002) 'Feminist and postcolonial challenges to development' in U.

Kothari and M. Minogue (eds) *Development Theory and Practice: Critical Perspectives*, Basingstoke: Palgrave

Larsson, A., Mapetla, M. and Schlyter, A. (1998) *Changing Gender Relations in Southern Africa: Issues of Urban Life*, Roma, Lesotho: Institute of Southern African Studies

Letuka, P., Matashane, K. and Morolong, B. (1997) *Beyond Inequalities: Women in Lesotho*, Maseru: Women and Law in Southern Africa

Mapetla, M. and Schlyter, A. (1998) 'Introduction' in A. Larsson, M. Mapetla and A. Schlyter (eds) *Changing Gender Relations in Southern Africa: Issues of Urban Life*, Roma, Lesotho: Institute of Southern African Studies

Metcalf, K. and Gomez, G. (1998) 'Gender and REFLECT' in *PLA Notes*, 32, London: International Institute for Environment and Development

Phnuyal, B., Archer, D. and Cottingham, S. (1998) 'Reflections on REFLECT' in *PLA Notes*, 32, London: International Institute for Environment and Development

UNDP (1997) *Human Development Report 1997*, New York: Oxford University Press

9 Closing the gap

Issues in gender-integrated training of adult literacy facilitators – possibilities, progress and resistance

Juliet McCaffery

This chapter explores how the gap between gender policy and practice was addressed through the training of adult literacy facilitators in gender-integrated literacy programmes in north-eastern Nigeria and Upper Egypt. The successful resolution of initial gender difficulties in the programme in Nigeria led me to look closely at the gendered interactions during the training in Egypt. It is my contention that though gender issues were not included in the design of the training, they emerged, were discussed, debated and contested and were the catalyst in a slowly changing dynamic which ultimately led to positive gender outcomes.

In this chapter I briefly describe the programmes, the socio-cultural context, the ideological and theoretical basis of the literacy programmes and the methodology used. I then consider the gendered profiles of the training programmes – trainers, trainees and the structure – before exploring gendered interactions, dialogue and debate.

Since the 1980s and the recognition that development did not always improve the lives of women, there has been increasing and well documented attention given to gender issues. The Millennium Development Goal 'to promote gender equity and empower women' with the target to eliminate gender disparity by 2015 gave an impetus to initiatives to raise the educational levels of women and girls. As over 600 million adult women are unable to read, adult literacy programmes for women should be an important component in this strategy. Research suggests that enrolling in adult literacy classes can have a significant impact on raising women's self-esteem and social confidence, which results in positive changes at household and community level (Bown 1993). Unfortunately there is still a significant gap between gender policy and practice. Many programmes and projects contain excellent gendered goals, which disappear in the details of implementation. At one stage in the Nigerian programme, the focus on women and girls was in danger of being subsumed into gender-blind processes and outcomes.

The programmes

In both Upper Egypt and north-eastern Nigeria the purpose of the programmes was poverty reduction through raising the level of literacy in targeted districts and communities.[1] The objective was to enhance learning
achievement, particularly among girls and women, by improving quality
and increasing access to basic education. The programme in Egypt
extended and developed the participatory and interactive approaches
developed during the previous project.[2] It operated in twenty-two
communities in six governorates in Upper Egypt addressing the literacy
needs of 100,000 people. In Nigeria the programme operated in three
states and with pastoral nomadic communities[3] and aimed to double the
number of male and female literacy learners. Selection of project areas in
both programmes was according to economic and educational indicators
– low incomes, low literacy levels and significant gender disparity. Individual projects in the programme were in rural areas or small towns.

Upper Egypt[4] is an integral part of the Arabic culture of the Middle
East, while north-eastern Nigeria is situated on the edge of the Sahara
between North and sub-Saharan Africa. Though there are strong differences in the history and organisation of the countries at macro-level, the
two project areas discussed here are both strongly Islamic, with small
Christian minorities. This has created a system of beliefs and way of life at
the micro-level of rural communities with many similarities between the
two contexts. Both these societies are strongly patriarchal with women
largely excluded from decision-making processes at all levels. Power in the
family, the community, the state and at national level is held by men. In
both northern Nigeria and Egypt, women's mobility was restricted to a
greater or lesser extent, depending on community traditions and the wish
of individual husbands. Polygamy was common in the project areas in
both countries. Seclusion was practised more commonly in Nigeria than
in Egypt, though not among the nomadic Fulani. The *hijab* was worn by
both Moslem and Christians in Egypt, but faces were not commonly
veiled. In both countries, literacy levels are low and the number of illiterate women is almost twice that of men.[5] Among the nomadic Fulani, it was
estimated that less than 10 per cent of men were literate and less than
1 per cent of women.[6] Men and women receive instruction in the Koran
from traditional community religious teachers and learn to recite the
Koran in Arabic.

Theory and practice

In both programmes a participatory approach drew on the theories of the
New Literacy Studies, the literacy events and practices of the communities

(Street 1984, 2001; Barton 1991; Heath 1982; Maddox 2001; Papen 2001). This approach locates literacy in the context of the community and focuses on the literacy and numeracy people require in their everyday life. Knowledge of the communities' economic, social and cultural practices was a prerequisite. PRA surveys were carried out before establishing literacy classes in order to ensure the literacy programmes were relevant. The use of primers was discouraged in both programmes.

In Nigeria the participatory approach was termed 'Learner Oriented Community Adult Literacy' (LOCAL)[7] to denote the learner and community-centred focus. The approach was systematised into a nine-stage framework, identifying the learners' hopes, aspirations and motivation in attending literacy classes. From this information the facilitator and learners jointly identified learning priorities and agreed a curriculum. In the Egyptian programme a new *Teachers' Guide* was written to provide a framework for a locally determined negotiated curriculum.[8]

The data on which this chapter is based were collected in various ways at different times. In Nigeria the detailed field notes I took during the training courses, advisory and evaluative consultancies were the basis of reports to the British Council and this chapter. In Egypt I had the luxury of simultaneous translation and took a detailed, almost verbatim transcript of the proceedings in two initial training courses for literacy facilitators. My interest was in exploring perceptions, actions and interactions, adopting ethnomethodological and phenomenological approaches. Discourse analysis was used to understand and interpret linguistic interactions.

As a participant in the training and a consultant on both programmes, my position as a researcher was not one of uninvolved neutrality. As technical adviser and trainer, I was an actor with some agency. My own identities of wife, mother and worker led over many years to my interest in gender issues and women's empowerment and enabled me to understand the contradictions and dilemmas with which both men and women were grappling. My position and experience as literacy consultant and sometime researcher and experience of working in other cultures gave me a broad perspective and an appreciation of how both positive and oppressive values are differently expressed in different cultures.

In Egypt my direct influence during the courses was small as the training was carried out in Arabic. I made few interventions, allowing the discourse to proceed in its own way. In describing and analysing the training I am not attempting 'to give voice'; the subjects speak for themselves. I am trying to understand how ideas on gender emerged, were expressed and contested.

Training methodology, purpose and structure

The training of literacy facilitators takes place, like the literacy programmes, in the broader context of 'The institutional structures, social
relationships, economic conditions, historical processes and the ideological formations in which literacy is embedded' (Street 2002: 21) and in
the ideologies surrounding gender roles in the community (Zubair 2001).
The purpose of the training was to provide literacy facilitators with sufficient knowledge and skill to enable them to develop an appropriate and
relevant negotiated curriculum. Also emphasised were the importance of
a positive attitude and an awareness of the skills, knowledge and life
experience that adult learners bring to the learning situation.

This modelling of practice was achieved in very different ways owing to
the difference in size of the programmes. In both programmes two states
or governorates combined for reasons of time and money. In Nigeria
thirty was the maximum number of people on any training course. In
Egypt there was an urgent need to train a large number of facilitators very
quickly to open 50 per cent of the classes by a certain date or the funding
would be withdrawn. In two months 175 women and 110 men were
trained on three courses. In addition between twelve and twenty-five trainers participated in each training. The high numbers provided a challenge
to the principle of participatory training and a complex training structure
was devised. Groups of thirty, each supported by a training co-ordinator,
were subdivided into three smaller working groups, each assisted by training facilitators. In this way the training became interactive, addressed the
needs of the individual and modelled facilitating learning.

In many literacy programmes, two weeks' training is deemed sufficient.
In Nigeria initial training was the first step in a four-stage process of initial
training, operationalisation, monitoring and follow-up training, followed
by courses on developing local materials, training trainers and monitoring
and evaluation. A range of training courses is planned in Egypt.[9]

Training in gender awareness or gender planning (Levy 1991; Moser
1993) was not considered appropriate to the cultural context. However
the training had to ensure that the focus on women was not subsumed
into a gender-blind implementation process. Exercises and activities were
included in the training to raise issues and provide opportunities for discussion. These included identifying the literacy hopes, aspirations and
needs of both women and men, and using PRA techniques to identify
daily tasks and economic activities, which drew attention to gender issues
and the often unrecognised contribution of women's paid and unpaid
labour.

Who is trained?

In gendered societies it is highly desirable, if not essential, that women are taught by women and men by men. This necessitated training women facilitators. In the southern Nigerian projects men and women participated in roughly equal numbers. In contrast, only four women attended the initial training for the two projects in the north-east and the facilitators among the nomadic Fulani were all men. In Egypt the numbers of men and women attending the initial training reflected the larger number of classes to be opened for women, with almost gender parity in the first training and significantly more women in the second and third, reflecting a higher gender differential in literacy levels in those communities.

Trainers

The attitude of the male trainers in both projects was complex. The gender imbalance in the training team in Egypt accurately reflected the gendered power structure in the organisation, in which men made the decisions. Senior literacy personnel at central and branch level were predominantly senior ex-army officers. Though civilians were also employed, there were very few women in the central or branch cadres at any level. The training team consisted of a university professor, national consultants, senior literacy staff and myself. They were supported by governorate literacy staff and by the programme's field co-ordinators whose responsibility was to mobilise the communities and support the classes. Apart from me, only four people involved in training were women.

Their attitudes were complicated. The trainers strongly believed women and girls should have greater access to education. Though none of them overtly challenged patriarchal power structures, they supported the female facilitators in different ways.

Prior to the training, the team were concerned that the women they had selected would not be sufficiently competent to work effectively in the flexible, community-oriented approach to literacy that the programme had adopted. They had difficulty in recognising their potential intellectual level and agency. This was at least in part due to the highly centralised bureaucracy in Egypt. As a result Upper Egypt received few resources until relatively recently. Competence and capacity were assumed to reside in Cairo. The trainers were therefore surprised at the level of confidence and active participation some women facilitators displayed from the start of the training.

I, and two younger Nigerian men with considerable experience of working in NGOs, planned and carried out the training in Nigeria. In

Nigeria, age is greatly respected and rarely challenged. The combination of age and gender provided a balance of power, but my role as the older team leader was the deciding factor in terms of power relationships. The young Nigerian men accepted the principle of gender equity and were concerned at seclusion, lack of educational opportunities and early marriage with its potentially damaging effects of early childbirth. Their personal lives reflected this awareness. They had no concerns over the competence of the facilitators, whose level of education was generally lower than that of their Egyptian counterparts. Experience in working at community level in NGOs may have given them a realistic and more positive view of the potential of rural people.

Any challenge to the *status quo* had to come from within the culture. The lack of women trainers in both projects made this problematic. It was mitigated in both situations by the presence of powerful women closely associated with the training, but not trainers. Four women were on the LGA Education Project Committee on one of the north-eastern projects. These included the head of women's education in the town, who was quietly strongly supportive, and the head of women's development, a dynamic, effective and outspoken woman who never failed to challenge the gender imbalance and to remind her male colleagues of the importance of women. She proved a powerful ally. Two young interpreters assisted me in Egypt. One also worked in the field of human rights. Though not a trainer for the literacy programme she trained translators, a position which increased her status. We developed a close relationship owing to a mutual interest in women's empowerment. She was particularly interested in gender-biased language.

Childcare

No childcare was provided for trainers or trainees on either programme despite the high number of women anticipated. The question simply had not arisen. Neither project had budgeted for childcare. In both countries young children were brought to the training. On the first Egyptian training five women brought children under eighteen months and two men brought boys between two and three years of age. On the second, which was not residential, five women brought babies whom they discreetly breast-fed when required. Male participants and male trainers would quite frequently hold babies for the mothers. Several men and several women brought older children on different days.

If a baby cried continuously the mother would take it outside the room. Two women facilitators complained about the babies crying and asked for 'the problem to be solved'. The ex-brigadier in charge of the training responded immediately:

BRIGADIER: Do you have children here?

FEMALE FACILITATOR: No.

BRIGADIER: I thought not or you would not have said this is a problem. Think of it as music accompanying the film. We will have children in the class, as they will need to bring them. This is the reality and we have to deal with realities.

A senior manager was proactive. On seeing no children at the second training course, he made enquiries and discovered that the facilitators had been discouraged from bringing the children. He invited them to do so, saying to the trainers, 'I expect a lot of children will come tomorrow. I want us to welcome them. The more the mothers feel we are welcoming the children, the more they will participate. It is very important at the humanitarian level that no mother will suffer because of her children.' Children tended to sit quietly on their mothers' or fathers' laps or on chairs often falling asleep.

Three of the female trainers in Egypt had very young children. One had a baby only three months old. Neither had ongoing permanent childcare. In both cases their mothers, who had previously worked in professional occupations, accompanied their daughters to look after the children. While the participants' children were incorporated into the training, the trainers' children were not seen during the day and only occasionally included in social interaction in the evening.

In private conversation these trainers agreed that working with young children was very hard. The impression throughout was that there was no bar to professional working women but they were expected to participate fully and did so. No concessions were given, and none was taken. The possibility of organised childcare for either participants or trainers was not mentioned.

Education, marriage and 'security'

In both countries the levels of female illiteracy reflected the gender disparity in school enrolment and achievement. The difficulty in finding culturally and linguistically acceptable female teachers was one issue, particularly among the nomadic Fulani in north-eastern Nigeria. Only a tiny minority of nomadic girls went to school, and non-Fulani teachers neither understood their culture nor spoke their language. Attempts were made to overcome this in the primary component programme with limited success.

One community in Egypt had retained many of their customs and their Libyan accent, of which they were very proud.[10] Teachers from inside the community who could understand them were needed. Whilst this may have been an issue, it was not mentioned in the PRA surveys carried out during the project design phases. In both countries these demonstrated that some families believed in educating girls, poverty forced others to make choices, some considered educating boys more important than educating girls and, in some very traditional communities, parents insisted their girls were not educated.

Discussions in the training reflected a similar range of attitudes and became intertwined with issues concerning marriage: 'Parents get their daughter married early so they won't spend much on her school fees – they need certain things like bags and so on. Parents won't spend that amount.' A daughter's 'security' was frequently mentioned. The phrase implies the importance of the girl's chastity before marriage, her behaviour in relation to feminine modesty and appropriate conduct. Women's behaviour is a key component in determining family honour and social status. Withdrawal from school, close supervision and early marriage are more likely to secure the desired outcome than attending prep or secondary school away from the vigilance of the family and community.

Male attitudes could be contradictory. One of the male national consultants said, 'When the girls are at home they are good, but when they are out of the house, they become irresponsible.' He went on, 'The schools should therefore be placed so as to ensure safety and accord with cultural perceptions.' His accounts of his own behaviour indicated that he was not averse to taking advantage of what he considered girls' 'irresponsible' behaviour.

Group members from one village stated that 'There are – a lot of fears about our women – in the old days the school was five kilometres away from the village – that was the primary – even those who went there couldn't continue to prep.' This fear of distance was reinforced by the story of one girl who had entered an 'unofficial marriage' to the bus driver without her parents' knowledge.[11]

The following extract from the transcript of a discussion during training in Egypt in the form of question-and-answer demonstrates some uncertainty and reflection on the subject of early marriage:

> TRAINER (M.): What is early marriage? How old are girls in your community when they get married?
> FEMALE FACILITATOR 1: Twelve.
> TRAINER: Do you think twelve, thirteen or fourteen are a suitable age?
> FEMALE FACILITATOR 1: No, it's not.
> TRAINER: Do you agree?
> MALE FACILITATOR 1: *(pause)* I wasn't paying attention.
> TRAINER: Do you agree with her?
> MALE FACILITATOR 1: No, it's not suitable.
> TRAINER: What is a suitable age for marrying?

MALE FACILITATOR 1: Twenty-five years, so she is a suitable age for responsibility.

TRAINER: Why not earlier?

FEMALE FACILITATOR 1: Too early.[12] Children are not strong enough, the mother becomes weak.

FEMALE FACILITATOR 3: I married when I was fourteen and I have two children. My health is weak now and I can't help them.

TRAINER: Will the children suffer if the mother is too young?

FEMALE FACILITATOR 4: When I got my second child before the first one was a year old, I was not able to breast-feed my older child.

TRAINER: As residents we are becoming more, is this related to early marriage?

FEMALE FACILITATOR 3: Yes, because she will have more babies.

TRAINER: Is there a relationship with illiteracy?

FEMALE FACILITATOR 2: Yes, because it makes boys and girls drop out of school.

FEMALE FACILITATOR 3: Also when a girl gets married early, she gets more children and she cannot educate them all.

FEMALE FACILITATOR 1: Also they do not send the older children to school, because they want them to help with the younger children.

TRAINER: We now know that early marriage causes ill health with the mother, more children. How can we solve it?

FEMALE FACILITATOR 1: Educate girls.

TRAINER: How will that help?

FEMALE FACILITATOR 3: If she is educated she will not get married until she finishes school.

It was noticeable that no counter arguments were put forward, despite the fact that early marriage is the norm in this community and it might be assumed that the group disapproved of early marriage. If the conversation is analysed in terms of the sequential positions, justifications and excuses, preferred and 'dispreferred' responses (Potter and Wetherell 2002: 76–85), a different interpretation of the conversation emerges. The second facilitator, a man, is directly addressed by the trainer, but he delays and tries to avoid the question. His social position as a professional in the context of the literacy programme requires him to give a particular answer – that marriage at twelve, thirteen or fourteen is too early. When the question is repeated he is unable to resist the pressure but the pause before replying suggests he has given a 'dispreferred' response, the response expected, but one he does not agree with. Having provided one response he has no hesitation in providing a second answer 'twenty-five years ...'; the lack of a pause for thought suggests an automatic answer.

An analysis which suggests the answers are strongly influenced by the context is reinforced by a comment from one of the field co-ordinators, who said it was a topic they were unable to explore effectively in the village when undertaking the PRA survey, as people did not want to talk.

In the second part of the dialogue the trainer moves on to the issue of family size. This is a topical issue in Egypt, as there is a government programme to reduce population growth and to encourage family planning. The men are silent during this part of the conversation. The subject of marriage, roles and power structures within marriage was a delicate issue. In some countries one of the reasons for educating girls was to secure a better husband.[13] The comment by a male facilitator suggests that this did not apply, at least in his community: 'The father chooses the husband for the girl and [it] doesn't matter that he is educated or not.'

The issue of polygamy was also raised and the following comment made by a female facilitator:

> Men marry two or three women. There are lots of girls in the village. It is not expensive. Eight hundred Egyptian pounds or so – gets the bedroom. (They) marry girls when they are young. Even if she's notorious (they) will still marry them.

She is countering the possible assertion that marrying several women is expensive or difficult and in a sense providing an excuse for men taking several wives, but then goes on to say that:

> Polygamy affects education. If he's got two women, if one has a strong character, she will discourage him from educating the other's children.

The obedience of the wife to the husband was the accepted norm, but there were exceptions:

FEMALE FACILITATOR 1: The wife obeys the husband.
FEMALE FACILITATOR 2: I came to the training though my husband said I shouldn't.
FEMALE FACILITATOR 3: Perhaps the husband should obey the wife . . . [*laughter*].

A woman facilitator in Nigeria also disobeyed her husband in order to attend the training programme.

Language

In both the programmes, language directly or indirectly gave rise to misunderstanding and conflict. Language use is a difficult issue. Discourse theory states that language frames action, not only expressing our thoughts and emotions but determining our thoughts and actions. Feminist analysis of language has resulted in changes in language use, particularly in respect of the assumption that female is incorporated and included in masculine terminology such as 'mankind'.

In Nigeria the neutrality of English, in relation to masculine and feminine, assisted in obscuring the gendered nature of the objectives, leading quite reasonably to a genuine misunderstanding. The language in much of the CEP Logical Framework, particularly in the primary sector, was gender-neutral, referring to 'children', to 'pupils', to 'facilitators' and to 'adult learners'. The number of facilitators and adult literacy instructors to be trained was not gender-specific though the target was to double the number of men and women attending literacy classes. This target was gender-specific. Without such specificity, it is unlikely the project purpose in relation to 'a focus on women' would have been achieved, at least in the northern projects.

In line with the project philosophy of community participation, the project manager asked the village and ward chiefs to send someone to be trained as a literacy facilitator prior to opening a class in the village. The chiefs were men, the course was residential and most chiefs asked men to represent their village or ward. The neutral English 'literacy facilitator or instructor' for both men and women had naturally been translated into the masculine form. The problem of training men to teach women was pointed out. By calculating the number of literacy classes required to double the number of women attending literacy classes, it was clear to all concerned, including the project manager and his Education Project Committee, that more women facilitators were required. They very much wanted the project to succeed. After some discussion it was agreed that two training courses would be organised for women only. Women with sufficient education were found, invited, attended, were trained and opened classes.

The language issue in the Egyptian project was also around the use of the masculine and feminine forms. The area of contestation was the use of the masculine or feminine form for the Arabic of both learners and facilitators. Over two-thirds of the classes to be opened were for women; thus women were in the majority on all training courses, yet the masculine forms of both facilitators and learners were commonly used. There were some exceptions. One of the national consultants consistently used both male and female learners in a session on communication: 'Building the education curriculum according to the needs of male and female learners'. On one occasion when he only used the feminine form he was asked why. He replied: 'We have a purpose – because our project is targeting females.' Another trainer referred to male and female facilitators at the beginning of his input, but then said he would use the male form 'and this would include females as well'. Later he referred to 'pupils' in the masculine form. Both the use of the feminine form and an explanation for the use of the male form were the exception rather than the rule.

The prime example of the inappropriateness of the use of the masculine was a male facilitator performing a teaching/learning role-play with three women. They were standing in front of him as he referred to them as 'learners' in the masculine. The interpreter challenged this:

INTERPRETER: Why do you use the masculine when they are women standing in front of you?

FEMALE FACILITATOR [*acting as a learner*]: It refers to both.

INTERPRETER: But you are a woman. How come you are accepting being addressed as a man?

FEMALE FACILITATOR: It's just that he is a male teacher and he is addressing learners.

INTERPRETER: But the learners in front of him are female.

The dialogue continued, and then crossed gender lines:

INTERPRETER: Why are you using the male form?

FEMALE FACILITATOR: I am used to teaching both men and women.

INTERPRETER: Do you teach males or females?

FEMALE FACILITATOR: I said 'men' without thinking.

INTERPRETER: I want to ask you a question. Do you teach males or females?

FEMALE FACILITATOR 1: It should be women to include me.

MALE TRAINER [*interrupting*]: Both are included in the male ... but woman is created from man's rib, so men come first.

INTERPRETER [*aside*]: The Genesis story originates from Babylon. The man is ill, the woman is trying to treat his rib. It was altered.

FEMALE FACILITATOR 2 TO TRAINER: But you are using the male form.

MALE TRAINER: I am sorry.

MALE FACILITATOR: But the male form is also used in the *Teachers' Guide.*

MALE FIELD CO-ORDINATOR: When we have a man, we talk about malelearners and when we have a woman we also find they talk about male learners, so both men and women need to think about this.

The facilitator was correct in stating that the newly published *Teachers' Guide* used the male form throughout, but any departure from this was still unusual (Mernissi 1983: 177). The interpreter was particularly annoyed at this. 'I went through the *Guide* and made the references to male and female teachers and male and female learners. It took me a long time, but they have all been taken out.' A day later a further conversation took place:

> INTERPRETER: Who will you be teaching?
> FEMALE FACILITATOR 1: Women.
> INTERPRETER: So why do we keep referring to male facilitators and male learners?
> FEMALE FACILITATOR 1: But male refers to both.
> INTERPRETER: No, we have a word for female facilitators.
> FEMALE FACILITATOR 1: But if I go back to the village, people will be very upset if we say female learners . . .

This woman's anxiety at defying linguistic conventions by using the feminine noun was apparent. The interpreter ignored the next speaker's attempt to discredit her argument by challenging her sexuality and placing her as outside the generality of women.

> INTERPRETER: How can you call for equality if you are giving up your right to be called a woman?
> INTERPRETER: How many of you are married?
> INTERPRETER: Who does the cooking?
> FEMALE FACILITATOR 2: Me.
> INTERPRETER: Who looks after the children?
> FEMALE FACILITATOR 2: Me
> INTERPRETER: Who goes out to work?
> FEMALE FACILITATOR 2: Both of us.
> INTERPRETER: What does your husband do when he cones home?
> FEMALE FACILITATOR 2: He is tired.
> INTERPRETER: But you are tired.
> FEMALE FACILITATOR 2: But if I go somewhere, he will stand and give me the chair.
> FEMALE FACILITATOR 3: Why then, should we be equal?
> FEMALE FACILITATOR 2: But this doesn't happen now . . .
> INTERPRETER: She should be recognised and referred to as a woman. If you do not, you will not be able to see learners' perspective . . . Male learners need to farm, and so on. Do women have the same needs?
> FEMALE FACILITATOR 2: Of course not.

    INTERPRETER: So if you don't pick up the needs you won't be able to
    help them.

The interpreter then referred to a famous case in which a woman was
beaten up by her husband. When asked, the woman had replied, 'But he
is my husband: he can beat me up.' This caused the women to reflect, and
one said:

    FEMALE FACILITATOR: But how can we get equality?
    INTERPRETER: You have to do it intelligently.
    FEMALE FACILITATOR: But some women can do everything.
    INTERPRETER: But you have to limit to your own reality, to you, your
    homes and your village.[14]

In this dialogue the speaker is beginning to move from the position of
a subject complicit in the construction of marginalisation to the begin-
nings of reconstructing the self, a process successfully achieved by the
female facilitator from a nearby small town who declared her wish to be
mayor.

These exchanges illustrate the social construction of identity through
discourse, the perception of the self with or without agency and how
agency can be acquired. As was pointed out, this has to be done in the cultural context of what forms of discourse are acceptable. Culturally unac-
ceptable discourse may be ineffective and have a negative impact.

The consistent use of both masculine and feminine is clumsy, as the
verbs as well as the nouns also have to be gendered. So the sentences
might read: 'Male facilitators and female facilitators planned (m.)
planned (f.) an outing with male learners and female learners.' While this
linguistic clumsiness is acknowledged, consistent use of the male form
frames thought, images and therefore action. It maintains the power relationships and patterns of domination and subordination (Potter and
Wetherell 2002: 109).

When considering learners' aspirations, literacy requirements or difficulties, an equal number of examples of men and women were given.
However male occupations, such as carpenter and fisherman, were mentioned more frequently than female occupations. If women are not kept
equally in mind, the literacy needs and aspirations of the male learners
dominate and the curriculum becomes male-oriented. The stories of
embarrassing encounters due to inability to read or calculate were predominantly female, but there were also positive and personal examples of
the capacities of non-literate women: 'Some of our mothers are illiterate,
but they have raised us well and educated us. Just because they cannot
read and write does not mean they are ignorant.'

Production of materials

Training in the creation and production of learner and facilitator-generated materials (LGMs) has the potential to provide opportunities for self-expression. The level of reflection and self-expression in the women's writing varied considerably. In north-eastern Nigeria many of the facilitators' stories were impersonal community histories or folk tales. Stories by women reflecting on their lives, particularly unhappy lives, initially received disapproval. During one training course in Egypt two women facilitators chose to read out their experiences of how they had been denied education, demonstrating their own search for voice and identity through writing reflecting the same process that takes place in the literacy class.[15] This writing also enabled men to comment on difficult issues, such as the psychological impact of seclusion on women and the difficulties men may experience when faced with competition between two wives. A few began to reflect that changes in the construction of gender relations offered some advantages for men as well as women.

While the interpreters were able to raise issues and challenge views at an intellectual level, the weight of tradition and moral probity was harder to ignore. The interpreter and the young administrator still felt unable to use the hotel swimming pool when the male trainers were present. The use of the pool on alternate evenings was negotiated. Calling it a joke, some of the men broke this agreement and turned up when we were swimming. The women held their ground but were extremely embarrassed and rarely used the pool afterwards. The men had successfully reclaimed ground.

Critical events

There was no overtly 'gender' element in any of the training described above, the introduction of issues relating to literacy led directly into discussions on gender. The discussions on the use of masculine and feminine forms were particularly critical in Egypt in opening up the debate. The views expressed by both men and women gave women permission to ask questions and begin to appreciate that the norm in their particular community was not necessarily universal. The contributions of some showed considerable reflection.

In Nigeria the critical event was the low number of female trainers for the first training for the north-eastern projects. The realisation that language use was a contributory factor resulted in unambiguous communication and requests for women with enough education to train as facilitators. It also led to the formation of a clear gender strategy. A gender analysis of the two north-eastern projects was undertaken, resulting in a ten-point

Gender Action Plan (McCaffery 1998). This included specifying gender targets for participants and trainers in all training, organising women-only training courses, setting gender targets for membership of all committees and all PRA survey teams and organising gender training for programme managers and committee chairs. Women trainers from regional NGOs were invited to make specific gender inputs to the literacy training, which further opened up the discussions and led to facilitators analysing their communities and developing their own gender action plans, including challenging 'negative practices'. A month before the end of the project, the target to double the number of women attending literacy classes in one of the north-eastern projects had been exceeded by 30 per cent and thirty-four women had been trained as facilitators, as well as twenty-four men.

The nomadic project in relation to women was also successful, though the causes and the 'critical events' responsible for this were more diffuse. One factor appears to have been the policy of not challenging community cultural norms. Gradually a slow change took place. The clan leaders led by example and sent their wives to literacy classes. A male relative was allowed to teach the clan women. Two and a half years after the project started, fourteen male instructors and ten female instructors had been trained and 162 women were attending classes, comparing well with 209 men. A class for young married girls was also established.

Conclusion

In Nigeria an analysis of the three-year programme had shown that the training of the facilitators played a key and critical role in enabling literacy facilitators, project staff and communities, particularly community leaders, to recognise, support and promote education for women and girls. The report from the British Council (2002) summarised the situation:

> The Project Managers had two incompatible demands made on them, to implement the gender policy of the programme, and to work within the culture of the community, respecting community members' opinions. In all the projects there was the issue that the power in the communities was held by men. To insist that women should participate equally in the project activities meant insisting on change in the culture . . .
>
> Working for change that involved some change in the role of women was successful when the community members who held power were willing to let them participate . . . working within the power structures, the projects were able to bring about a certain amount of change in the status of women in their communities.

In Egypt the support given to women by male trainers and the discussions and debates, particularly those on marriage and language use, started the reflective process.

The training of adult literacy facilitators can provide the spaces for women to reflect, to struggle and to begin the construction of independent identity and agency. It can provide the opportunity for men to consider the social construction of gender and gendered power relationships in their own households and communities This leads to a slowly changing gender dynamic, better gender-related programme outcomes and perhaps in time to increased gender equity.

Notes

1 The Community Education Programme (CEP), Nigeria, 1997–2000, and the Capacity Enhancement for Lifelong Learning (CELL), Egypt, 2001–4, were both managed by the British Council and financed by the Department for International Development.

2 The Adult Literacy Training Project, 1996–9 operated in two governorates, Menoufia and Qena.

3 Local government project areas were in Akwa Ibom, and Abia States in the south-east, Borno State, and among two nomadic Fulani clans in Tarabawa and Adamawa States in the north-east.

4 The Nile area north of Cairo to Luxor is generally referred to as Upper Egypt.

5 According to the statistics from the Federal Government of Nigeria, when the Community Education Programme started in 1993, 70 per cent of women were illiterate compared with 46 per cent of men. In Egypt 60 per cent of women are illiterate compared with 35 per cent of men (World Development Report 2000).

6 A survey of 900 nomadic pastoralists in southern Borno State (Sa'ad 2000) found only 4 per cent of the men had either Western or Koranic literacy and the literacy rate for nomadic women was considered to be less than 1 per cent.

7 The term LOCAL was first used in the ALTP in Egypt to emphasise both the learner and the community focus of the programme.

8 The CELL *Teachers' Guide* proposed five themes into which specific issues could be incorporated: 'How to Learn, My Family, My Village, My Community, My District.'

9 Training courses on the second 'Pathway' stage of the programme and courses in monitoring and evaluation are planned as of November 2003.

10 The programme social development adviser explained that many of the communities along the Nile have very different histories and some were formed by in-comers from other parts of Arabia at different times. Some of the original customs were maintained and are now reinforced by outward temporary migration. Field notes, August 2003.

11 A unofficial marriage is recognised by a statement from both parties. This shows the woman has consented and it bestows responsibilities on the man for any children resulting from the union.

12 The word 'early' translates also as 'premature'.

13 Research undertaken in Pakistan in 1993 as part of a secondary education programme funded by the World Bank.

14 Field notes (August 2003), Book 2: 95–7.

15 Seventy small books were published in five languages, Hausa, Fulfulde, Ibo, Ibibio and English. Two books of stories by women written in colloquial Arabic were published in Egypt under ALTP.

References

Barton, D. (1991) 'The social nature of writing' in D. Barton and R. Ivanovic (eds) *Writing in the Community*, London: Sage

Bown, L. (1993) *Preparing the Future: Women, Literacy and Development*, London: ActionAid

British Council (2002) 'Nigeria Community Education Project', Manchester: British Council

Cantor, N. and Mischel, W. (1979) 'Prototypes in person perception' in L. Berkowitz (ed.) *Advances in Experimental Social Psychology* XII, London: Academic Press

CELL (2001) *Inception Report*, CELL and GALAE, Cairo: British Council

—— (2003) 'How to learn, my family, my village, my community, my district' in *Teachers' Guide*, CELL and GALAE, Cairo: British Council

Chambers, R. (1983) *Rural Development: Putting the Last First*, Harlow: Addison Wesley

Federal Government of Nigeria/UNICEF (1993) 'Situation and Policy Analysis of Education in Nigeria', Lagos: UNICEF

Fordham, P., Holland, D. and Millican, J. (1995) *Adult Literacy: A Handbook for Development Workers*, Oxford: Oxfam/VSO

Heath, S.B. (1982) '"What no bedtime story means": narrative skills at home and at school', *Language in Society* II

Kabeer, N. (1994) *Reversed Realities: Gender Hierarchies in Development Thought*, London and New York: Verso

Levy, C. (1991) 'Critical Issues in Translating Gender Concerns into Planning Competence in the 1990s', paper presented at the joint ACSP and AESOP International Congress, Oxford

Maddox, B. (2001) 'Literacy and the market: the economic uses of literacy among the peasantry in north-west Bangladesh' in B.V. Street (ed.) *Literacy and Development: Ethnographic Perspectives*, London: Routledge

McCaffery, J. (1998) 'An Analysis of Options for Addressing the Gender Priority in the Biu Project: Nigeria', report for the British Council, Manchester

—— (2003) Reports on the Training of Adult Literacy Teachers for Bene Suef and El Fayoum, and Luxor and Qena, CELL, Cairo: British Council

McCaffery, J., Obanubi, F. and Sanni K. (2000) *A Guide for Training Literacy Instructors: Learner-orientated Community Adult Literacy*, Manchester: British Council

Mernissi, F. (1983) *Beyond the Veil: Male–female Dynamics in Muslim Society*, London: Al Saqi Books

Moser, C. (1993) *Gender Planning and Development: Theory, Practice and Training*, London: Routledge

Overseas Development Administration (1996) 'Nigeria Community Education Programme', London: West and North Africa Department

Papen, U. (2001) 'Literacy – your key to a better future? Literacy, reconciliation and development in the National Literacy Programme in Namibia' in B.V. Street (ed.) *Literacy and Development: Ethnographic Perspectives*, London: Routledge

Potter, J. and Wetherell, M. (2002) *Discourse and Social Psychology: beyond Attitudes and Behaviour*, London: Sage

Preston, R. and McCaffery, J. (2003) *Partnerships and Expertise: Implications for Communications in Complex Projects in International Human Development. Case Studies from Sub-Saharan Africa, Eastern Europe and Latin America*, Coventry; University of Warwick/INCED

Robinson-Pant, A. (2001) *Why Eat Green Cucumber at the Time of Dying? Exploring the Link between Women's Literacy and Development in Nepal*, Hamburg: UNESCO Institute of Education

Sa'ad, Abdulmumini (2000) 'Nomadic Fulani and Family Life Education in Nigeria: the Case of the Southern Borno Nomads', paper presented at the Voice for Change conference, IEC, Cambridge

Street, B.V. (1984) *Literacy in Theory and Practice*, Cambridge: Cambridge University Press

—— (2001) *Literacy and Development: Ethnographic Perspectives*, London: Routledge

Tahir, G. (1991) *Education and Pastoralism in Nigeria*, Zaria: ABU Press

Wieder, L. (1974) *Language and Social Reality*, The Hague: Mouton

Zubair, S. (2001) 'Literacies, gender and power in rural Pakistan' in B.V. Street (ed.) *Literacy and Development*, London: Routledge

10 Women, literacy, development, and gender

A telling case involving an HIV-positive woman

Donna Bulman

In this chapter a 'telling case' is used to examine connections between health, HIV/AIDS, development, and literacy-related issues within the Canadian context. A 'telling case' refers to 'a situation in which circumstances surrounding a case serve to make previously obscure theoretical relationships suddenly apparent' (Mitchell 1984: 239). The 'telling case' used in this chapter is taken from research carried out as part of a study on how women in the Maritime Provinces of Canada learn about HIV/AIDS. This study was done in the context of a doctoral research degree programme. Prior to describing the case, a brief overview of Canadian literacy-related policy initiatives within adult education is provided. Following this, gender-related issues are briefly described. Next, the case utilised throughout this chapter is detailed and examined through a gender-sensitive lens in order to expose gender-related issues as they relate to health, development, or literacy education. This section concludes with the presentation of some options Sarah might consider if she chose to go forward with further developing her literacy skills. This includes a brief discussion on how a rights-based approach to literacy education or a programme based on a social model of disability might be helpful to the individual situation described within this chapter.

In the following section of this chapter I provide information on the general context in which literacy education is offered to women within Canada. This information serves as a background to the specific case that makes up the major portion of this chapter.

The context

Within Canada, much of public discourse surrounding literacy takes on a crisis tone (Veeman *et al.* n.d.). This discourse is often based upon statistics that attempt to describe literacy levels throughout the country and that compare literacy levels within Canada to that of other countries. According to Longfield (2003) more than 40 per cent of Canadians who are of working age lack the basic literacy skills necessary for participation in the changing labour market. In addition, Atlantic Canadians[1] and those who live within Quebec have fewer literacy skills than those people who live in Ontario and western Canada (Longfield 2003). However, as noted by Rogers *et al.* (see Chapter 7), statistics related to literacy should be viewed with caution, as in some instances statistics 'however carefully collected often get their facts wrong'. In addition, statistics can be interpreted in a variety of ways (Sussman 2003) depending upon different agendas and definitions of literacy. Regardless of the actual number of people who face challenges related to literacy within Canada, literacy-related issues have ongoing implications for Canada's economic, social, and cultural future.

Within Canada the National Literacy Secretariat comes under the auspice of Human Resource Development Canada (HRDC). This may imply that from a government perspective literacy is viewed primarily in terms of economic participation (Veeman 2002). The relationship between literacy levels and employment opportunities is one of the dominant literacy-related discourses within Canada. Oftentimes this discourse silences alternative discourses, including those that do not view people with literacy-related challenges through a deficit perspective.

Table 10.1 provides a brief overview of the history of public literacy-related initiatives within Canada. Prior to presenting this information, however, it is necessary to note that within Canada education is primarily a provincial and territorial, not a federal, responsibility (Selman and Dampier 1991; Shohet 2001). This provincial jurisdiction over education is defined originally in the British North America Act of 1867 and later reaffirmed in the Canadian constitution (Shohet 2001). It is, however, accepted that literacy problems are a national issue, so the federal government does have a role to play in addressing the challenge. Partnership agreements between the federal, provincial, and territorial governments are sometimes used to overcome constitutional obstacles. However, within these partnership agreements the federal government 'must recognize the constitutional predominance of both the provinces and territories' (Longfield 2003: 14). One result of this situation is that some provinces provide stronger provision for literacy education than others. Table 10.1 indicates that many initiatives have attempted to address literacy-related problems within Canada. Other services and resources not identified in the table include the National Adult Literacy DataBase, the Directory of Canadian Literacy Research, the Canadian Literacy Thesaurus, and Community Access Points.[2] Some successes have been achieved; however, as noted earlier significant literacy problems do remain.

Literacy programmes in Canada are often seen to be remedial and frequently are based upon ideas of communitarianism. According to Johnston (2000) communitarianism focuses on personal responsibility, the

Table 10.1 Overview of literacy-related public policy within Canada

1922	Frontier College, which had previously been referred to as the Canadian Reading Camp Movement, opened. A function of Frontier College was to provide adult basic education and thus address literacy-related problems
1960	The Technical and Vocational Training Act was passed in order to upgrade the skills of the Canadian work force
1967	The Adult Occupational Training Act was passed, leading to the development of the Canadian NewStart Program. The purpose of this initiative was to train 'educationally disadvantaged' adults (Selman and Dampier 1991: 166) thus illustrating a deficit model of literacy or adult basic education
1970s	Literacy began to be seen as a social justice issue among activists
1970	Laubach Councils were set up across Canada. These councils were made up of volunteers who provided mainly one-to-one literacy tutoring to those who requested it
1977	The first national conference on Canadian literacy was held, leading to the development of an advocacy organisation, the Movement for Canadian Literacy
1979	The Canadian Congress for Learning Opportunities for Women was founded. This organisation closed in the mid-1990s
1981	Laubach Literacy of Canada was established to co-ordinate the various Laubach literacy councils within Canada.[a] Although this organisation publishes literacy-related materials and establishes basic standards for tutor training, it has no control over the activities of local councils
1987	The Southam newspaper chain released a group of articles on adult literacy in Canada. This was the first time literacy in Canada was assessed by using 'real tasks' (Longfield 2003: 89) rather than years of schooling. This indicated that 5 million Canadians were illiterate (Calamai 1987). Following the release of these articles, the National Literacy Secretariat was created to fund literacy initiatives. The main purpose of the National Literacy Secretariat is to encourage and support research initiatives, increase public awareness of issues relating to literacy, develop educational materials, co-ordinate sharing of information, and improve access to learning opportunities (Shohet 2001)
1994	The International Adult Literacy Survey provided an updated profile on literacy in Canada. This survey measured prose, document, and quantitative literacy and divided people's literacy ability into four levels. According to this study 19 per cent of Canadians were at the lowest levels and 47 per cent did not have the skills necessary to meet everyday literacy demands (Quill Learning Network 2003)[b]

Table 10.1 Continued

1999–2000	Provincial and Territorial governments who did not have policy statements related to literacy developed them. Unfortunately this increase in policy statements did not directly translate into increased services for people
2002	The National Summit on Innovation and Learning took place. One recommendation from this meeting was the development of a pan-Canadian and essential skills development system supported by the federal, provincial, and territorial government

Sources: adapted from Shohet, cited in Longfield (2003); Selman and Dampier (1991).

Notes

a Most basic adult literacy work within the Maritime Provinces is done on a voluntary basis, making it difficult to ensure co-ordinated and accountable services are offered. Many volunteer tutors, who are often women, have limited training opportunities.

b Data from this survey should not be considered unproblematic as literacy skills are flexible. People continually develop and lose literacy skills depending upon the use made of such skills. In addition, the Canadian part of this study did not include the following groups of people: those who live in the Northwest Territories, Yukon, and Nunavut, people living in institutions, homeless people, people living on Indian reserves, and full-time members of the armed forces (Sussman 2003).

family, the community, and social cohesion. It has strong undertones of 'moral rearmament' (2000: 18), meaning that ideas within this framework such as the importance of the nuclear family and the traditional role of women is celebrated and in some cases seen to be normative. Johnston (2000) while writing in a British context notes that educational initiatives based on this often include family literacy projects. Interestingly, within Canada there is a focus on family literacy, intergenerational learning, and community learning. This is represented in recent policy documents such as 'Raising Adult Literacy Skills: the Need for a pan-Canadian Response', report of the Standing Committee on Human Resources Development and the Status of Persons with Disability (Longfield 2003). In this document one of the eighteen recommendations put forward to the House of Commons was that the National Literacy Secretariat 'extend support for community learning and family literacy partnerships' (2003: 79).

In addition to programmes based upon ideas related to communitarianism, Canadian literacy programmes are often built upon ideas that are based on humanistic perspectives. Programmes based on this type of philosophy often focus on issues related to self-esteem or motivation and make the assumption that people with literacy difficulties have had challenging and difficult lives and negative learning experiences (Quigley 1997). This approach has been criticised by a variety of educators such as Quigley (1997), who indicates that literacy programmes based upon such stereotypes may be harmful to learners. Literacy programmes based on such humanistic assumptions may also not recognise the diversity of literacy students and may view literacy skills as being very stable and thus neglect to ask critical questions, such as: how should people who have lost literacy skills through illness or accidents be best helped? Why is the retention in literacy-related programmes as low as 8 per cent among those eligible in Canada and the United States (Quigley 2000)? Does gender influence the type of literacy programming required? Why do many people eligible for literacy programmes not attend them, and does rurality influence attitudes towards literacy education?

A discourse that often surrounds literacy education within Canada is that improved literacy skills improve job prospects and earning power and hence are beneficial to both the individual and society. This is significant as currently one woman in five in the Maritime Provinces of Canada lives in poverty (New Brunswick Advisory Council on the Status of Women, 2002). Single women and unattached elderly women have the highest poverty rates among women from this area of Canada (Colman 2000). This discourse ignores the fact that literacy skills take a long time to develop and that improving technical literacy skills by itself is seldom sufficient to be more competitive within the labour market within Canada or other industrialised countries with significant rates of unemployment. This is particularly true if the improvement in literacy skills is slight. Within a developed or industrialised country this discourse might be more accurately stated as 'the higher the educational attainment, the better the job and income prospects become' (New Brunswick Advisory Council on the Status of Women 2002: 5). In an industrialised country, upgrading basic literacy skills may not significantly improve job marketability or earning power.

Gendering literacy provision

Prior to discussing gender in the context of literacy, it is important to examine the term 'gender' from a critical perspective, as this term is quite problematic. Traditionally the term 'gender' referred to the cultural difference between men and women 'based on the biological difference between male[s] and female[s]' (Connell 2002: 8). However, some researchers view the term as heterosexist (Bella and Yetman 2000) as it is based on a binary concept in which women and men are compared to one another and women are viewed as 'other' or inferior to men. In addition Connell (2002) notes that most of us combine masculine and feminine traits and that the boundaries between genders are not clear. Connell (2002: 10) redefines gender as 'the way human society deals with human bodies, and the many consequences of that "dealing" in our personal lives and our collective fate'. He also notes that gender patterns differ among cultures, that gender is dynamic, that gender relations are socially reproduced, and that gender as we know it may not exist in the future. Although these arguments may seem very academic in situations where women experience severe oppression, they do have long-term consequences in how gender is thought about and what this may mean for the future.

In addition to critically examining the term 'gender' it is important to review other gender-related issues in Canada that may influence women's ability or desire to take part in literacy programmes. Some of these issues are as follows:

- As noted earlier, one woman out of five in Canada lives in poverty (New Brunswick Advisory Council on the Status of Women 2002) thus making it difficult to afford childcare and transport to attend literacy-related events.
- In Canada, women do two-thirds of the unsalaried work. This is equivalent to between 32 per cent to 54 per cent of the gross national product (ibid.). The end result may be that women sometimes lack the energy to engage in literacy activities, particularly those that may be participatory or ongoing in nature or those which require a lot of preparation time outside the actual programme setting or which require women to travel long distances.
- Within Canada, more than $1.5 billion a year is spent on health care costs resulting from violence against women (Health Canada 1999). One result is that women are sometimes living in situations where they are not free to make choices about their own lives, including whether or not they wish to attend literacy classes.
- One result of the underemployment or unemployment of women is that in some instances women who do not meet the criteria for employment insurance through Human Resource Development Canada are ineligible for certain literacy programmes sponsored by this government department. In addition, many women are employed in small organisations, with few benefits and high turnover rates. These organisations may have few incentives to provide workplace literacy training, much less the higher-level training which may be needed if Canada is to remain competitive within the world market.

All of these factors must be taken into consideration when developing literacy programmes for women.

Literacy education programmes within Canada tend to be learner-centred, as opposed to women-centred, with the result that little emphasis is placed upon whether women experience problems with literacy differently than men (Horsman 1996). Finally much literacy work is carried out by women and is often ghettoised with resultant low pay and few benefits. This has long-term implications for literacy programmes, as the turnover of tutors is high and in many situations student retention is low.

Oftentimes violence against women is silenced and the issue of how violence interferes with learning in both literacy programmes and adult basic education is not given the attention it deserves. Various justifications for silencing discourses related to violence exist. Horsman, who does not agree with many of these justifications, indicates literacy tutors may silence this type of discourse within learning situations in the belief that the issue of violence is a 'can of worms' (Horsman 1997: 15) and best not discussed or that tutors are not therapists and therefore should discourage such conversation (ibid.). This rationalisation makes the faulty assumption that silence on these issues is neutral. Horsman (n.d.) also indicates that discourses of violence which are not silenced may be medicalised. Tutors with this viewpoint may frequently refer students to members of the helping professions such as to counsellors and doctors. This is not necessarily unhelpful, however for some students it is inappropriate owing to past experiences with such people. Thus, tutors wishing to make such recommendations need to be cognizant that a referral like this is not appropriate for all people.

Horsman (1996) also critiques the gender implication in family literacy programmes in that these programmes suggest literacy for women can be justified only for children's sake. It also reinforces traditional roles of the family and perhaps suggests that literacy education is a duty for women wanting to be good parents instead of being a right for every citizen. It may also exclude women who do not have children or those who do not live in traditional families, such as Sarah, who is described in the 'telling case' in the next section of this chapter.

A 'telling case'

The case discussed in this chapter involves a woman[3] who is from the Maritime Provinces of Canada and who is HIV-positive. This individual, who will be referred to as Sarah, has challenges associated with understanding and remembering both written and verbal instructions. This could potentially have harmful affects on her health and other aspects of her life. In addition, Sarah has problems in group situations as she tends to repeat information and thus often experiences unkindness from other group members who become impatient with her behaviour.

I first met Sarah when I worked in a community-based AIDS organisation. Our initial meeting took place at a workshop designed for HIV-positive people who were considering returning to the work force after an extended period on disability insurance. I later interviewed Sarah as one participant in my postgraduate studies which focused on how women in the Maritime Provinces of Canada learn about HIV/AIDS.

Sarah was a fifty-two-year-old woman at the time of our interview. In the formal school system she entered grade 8 but did not complete it as she was in a car accident with the result that she acquired a head injury. However, she was sixteen years old when she entered grade 8. The average age of entering grade 8 in Canada is thirteen years of age, so Sarah had experienced difficulty within the school system prior to her accident. In our conversation Sarah indicated she had repeated grade 1, as her teacher felt she was 'too stubborn' to move on to grade 2. This would seem to be an inappropriate reason not to promote someone to the next grade if they are meeting acceptable benchmarks. Indeed, Sarah's 'stubbornness' has been very beneficial to her as she copes with complex health problems, HIV-related discrimination and gender-related discrimination. Sarah also repeated grade 8 and indicated that 'her teacher did not like her'. These difficulties may have resulted partly from Sarah's other physical health problems, which included petit mal seizures, a blood clotting disorder, and thyroid problems.

Many of Sarah's memories of school are unpleasant. This may be one reason she has not attempted to attend additional literacy classes now that she no longer has childcare responsibilities. Interestingly, Ziegahn (1992), Imel (1996), and Quigley (1997) all suggest that non-attendance at literacy or adult basic education classes may be related to previous school experiences. Kerka (n.d.) notes non-attendance may be related to the realisation that much of the content in school is unrelated to the situations in which many people live.

After leaving school Sarah worked in a variety of low-paying jobs that women with few opportunities for gaining educational qualifications often find themselves in. This included babysitting, bartending, and house cleaning. Sarah describes a lot of communication problems within her own family. She also indicates her family has rejected her in part owing to her HIV diagnosis and in part owing to her personality and frankness on family-related matters. She indicates she gets little support from her family and has been disinherited.

As an adult, Sarah has experienced serious violence from three of her four husbands. For example, one husband hit her so hard she permanently lost a significant portion of her hearing. This hearing loss contributed to later literacy-related difficulties. In another incident, her partner became emotionally abusive owing to her HIV status.

When Sarah was married to her first husband she attempted to attend some further schooling. While in this programme she was 'tested' and explained that from this she was told she was 'suitable' to complete a grade 10–12 education programme. Notwithstanding the reliability of such testing, Sarah was not able to continue in this programme because she had a small child and her husband refused to parent when she was not available. This type of situation is supported by Horsman's (1990) research that describes a variety of situations and strategies that men who are resistant to women improving their literacy skills utilise. This resistance may occur as increased literacy skills, as well as the opportunity to talk regularly with other women, may lessen the isolation certain women experience – thus making them less dependent upon their partner with the result that the power balance within the relationship shifts.

Sarah clearly does have some literacy skills but seems to have ongoing difficulties related to comprehending what she reads and to health-related literacy. For example, although Sarah indicates that much of what she has learned about HIV she learned through reading, she lacks basic information about a disease she has lived with and managed successfully for twenty-one years. For example in our discussion she did not know what the initials HIV stood for and was not aware of any specific symptoms HIV-positive women might have that men did not. She described HIV as 'your white blood cells eating your red blood cells'. She also believed the criteria for beginning on antiretroviral drugs was a CD4 count of less than 350. While this is a factor that is considered when deciding among treatment options, other complex factors also go into deciding whether or not to start on antiretroviral medication. Sarah seemed to experience difficulty when switching between concrete and abstract thought and this may have contributed to her lack of understanding of some of the medical aspects of her disease. However, it must be acknowledged that Sarah has developed a variety of decoding skills necessary to cope successfully with her disease. This situation may serve as a reminder that many people have developed literacy or decoding skills specific to their particular needs (Barton and Hamilton 1998) regardless of their formal literacy level.

Sarah indicated that while she does not have difficulty reading the labels on medication bottles she does have problems remembering what is written on them. However, Sarah has already designed strategies to cope with such situations, including asking her current partner to remind her when the medication is due, using a timer if necessary, and talking with a chemist she particularly trusts. All of these strategies suggest that Sarah is not dependent on others, although many stereotypes about people with reading difficulties would suggest this is true of many people in this situation.

Sarah does have a lot of strengths that could be utilised within a literacy programme should one become available which would meet her needs. For example, she is street-smart, as shown by her ability to survive on the streets during actual periods of illness, while at the same time being acutely aware of resources available to her should she need them. Through networking she is able to meet many of her literacy needs. For example, through utilising the services of both HIV/AIDS activists and professionals Sarah was able to deal with the paperwork involved in getting the Canadian government to recognise that she had received tainted blood and was thus eligible for compensation. She is also an able fund-raiser for a variety of causes and raised over $7,000 for a community-based organisation she supports. She is able to keep accurate records of her fund-raising work.

Sarah lives in a city that has a population of approximately 61,046. However, this city is still very rural in many of its attitudes and characteristics. For example, Sarah has been barred from several social activities because she is known to be HIV-positive and does not always conform to gender-specific norms. This city is also limited in the resources available for people with complex challenges associated with literacy. For example, the Community Academic Services Programs which provide adults with GED preparation and adult basic education are very poorly resourced and are currently not suited to Sarah's needs owing to her high levels of fatigue and problems with physical mobility. This situation is an example of the gap which may exist between policy-related rhetoric and actual service capability or provision.

Sarah does not fit many of the images that exist within Canada about people with low literacy skills. For instance she does not live in poverty, as she receives both disability pension and yearly payments from the federal government due to receiving tainted blood. In addition, Sarah is not passive. Through networking she is able to have many of her needs met. In addition, even if Sarah were to improve her literacy skills she would not be able to work or improve her income owing to her many health problems.

It is my argument that Sarah could be helped to regain and improve her literacy skills if a rights-based approach to literacy education was offered. This approach has been used successfully with marginalised people in a variety of countries. Within a Canadian context, a rights-based approach would view adult literacy education as right rather than a second chance for those who were not successful within the formal school system. In Sarah's case it could also mean that although she has complex health problems she would have the right to assert that her specific needs were an integral part of her entitlement to literacy education. Most important, it would allow Sarah access to high-quality literacy education should this be her desire.

Sarah's situation could also be improved if the philosophy around literacy programmes was based on a social model of disability rather than a deficit model. A social model of disability model assumes that people with disabilities experience problems due to deficits within society rather than within themselves (Leicester 1999). This approach could also contribute to a lessening of the stigma associated with literacy-related challenges.

Conclusion

This chapter has provided background information on literacy within Canada seen through a gender-sensitive lens. Through the use of a 'telling case' it has attempted to show how one individual does not fit into dominant gender and literacy-related stereotypes. For example, this individual is not dependent on others, does not have low self-esteem and does not identify as a person with low literacy skills. She does however experience multiple other identities that would have to be taken into consideration in developing a literacy programme that would be beneficial to her, particularly if it was based upon a social model of disability and a rights-based approach. In fact the individual concerned is independent and is able to have many of her needs met through networking and mutually beneficial exchanges with other people.

Notes

1 Atlantic Canada refers to Nova Scotia, New Brunswick, Prince Edward Island and Newfoundland.
2 Currently many Community Access Points contain dated computer equipment and have limited staffing.
3 Pseudonyms are used throughout this chapter when referring to HIV-positive individuals.

References

Barton, D. and Hamilton, M. (1998) *Local Literacies: Reading and Writing in One Community*, London: Routledge

Bella, L. and Yetman, L. (2000) *Challenging Heterosexism: towards Non-heterosexist Policy and Regulation in Health and Social Service Agencies*, Halifax NS: Maritime Centre of Excellence for Women's Health

Calamai, P. (1987) *Broken Words*, Toronto: Southam Newspaper Group

Colman, R. (2000) *Women's Health in Atlantic Canada: a Statistical Profile*, Halifax NS: Maritime Centre of Excellence for Women's Health

Connell, R. (2002) *Gender*, Cambridge: Polity Press

Government of New Brunswick (2003) 'About New Brunswick – Population', http://www.gnb.ca/cnb/nb/Pop-e.asp (accessed 19 July 2003)

Health Canada (1999) *Violence Against Women*, Ottawa: Author

Horsman, J. (1990) *Something in my Mind Besides the Everyday*, Toronto: Women's Press

—— (1996) 'Literacy and Gender', http://www.jennyhorsman.com/ymca.html (accessed 7 July 2003)

—— (1997) *But I'm not a Therapist: Furthering Discussion About Literacy Work with Survivors of Trauma*, Toronto: Canadian Congress for Learning Opportunities for Women

—— (n.d.) 'Creating Changes in Literacy Programs: Talking About Taking

Account of Violence', http://www.jennyhorsman.com/creatingchange2.pdf (accessed 7 July 2003)

Imel, S. (1996) 'Adult Literacy Education: Emerging Directions in Program Development', http://www.ericfacility.net/databases/ERIC_Digests/ed402475.html (accessed 14 September 2003)

Johnston, R. (2000) 'Community education and lifelong learning: local spice for global fare?' in J. Field and M. Leicester (eds) *Lifelong Learning: Education Across the Lifespan*, London: Routledge

Kerka, S. (n.d.) 'Family and intergenerational literacy', *ERIC Digest 111*, http://www.ericae.net/ED334467.htm (accessed 14 September 2003)

Leicester, M. (1999) *Disability Voice: Towards an Enabling Education*, London: Jessica Kingsley

Longfield, J. (2003) 'Raising Adult Literacy Skills: the Need for a Pan-Canadian Response', report of the Standing Committee on Human Resources Development and the Status of Persons with Disabilities', http://www.parl.gc.ca (accessed 7 July 2003)

Mitchell, C. (1984) 'Typicality and the case study' in R.F. Ellen (ed.) *Ethnographic Research: a Guide to General Conduct*, London: Academic Press

New Brunswick Advisory Council on the Status of Women (2002) *Women and the Future of Health Care in Canada: Brief to the Romanow Commission on the Future of Health Care in Canada*, Fredericton NB: Author

Quigley, A. (1997) *Rethinking Literacy Education: the Critical Need for Practice-based Change*, San Francisco: Jossey Bass

—— (2000) 'Beyond Participation and Stereotypes: towards the Study of Engagement in Adult Literacy Education', http://www.edst.educ.ubc.ca/aerc/2000/quigleyal-web.htm (accessed 9 July 2003)

Quill Learning Network (2003) 'What is Literacy?' http://www.quillnet.org/stats.html (accessed 7 July 2003)

Selman, G. and Dampier, P. (1991) *The Foundations of Adult Education in Canada*, Toronto: Thomson

Shohet, L. (2001) 'A Brief Overview of Literacy and Adult Basic Education in Canada 2001 with Implications for UK Adaptations where Appropriate', http://www.usask.ca/education/alcs/papers.htm (accessed 12 January 2004)

Sussman, S. (2003) *Moving the Markers: New Perspectives on Adult Literacy Rates in Canada*, Ottawa: Movement for Canadian Literacy

Veeman, N. (2002) 'Improving Adult Literacy Levels: a Critical Look at Government Strategies and Public Awareness Campaigns', http://www.usask.ca/education/alcs/papers/veeman1.pdf (accessed 12 January 2004)

Veenam, N., Walker, K. and Ward, A. (n.d.) 'Educating Rural Youth in Today's Society: Schools and Learning Capacity at the Community Level', http://www.usask.ca/education/alcs/papers.htm (accessed 12 January 2004)

Ziegahn, L. (1992) 'Learning, literacy, and participation: sorting out priorities', *Adult Education Quarterly*, 43 (1): 30–50

Part III

Learning from experience

This part of the book brings together case studies of literacy programmes from India, Uganda, Mexico and South Africa, analysing how processes around literacy learning in the classroom and in everyday life interact with changing gender roles and relations. The writers in Part III take a gendered perspective on innovative approaches to literacy teaching (such as ActionAid's REFLECT programme), as well as exploring how individual women view literacy in their daily lives. Khandekar refers to the 'multidimensional' oppression faced by women who are low-caste and poor – as in the earlier accounts in this book (e.g. Bulman, McCaffery), coping with violence is an integral part of many women's lives which influences how and why they participate in development programmes. These first-hand accounts of how various innovative literacy approaches were implemented illustrate how the participants 'took hold'[1] of the intervention and in most cases, transformed the programme's intended strategies.

The idea of the literacy class as an important social space for women to discuss their lives comes through in all these accounts. Sujata Khandekar describes how the CORO classes provided the women in Santosh Nagar 'with mental spaces to think about themselves' and a chance to come together, not related to their familial responsibilities. Coming together in this way allowed the women to think about the issues that concerned them most and the 'togetherness' later turned into solidarity and social action against illegal liquor dens. In the Muthande Literacy Programme too (Juliet Millican's chapter), the classes provided a space for the elders of the community to talk about their problems. In both these cases, the social function of the class appeared to be an unintended outcome of getting together to learn literacy – in contrast to the REFLECT circles in Uganda (see Marc Fiedrich's chapter) where the planners' primary objective was to create a forum where women could discuss issues around gender inequality. By analysing the use of the gender workload calendar, a tool used for facilitating discussion in REFLECT circles, Fiedrich suggests that 'circle debates are inevitably contrived'. Though the women participate in the circle discussions and appear to agree with the health education messages, their actions suggest that they value not the content but the ability to '"parade" prestigious forms of knowledge'. In all the above cases, what the participants took from the programme may not have been what the planners originally intended.

The Uganda case study illustrates issues around ownership of the REFLECT methods, as raised by Attwood *et al.* in Part II. Similarly, Juliet Millican describes the difficulties of 'translating theory into practice' when a social literacies approach was used to inform the Muthande Literacy Programme in South Africa. Not having a primer placed huge demands on relatively inexperienced facilitators who were expected to create their own materials. However, working with a concept of local literacies enabled the programme to implement dual language literacy (English and Zulu) as participants needed to read both languages in their everyday lives. The role of the outsider and outside agencies in implementing literacy programmes is brought under scrutiny in these case studies. As Millican concludes, 'participative approaches, while attempting to transfer power, can be seen as an abdication of responsibility'. Though the innovative approaches described in this part aim to be more bottom-up, these experiences could suggest that just the act of bringing methods of facilitation from 'outside' may prevent people from shaping the programme's objectives.

These chapters highlight the symbolic importance of learning literacy or attending literacy classes to the women concerned. Claudia Flores-Moreno's account relates women's motivation for attending literacy classes in La Paloma, Mexico, to the fact that they had been excluded from school as young girls. They now want to 'learn something ... to be someone in life' through joining the literacy group. Similarly, though the Muthande programme was intended to focus on 'literacy for information' and help with everyday literacy support, the older women participating were more interested in attending 'school' as 'the fulfilment of a dream': 'school-based literacy was for them the literacy of power'. Rather than learning to read and write as the means to future employment or a better life, the women wanted to 'construct an identity that they could pass on to their grandchildren' by providing a positive role model. The fact that they were not learning literacy for any specific functional purpose also meant that they did not want the programme to be time-bound as originally envisaged: 'I will stay here until I die.' The writers in this part differ as to how far they suggest that participants 'diverted the intention' of the programme planners (Fiedrich) or that the programme simply evolved in another direction (Khandekar).

So are these case studies about literacy at all? As Khandekar points out, 'it was not literacy *per se* but literacy learning as a collective process' that enabled the women in Santosh Nagar to take action. Though the women were initially concerned to talk and share their problems, as the social action evolved they became more interested in learning to read and write as just 'one part of their survival struggle'. Millican, like Khandekar, brings out the physical difficulties of older women learning to read and write, suggesting that these aspects are overlooked if literacy is not viewed as a 'skill'. In all the case studies, we are made aware that literacy is often used 'as a proxy for self-transformation' (Fiedrich), which can be regarded as a threat (in Flores-Moreno's case) by other family members in destabilising the existing power relationships. These in-depth accounts of literacy programmes illustrate that though literacy may be the entry point (as in Santosh Nagar), the women involved may have very differing reasons for coming together and equate literacy with a broader vision of 'education'.

Note

1 D. Kulick and C. Stroud, 'Conceptions and uses of literacy in a Papua New Guinean village' in B.V. Street (ed.) *Cross-cultural Approaches to Literacy*, Cambridge: Cambridge University Press (1993).

11 'I will stay here until I die'

A critical analysis of the Muthande Literacy Programme

Juliet Millican

This chapter provides a critical analysis of the Muthande Literacy Pro-gramme that was joint-funded by the Department for International Devel-opment (DfID) and the European Commission and run in Clermont, a township area near Durban in South Africa, between 1997 and 2000. The programme was devised for a particular group of elders attending a welfare lunch club run by the Muthande Society for the Aged (known as MUSA), a member of Help Age International. Although not established with a gender focus, 90 per cent of the participants were female and all were of pensionable age. An analysis of it raises some interesting questions for policy makers and for educationalists around how programmes are played out 'on the ground' and the difficulties associated with the transfer of theory into practice. It is also a good illustration of the social and sym-bolic aspects of literacy and their implications for notions of power.

It is one of very few programmes nationally and internationally that has been designed with and by older people and has also been referred to as OPL (Older People's Literacy, Street 2000). As such, it provides a useful example of the value of literacy to a group who are generally not wage earners. Literacy programmes tend generally to attract larger numbers of female participants but in a programme targeted at older people, where women have a longer life expectancy than men, they were the teachers, the managers and the participants. Their priorities reflect those of a group who for the first time in their lives had achieved some power, as carers of grandchildren, drawers of pensions and active in greater numbers than their male counterparts.

The programme also illustrates concerted attempts to feed new think-ing around literacy practices into literacy programmes, and the longevity of the dominant and autonomous model. In design and conception it was intended to be 'unique and ambitious' and yet, despite its success, it reverted within its three-year life span to look much like a traditional liter-acy programme. The impetus of the learning group to 'recreate school' and to be part of a school environment outweighed many attempts by the convenors to focus on communicative practices. The problems encountered locally of available and adequately trained personnel, proper budget management and difficult internal relationships were similar to those of many development projects and, combined with the expectations of participants, served to limit many of its original ambitions.

The title 'I will stay here until I die' was suggested by Elda Lyster, who worked as evaluator to the programme. The phrase seems to capture a particular aspect of it, a sense of arrival or wish-fulfilment among the participants from being there at all. To them literacy seemed to represent, not the means to achieve an end, but, as in Kate Rockhill's 'Literacy as threat/desire' (1987) – achievement itself. Most older women from township areas had grown up with strong pressure from their families to assume a caring role and in many cases to enter domestic service. The majority of them had been serving others almost since childhood, and access to education was the preserve of the rich and a validation of personal status. Having been denied that access for most of their lives, they were now determined to hold on to it for as long as they were physically able.

I was appointed as consultant to the project to work with the group on the design of the curriculum, methodological approaches and an outline for facilitator training. As an educationalist with a background in literacy and experience in different cultural contexts, I had a range of experience to draw on. As an outsider, resident in the United Kingdom and visiting South Africa only once or twice a year, I was subject to the constraints of most consultants – of having advisory responsibility but no implementing authority. Despite a person-centred approach, I was bringing with me thinking that had been developed outside of the experience of the participants (on the principles of androgogy, multiple literacies, learner-centred programmes, facilitator style) and attempting to integrate these in a participatory way with people to whom learning meant 'school'.

The project was conceived of during a participatory needs assessment exercise, facilitated by Help Age International (HAI) as part of a joint planning exercise with Muthande. A group of elders were trained in the use of PNA[1] tools and subsequently carried out mapping exercises and semi-structured interviews with around 100 MUSA club members to determine their needs. The exercises concluded that they, as older people in South Africa, needed *imfundo yabadala* or adult education in order to deal effectively with their pensions, their families, the democratic process and the rigours of modern life. However, although this suggests a request for an empowerment focus, most of those consulted had no experience, even indirectly, of adult education and no model of alternative approaches to learning.

Help Age International wrote the funding proposal and approached

DfID and the EC (European Commission) for joint funding and the criteria inherent in it could be summarised as the following:

- The programme should be fully participatory and follow the PNA code, i.e. the participants should determine the structure, the content and the process for running the programme, from knowledge of their own needs and social preferences.
- The programme should include some provision for the development of learner-generated materials: learners should be encouraged to write and produce their own materials, which might be published for use by others at a later date, and reflect their own priorities.
- The project should be seen as a pilot, attempting to develop a model that might be used with other groups of older people in South Africa, if not throughout other regions in which HAI works. Time and thought needed to be put into the documentation of learner workbooks, learner progress, etc., which should be collated for future research.
- The project should begin with an investigation into local literacies: those that were used by older people and those that both provided and denied access to different services and facilities. By focusing on communicative practices, it should move away from the autonomous model of a single school-based literacy and towards recognition of a multiple literacies approach.
- The ethos of the programme would be Amandala Kubantu Abadala – Power to Older People. The project as a whole should aim to assist older people in reclaiming their right to a sense of power, and in exploring those literacies that provide access to power.

All these, in differing ways, proved contradictory and problematic, but ultimately provide some useful lessons. I will use an examination of each of them in turn as the framework for the rest of this chapter.

Participation

The importance of participation or participatory approaches has dominated the field of adult education and development since the early 1980s. PNA with its basis in Rapid Rural Appraisal (RRA) or Participatory Rural Appraisal (PRA) has formed the key to much recent development planning and used to formulate an approach to literacy work particularly within REFLECT. In this project the request for literacy and adult education was an unexpected outcome of an earlier needs assessment among older people in the townships, and what they saw as necessary to deal with many of the presenting problems in their lives. Those elders trained to carry out that first PNA worked with us again to investigate older people's perceptions of literacy and the literacy practices that they engaged with. We devised a number of exercises for them to carry out with Muthande members – recording people's 'literacy life stories' – or getting them to talk about what literacy meant to them, what education and adult education meant to them, where and how they learned to read anything, what could they read, what could their parents read, what had influenced their views of literacy, reading and education in the past. Timelines were used to document the times in a day when people used literacies, or needed to, looking at a clock, listening to the radio, reading the Bible, going to the *spaza* shop. Maps were used to record mobility – where did people travel to or need to go – and people's conception of the different buildings in their locality where literacies 'happened': the post office (letters, stamps and telephones), the doctor's (prescriptions and health cards), the shop, the pension pay point, the church and the home. We used a 'bean voting' exercise to gather people's priorities: out of the different things people wanted to learn, which did they feel were most important? We asked for their own criteria for literacy facilitators who they felt 'should be enthusiastic, of a similar age, and not come to class drunk'. We were swayed by their preference for a project co-ordinator who, while knowing little of literacy programmes, was 'sympathetic and kind'.

All this led to a programme which had no prototype, which reflected the voice and needs of older people and which as an outsider I was reluctant to actually 'fix' with my own particular vision. It also led to a group of facilitators who identified with their groups but who had notions of education rooted in the Bantu system and very little experience themselves. My expectation, that they would adapt my examples to fit in with local practices, be creative and flexible within pedagogic guidelines, was an unreasonable one. Similarly the adult education organisation which provided the initial training, though expressing a commitment to the 'uniqueness' of the programme and working to guidelines I set them, was swayed by its own budget constraints and the availability of staff. In the end it delivered an extended training course for tutors that differed very little from its general tutor training, and which, while it ended in the wearing of full academic regalia by trainee teachers, involved content that was in many ways beyond their grasp.

In Street's visit report of 1997 he writes, 'a social literacies approach places great faith in the knowledge participants have of each other and sees the common links between facilitators and learners as a strength that may counter any weakness in educational knowledge'. However he also acknowledges the need for some subject knowledge over and above social knowledge to avoid 'the blind leading the blind'. The training programme that was delivered seemed to represent a collision between these two aspects, a subject-driven programme delivered to people selected entirely on their social relationships, with a tenuous fit between them.

In retrospect, a stronger but sensitive outside voice determining minimum criteria for facilitators, an experienced if enforced co-ordinator and a more rigid insistence on the content of tutor training (even if it meant breaking the participatory code) might have been preferable. Certainly, by the second year of the project, facilitators were struggling and overwhelmed by the expectations placed on them. As Lyster summarised at the end of year 1, 'a good primer at this stage would be better than a bad facilitator with no primer at all!'

Learner-generated materials

The initial proposal had made provision for the development of learner-generated materials, and anticipated that tutors would acquire 'material development skills' during the second year of the project. It envisaged that groups would work with local advice agencies to compile booklets on matters of interest: these might be health care, pensions and the rights of the elderly. It was suggested that these would then be printed in the township. Again this generated intense debate between ourselves. Rogers (1994) has written extensively on the value of learner-generated materials, but Lyster felt strongly that developing good, readable materials for new learners was a complex task. Street warned against tutors experiencing 'overload' in trying to learn too many professional tasks, and in reality they would not have coped with it. Instead we circulated booklets published by the New Reader's Project at the university on pension rights and heath care, but the participants' preference was strongly for stories. The centres were given small libraries of stories, which were loaned out and read again and again, and during the third year they worked with the New Reader's Project and a reminiscence facilitator to produce their own group of stories. These stories or personal histories, recounted orally, transcribed and produced as a book, for many formed the high point of the project. And yet reading or the oral recounting of stories had not been mentioned in our early analysis of local literacy practices and would probably not have been identified as part of a local communicative repertoire. Their value I feel was in their affirmation of a sense of identity among participants and recognition of their personal memories and individual voice. That alone may have done more for people's confidence than anything they actually learned to do. The symbolic importance of literacy was as great, if not greater than, its instrumental importance.

Documentation of a unique programme

There was a great deal of focus in the early days of the project on its uniqueness – because it was dealing with older people, taking a participatory approach and using a social literacies perspective, and Street in particular stressed the need for documentation. The evaluators collected facilitator diaries, student writing, project reports, workbooks, minutes of committee meetings ... to the extent that they became unwieldy. Some learner writing was reproduced in the final evaluation, but the struggle to produce facilitator diaries is probably not justified by their subsequent use. Faciltators and local project staff seemed to be very aware of the division between academics who 'came to look at and write about the project' and their own daily struggle to cope with the tasks they had. Looking at some of these materials in retrospect they indicate to me one or two important things:

- A focus on literacy practices and the reluctance to see literacy as a skill often ignores the amount of actual practice it takes someone to write something for the first time. Most of the elders' workbooks don't look very different from those of a first or second-year primary school pupil: the same shaky handwriting, the same stiff attempts to produce curves and straight lines. This is exacerbated for elderly people with fading eyesight who have spent a lifetime on heavy domestic or agricultural rather than more manipulative tasks, and the provision of adequate reading glasses was something we struggled to get right throughout the project. But in a sense we knew that already, there were no great surprises.
- Identifying and responding to the needs of learners is not an easy task for tutors inexperienced in analytical skills. Facilitator diaries are full of statements such as 'We are happy we come to class every day, the learners enjoy, we are happy to have new learners' and almost never critical. Their reports on learners echo such statements as 'She is a nice lady but she cannot remember, she is very clever and progressing well, her writing is good' – they are essentially descriptive rather than analytical.

What they tell me above all is that learners and facilitators enjoyed their programme for the social and symbolic aspect of schooling it provided them with, and as such did not want to say anything to jeopardise it. And, additionally, that adults who have experienced a lifetime of oppression are far more used to being told what to do or think than to think or initiate for themselves. It often takes a radical and free thinker to break out of that oppression: it is not something that would fit easily with a group of elders who have had few opportunities to question during their lives.

Local and multiple literacies

The second PNA exercise looked at the local literacies which people were aware of, and, though limited, it was reasonably successful. It provided us with an outline training programme based on a series of themes and broken down into specific tasks. Areas such as helping children with homework and home/school literacy, church literacy, Bible and hymn sheet reading, pension and governmental literacies and market literacy provided us with natural groupings for a theme-based curriculum. Constructing a programme that had a broader adult education base gave scope for discussion of alternative belief systems, visits to a local mosque and synagogue, assertion training around pension pay-out issues, and prevented the programme from assuming a more narrow functional approach. People enjoyed the outings, saw and learned things about their own locality that they had never had the opportunity to see before and in many ways were beginning to question things for the first time in their lives.

The theme-based curriculum enabled us to look into the different kinds of literacies that existed in people's lives, and to focus on the tasks they needed literacy for, which became the starting point for learning. The decision to teach dual language literacy or the literacy of use, and to look at writing and reading in Zulu and English alongside each other, was an important and useful one. Nor was it difficult for facilitators to grasp. As people used to moving between two languages even in one sentence, they knew almost instinctively whether in filling in a form you needed to understand words in English or in Zulu, and working within the same script it was possible to decode both and discuss their significance. Facilitators brought in advertising coupons from 'Pick and Pay' and learners carefully copied out their names beside the word Name (in English) in one of their first lessons, and then went on to letter recognition exercises with slogans like 'Special offer' or 'Two for the price of one'! The main aim for many of them was to be able to sign rather than thumbprint their pension receipts. Robinson-Pant (2001) has also done some work on multiple language use, and tends to agree that with a similar script it is less problematic for learners than has been imagined.

We also designed into the programme a slot for learners to bring into classes their actual daily literacy problems, which from initial research we had anticipated might be letter reading or understanding bank statements – issues of a private nature that people might not want to disclose to neighbours. This was envisaged as a one-to-one drop-in session in which facilitators could help learners to read their texts by mediating them, rather than reading for them as a neighbour or child might do. Very quickly this lost the format of an individual tutorial and turned into a time when people could talk about what was happening in their lives – their personal problems. Facilitators soon grasped that if problems were harboured and not shared, members would not be able to concentrate, and members felt that problems were best shared between the whole group. Besides, if something that looked like school was going on – they didn't want to miss any of it. However the issue of needing someone trustworthy to read or interpret documents for them seemed less important than suggested in the initial Participatory Needs Assessment: people had already developed these support strategies in their lives, which they continued to use.

Literacy and identity

Much of the theory that attempted to inform this programme stems from an analysis of communicative practices and an understanding of a communicative repertoire. The DfID Literacy and Livelihoods policy that followed it defined literacy in terms of communication and access to information. However, what emerges from this programme is the greater importance attached to the symbolic nature of literacy and its effect on personal identity. This may be particularly so as the participants were overwhelmingly older women.

Although they were having to take on new roles in a world that was undoubtedly changing around them, the majority of them had support structures in place to deal with their changing information and communication needs. The initial needs assessment had indicated some of these, such as the privacy to read a letter, the ability to help with homework, the need to budget with pensions, but an evaluation of the programme brought out other concerns. The ability to sign rather than provide a thumbprint when receiving a pension is personally and socially significant, even though the thumbprint is functionally as efficient. Having your own stories captured and written down similarly provided a symbolic sense of value. And above all, being a participant in school, and in a school that to the outside world replicates traditional schooling, provides the identity of an educated person. All these contribute to a sense of personal power that is far greater than any actual access to power they might provide. For women who had been used to pleasing others, making do, getting by, finding ways … this sense of power and pride was ultimately what they sought.

Amandala Kubantu Abadala

The slogan 'Power to older people' was coined and reiterated by Muthande members during the first needs assessment, and interviews during the final evaluation with members and their family testify unanimously to a new sense of well-being among those who participated. While we can theorise about what access to power literacy evokes, those involved clearly felt more powerful. And surely if you *feel* more powerful your personal power *is* extended. In almost every case this feeling of power came from finally being at school. As adults who, as we know from their literacy life stories, were generally denied access to schooling for more than if anything a very few years, attending school was the fulfilment of a dream. And because of this, learners wanted the experience of being at school, of a teacher who told them what to do and who they could refer to as Ma'am, sitting in rows at desks, exercises from the blackboard, homework and inevitably exams.

However, as participants, they appeared able to combine this with choosing a teacher who was sympathetic and who they could talk to, an initial sharing or off-loading of personal problems, a social group they could interact with and the opportunities for outings and broader discussions. In short, despite problems of implementing the programme on the ground, the participants ended up with what they felt was most important, an opportunity to enhance their social and identity needs.

In my second visit report I quoted from Liezl Malan's article (1996: 152): 'Learners hold on to pedagogical notions of literacy because of the promise of social transformation they associate with schooling.' Malan concludes that learners persevere in attending classes because they simulate schooling and are associated with the social and economic benefits of school education. Her implications are that the goodies that may go with schooling – employment, improved health, social status – are for many unrealistic. I would like to suggest the opposite: Muthande members continued to attend classes because they provided that social transformation in the here and now. As older people they were not striving to build a future so much as realising long held dreams and constructing an identity that they could pass on to their grandchildren. School-based literacy was for them the literacy of power. Learners enjoyed the company of each other, felt a sense of purpose and 'arrival', noticed some if very small progress in writing but definite improvements in their sense of health and well-being, from being out, getting exercise, both physical and mental, and from being seen and heard. As such they wanted to stay in the programme 'until I die' and saw no reason to leave.

In the townships of South Africa, where a generation of people are being decimated by AIDS and where grandparents, particularly grandmothers, are becoming prime carers, many felt the example they set by attending school was crucial to their grandchildren. At a time when social and technological change was so rapid grandmothers also wanted to reexamine the situation in which they found themselves, in order to participate in it effectively.

Conclusion

The literacy needs and aspirations of an older, non-productive generation can be determined only by planning with them, and taking into account the social and identity issues associated with learning, and in this respect the MUSA programme contains a number of useful lessons for us as planners from outside:

- The importance of structure, to participants and facilitators, and the design of a programme that is manageable will of necessity limit its flexibility to respond to local context.
- The challenges of planning without a textbook – particularly for people who have not had the opportunity of creative thought – can lead to the use of examples as models and dependence on a limited number of ideas. People will not think independently until they are secure in what they are doing; clear guidelines are crucial when doing things for the first time.
- Participative approaches, while attempting to transfer power, can be seen as an abdication of responsibility. Insiders are aware of their felt needs, but not always of the pitfalls associated with following them. These lessons come only from experience and an outsider's role is to make that experience available.
- The unconscious assumptions of participants are often difficult to discover in advance, and yet form a strong force in how any project evolves in practice. Encouraging people to explore these and make them visible may enable people to question their validity.
- The constraints of human and material resources available on the ground can never be overestimated and will impact on a project despite policies put in place to guard against it. Theoretical perspectives form only a starting point, but if held on to too tightly can detract from a proper understanding of what is actually going on.
- Women in particular tend to be led by social and familial needs; the concrete outcomes of literacy may be less important than the social and personal contacts that are offered by the programme as a whole.

All these are lessons that emerge again and again from women's literacy programmes throughout the world.

Although the project ended in 2000, the materials developed throughout its life are still in use by MUSA, which is continuing a smaller programme with its members and without external support. The book of transcribed stories, *The Power of the Drum*, is available from the New Reader's Project, University of Natal. The facilitator support manual, *Older People can Learn*, is also available through the University of Natal and guides tutors through the development and management of a curriculum based on a series of themes and related skills and practices. Written under the working title of 'Granny goes to school', it is in admiration of the programme's participants. They, like Dudizile, were the real life of this project. A large, elderly woman, who had experienced a lifetime of working for others, of raising children and grandchildren, she would struggle up the hill to the centre with arthritis and bad feet carrying books and saying with pride, 'Look at me. Can you believe it? Granny goes to school!'

Note

1 Participatory Needs Assessment, a term coined by the team during this exercise and based on the tools and philosophies of PLA/PRA.

References

Lyster, E. (2000) Evaluation Reports, 1996–2000, London: Help Age International

Malan, L. (1996) 'Theory and practice in contemporary South Africa' in M. Prinsloo and M. Breier (eds) *The Social Uses of Literacy: Theory and Practice in Contemporary South Africa*, Amsterdam and Johannesburg: Benjamins/SACHED

Millican, J. (2000) Visit Reports, 1996–2000, London: Help Age International

Robinson-Pant, A. (2001) *Why Eat Green Cucumber at the Time of Dying? Exploring the Link between Women's Literacy and Development in Nepal*, Hamburg: UNESCO Institute of Education

Rockhill, K. (1987) 'Literacy as threat/desire: longing to be somebody' in J.S. Gaskill and A.T. McLaren (eds) *Women in Education*, Calgary: Detselig

Rogers A. (1994) 'Using Literacy: a New Approach to Post-literacy Materials', ODA Research Report, London: ODA

Street, B.V. (2000) Visit Reports, 1996–2000, London: Help Age International

12 'Literacy brought us to the forefront'

Literacy and empowering processes for Dalit community women in a Mumbai slum

Sujata Khandekar

Introduction

This chapter examines emergence of collective activism out of literacy learning among underprivileged (Dalit) women in one of the slums of Mumbai (India). Against the background of a literacy learning programme, this ethnographic fieldwork aims to understand how gender is constructed, operated and reinforced through various structures in the community, what aspect of the literacy programme stimulated women to challenge prevalent gender norms and how these structures react to women's awakening *vis-à-vis* their position and situation.

Committee of Resource Organisations for Literacy (hereafter referred to as CORO), a Mumbai-based NGO, had initiated literacy programme in twenty different communities in north-east Mumbai slums simultaneously. As one of the founder members of CORO and as a literacy activist, I was co-ordinating and shaping up literacy learning programme in 'Santosh Nagar', a locale of this fieldwork. In the entire process of literacy learning in these communities I enjoyed two positions. One was that of an active participant and the other that of an outside observer. As an active participant I participated physically and mentally in planning, implementation and in activism that emerged in the literacy process, ranging from demonstrations to visiting administrative or police officials. As an outside observer (upper-caste, upper-class, well educated woman) I took extensive field notes and interacted extensively with community people in an effort to ethnographically understand the community.

The chapter is divided broadly into three parts. The first will sketch the profile of Santosh Nagar and deliberate about women's gendered position in this community. The second part will unfold various literacy processes and the third will discuss reactions of various elements to assertions of these women. Excerpts and information from some of the interviews that I did with literacy participants and secondary data obtained from CORO are used to support my analysis.

About CORO

Inspired by the approach of the people's movement advocated by National Literacy Mission Authority (NLMA) India, CORO was established for the propagation of adult literacy in Mumbai slums in 1989. Representatives of different organisations (all from Mumbai) working in different 'New Social Movements' (NSMs) came together as resource organisations to work for literacy under the auspices of CORO. These representatives were from women's organisations, People's Science Movement, Readers' Movement (concerned with promoting reading habits) and the University Teachers' Association. Two of these constituents were grass-roots groups. The founders of CORO were well educated, well employed and shared a common vision to generate developmental initiative from within marginalised people through life-related literacy learning. Many CORO founders were intellectually influenced by Paulo Freire's concept of 'conscientisation' (Freire 1972; CORO 1992).

In the initiation phase (1989–90) CORO's literacy programme was based on its founder's middle-class perception of education and literacy. However it developed into an integrated community development activity in the implementation phase (1991–5) in response to stimulus from the community people. CORO's extended initiatives included legal aid and counselling centres, a women's credit co-operative society, study classes for primary schoolgoing children, guidance centres for accessing basic amenities and capacity building of grass-roots activists. CORO's implementation phase was marked by heavy involvement of community women, both as learners and as instructors. Activism and capacity building gradually led to the emergence of women's initiatives to tackle issues of 'their' importance. CORO's effort became institutionalised (1995–2001) in a federation of around 300 grass-roots *mahila mandals* (women's groups). CORO's literacy efforts took place predominantly within the Dalit (Scheduled Caste)-populated slums.

Dalits

In India a stringent, rigid and hierarchical caste system prevailed for a sufficiently long period to have left deep traces in the minds and attitudes of people (Rangari 1984). Those now referred to as Dalits were earlier called 'Untouchables'. They were at the lowest position in the caste hierarchy and faced strong discrimination. They were denied the right to education and had to do polluting tasks as a service to upper-caste people (Kumar 1995: 63). Discrimination still prevails in the minds of people even though it is constitutionally forbidden since India became a republic in 1950. Dalits constitute the vast majority of the population in CORO's work area.

Like Dalits, women (of all castes, class, religion) were denied the right to education in Indian history.

Santosh Nagar

Santosh Nagar is a Dalit-populated slum of around 900 households situated in north-east Mumbai. Dalits from different rural parts of the state migrated here to make their livelihood in the severe drought of the 1970s. Owing to their non-existent or low education and lack of associated skills most of the people are marginally employed. They work for daily wages. There are no minimum basic amenities in the community. In spite of various efforts CORO could mobilise only non-literate women and not men to participate in the literacy learning programme. I was a regular visitor to these literacy classes as the main functionary of CORO, and participated in women's meetings extending well beyond literacy classes.

Women's gendered position in Santosh Nagar

Women in Santosh Nagar were at the lowest strata in social and cultural hierarchy. Forty-one per cent of community women were non-literate. The majority of them were either in regular (daily) or irregular marginal employment (as domestic servants or rag pickers or similar marginal jobs). Fifty-four per cent of community men were also marginally employed. Acute alcoholic habits in men had effectively rendered many families women-headed families. It is observed from the reasons and patterns of loan disbursement of CORO's credit co-operative society that women spent the money they got on children's health, education and food. Men with either permanent or temporary jobs spent more money on adult goods like alcohol, cigarettes and other such things. Effectively the family was caught in a vicious debt trap with exorbitant rates of interest. Women single-handed managed all household matters but considered themselves to be the subordinate sex and *adani* (unknowledgeable) whereas the fact was merely that their wisdom was not supported by alphabetical literacy. Women had accepted all social norms and practices that perpetuated their subordinate status. For example a typical response of women to wife beating was 'He is husband. He will beat his wife. Will he beat a woman on the road?'

There was a wide gender gap in the status of education in the community. Women were either non-literate or minimally literate. The drop-out rate of girls in primary education was high. Women attributed the reasons for their low or no education to poverty, negligence of parents, household chores and care of siblings. In contrast their 'brothers' were admitted to schools and efforts were made to retain them in school.

The gendered inequitable access to minimally available resources within the family due to poverty worsened a woman's position. Women were denied the right to education right through the history of India. In addition to her identity as a woman, her identity as a Dalit, who were oppressed under the caste system, further marginalised her. The higher percentage of non-literates among Dalit women and higher drop-out rates among Dalit girls in primary education could thus be explained to lie in structures of poverty, class, caste and gender.

Decisions related to 'marriage' were made by men for women. Older women in the community were married off as early as ages of ten to fourteen. Meerabai, a young widow, had lost her husband on the fourteenth day of her marriage owing to pneumonia. She was ten years old then and did not remarry. Daughters are generally not considered as part of the natal family once they are married off. Vijubai, a literacy learner, told in her introduction that she had three sons. When asked whether she had no daughter, she replied, 'Yes, I have. I have three daughters. But they are married, and no more belong to this family.' Most of the women did not know their own age. Kesarbai, a literacy learner, said, 'Maybe I am twenty to forty years old or maybe a hundred.'

Women manage household things and equate this with decision making in the family. Shakuntalabai in one of the discussions said, 'We are decision makers in the family. They [husbands] give money to us, and we have to manage everything by ourselves. They don't ask us what we did with it.' When probed further by asking how would the husbands react if women gave some money to their needy relatives or spent it on things other than family needs, another woman learner reflexively answered, 'They would think us to be the thieves and would snatch all money that they gave us.'

Gendered division of household labour was explicit in the community. All household work including childcare was the woman's responsibility, irrespective of whether she worked outside the house (as a wage earner). Interestingly, even women who were sole earners in the family said that their income was subsidiary and was only to supplement the main income of the 'male breadwinner'. Woman with her dominant identity as a mother, a sister, a daughter and a wife had confined herself to the four walls of the house.

Women's restricted mobility was the accepted norm. Ramabai's husband did not allow her to go out of the house. He was unaware of her joining literacy classes. She attended classes when he was out at work. Defying restrictions openly would have led to a major confrontation in the family. A seemingly self-imposed ban by women on their own mobility could easily be felt.

Violence against women was rampant. It was generally crude and physical in form, as was indicated by the cases registered in CORO's legal aid and counselling centres. Wife beating, desertion, harassment for dowry, rape, are some of the commonly noticed crimes against women. For lack of any alternative arrangement (parental or institutional support) women opted to stay in violent marriages. (Hardly five per cent of the total 2,000 cases registered in CORO's legal aid centres in the last seven years have sought legal help for divorce.) The rest all desired reconciliation with their husbands.

Thus the identity of a community woman in these slums is complex and multidimensional. She is a woman, a poor woman and a Dalit poor woman. The construction of her identity in each of these dimensions effectively results in lowered self-esteem and prohibits her from participation in public life. Her non-literacy is the legacy of her identity as a Dalit and also as a woman, which leads to lack of skills that can fetch her respect and good money. At home she is dominated because she is a woman and is culturally a subordinate sex. As a result she is confined to her home, always occupied with her mental and physical stress and thus does not participate in the public domain. Women are always included in the broad category of 'Dalit' or 'poor' by the political leadership. Women in the position of community leadership and as social actors were thus an unbelievable option for these women prior to CORO's literacy efforts.

Literacy processes

Before initiating the literacy programme, CORO conducted a detailed family survey in the community and tried to organise a literacy intervention with the help of local youth in a very linear way. CORO's middle-class notions of literacy and education were challenged by the perceptions of community women. In a small-group meeting of non-literates when an aspect of literacy, being able to read the bus numbers for easier mobility was emphasised, Savitri, a non-literate woman rose to say, 'I cannot read and write but I can take you to any corner of the city. Tell me where do you wish to go.' Savitri was absolutely right because she was a small fish vendor, travelling across the length and breadth of the city in search of fresh, cheap fish. She was managing her own accounts orally. The question thus encountered was why literacy – when it was not their perceived need? However, deeper interaction with community people and sensitivity to their needs and priorities shaped up CORO's literacy efforts later.

Literacy kits provided by the government failed to motivate women to acquire literacy *per se* skills because the contents of the kits were irrelevant to life in urban communities. Moreover the kit contained books, a notebook and a pencil. Women in all communities were very hesitant to write in the notebook with a pencil. 'You should give us slates. Then we can rub it easily when we make mistakes. We are afraid of writing on these books and notebooks,' represented Shakuntala. CORO then provided slates to all learners. This helped women to overcome the mental barrier: probably women equated writing on notebooks with higher literacy skills. They were afraid that somebody would look into their notebooks and ridicule them for their mistakes. While seeing me writing the field notes a learner remarked, 'Look, how her hands move swiftly. We cannot do that.' But when reminded of their extraordinary skill of making chapatis (Indian bread), which involves swift hand movements, they looked convinced that literacy skills could also be a matter of practice.

I also noted (mainly through the body language of many learners) that picking up a pencil and trying to 'draw' alphabets on a slate/notebook was a big event for learners. It took a lot of time to initiate this action as if there was a barrier from 'within' (cultural?) to do this. I feel it was a mental set-up or block that obstructed woman from taking this step. It could be a mixture of fear, inhibition, novelty, diffidence (that they lacked some 'respected' skill), confidence (that they were trying to catch the missed bus) and in the case of Santosh Nagar learners it could also have been an assertion of denied rights.

CORO, through many activities, made an effort to build a literacy environment in the community. While most of the people looked at libraries as a post-literacy activity, CORO started mobile libraries, one for fifty households (total 150 libraries) each in all the communities it worked in, as a pre-literacy learning activity.

Gross similarities in literacy learning programmes in all communities eventually turned into a community-specific literacy programme. In some communities it was the issue of Public Distribution System (PDS), in others it was a fight against violence towards women while in Santosh Nagar it was an anti-alcohol movement which generated and sustained women's motivation in literacy learning. Efforts were made to weave reading and writing activities in the classrooms around the activism generated outside the classrooms.

CORO developed its own literacy learning material acknowledging learner's emotions, needs and aspirations. CORO started its literacy learning programme with learners writing the name of Dr Babasaheb Ambedkar, an undisputed Dalit leader and a reformer who vehemently opposed the atrocious caste system that denied the discriminated castes even the basic human rights, including the right to learn. CORO also developed a literacy kit based on problems that women faced with the PDS system, which enabled women to lodge written complaints against the shopkeepers. This made literacy learning a relevant activity for many learners.

Regular visits of CORO activists to the community and their personal rapport with community women stimulated women to attend classes.

Classes were then marked more by discussions, experience sharing and less literacy *per se* learning. Discussions ranged from childhood nostalgia to cleanliness, their daily routines, their communications, health-related issues, domestic issues, superstitions, current realities, local politics, power relations, their aspirations and other relevant topics. Literacy classes in Santosh Nagar generated unusual excitement in the community. A total of twelve classes were running. Women were willing to attend classes but many worked all through the day so could not come. CORO started night classes (at 10.00 p.m.) in addition to the afternoon classes. Many women started attending night classes when all their domestic chores for the day were over and they could spend some time for their own. Gradually the attendance in night classes increased.

The homogeneity of groups was very helpful in building team spirit and cohesiveness among learners. All women in literacy classes had almost the same economic and social position. They were all Dalits and in the average age group of thirty to forty years. People coming from the same region or village formed clusters in the slums and thus each class had a homogeneous group of women coming from the same region. They shared common concerns. They came together only on religious occasions or family functions where other family members accompanied them. Their household responsibilities had offered them little time for deep interactions.

Initiation of literacy classes acted as stimulation to the women in Santosh Nagar. Literacy classes provided much-needed social and mental spaces for women learners, an opportunity to come together on a regular basis for reasons not related to their familial responsibilities. This totally new avenue generated a lot of excitement among them. In literacy classes, women interacted with other women of similar status, discussing their life experiences. This helped them to recognise, understand and reiterate the commonality of their problems in and out of the household. Literacy classes also provided them with mental space to think about themselves. Women needed some sort of change in their over-stressed lives. Socialisation through literacy processes helped them to think about the issues that bothered them most, and the togetherness (later turned into solidarity) rendered them courage to break the 'culture of silence'. While classroom activities provided much-needed social and mental space for women, the outside classroom activities built a conducive atmosphere for expression of their enhanced self-esteem and of togetherness.

Learners opined that they felt better because they attended classes. 'We have our own activity,' said a learner. It would be incorrect to say that they were longing to learn alphabets and numeracy, yet all of them looked forward every day to the literacy class. It was not literacy *per se* that enthused them, it was literacy as a process of coming together, sharing, constructing self-identity (through carving time out for themselves and thus asserting themselves) that triggered their latent potential. Who prompted them to attend classes? Sakhubai said, 'Our own mind brings us here. There was gossip about us "roaming" out during the night-time. But we paid no attention.' This coming together gave women the strength to assert themselves.

Gains of literacy which were initially limited to 'feeling better' at the individual level described as a lesser perspective of women's empowerment (Longwe 1997) were later transformed into collective action (described as the stronger perspective of empowerment, ibid.) that rocked the entire community. Literacy activity enthused not only women but also the sensitive youth in the community who were unemployed, little educated and were literally sitting idle. In literacy they found an activity that gave them respect, recognition and an opportunity of wider exposure.

Collective action

Women agitated against the alcoholic habits of men in the community. Alcoholism affected them economically and socially. It pushed families into a vicious trap of indebtedness. It was a frequent cause of violence, mainly against women. It affected the health of family members. Sonabai related that many men had sold the roofs (tin sheets) of their houses to buy liquor. Women used their collective strength to resist alcoholic habits in community men.

The social get-together organised by CORO to celebrate International Women's Day triggered the imagination of Santosh Nagar women who attended. They listened to the narrations of rural women from Pune district (in Maharashtra), specially organised for the occasion. The women from Pune shared how they resisted the alcoholic habits of their husbands and confronted liquor den owners. Charged with these narrations, followed by lengthy internal deliberations, women of Santosh Nagar collectively demolished all four illicit liquor dens in their community. They continued their fight (with waxing and waning) with den owners for nearly two years. They also faced the wrath of male family members during this period, but they did not give up their fight. The efforts by men in the community to break women's solidarity did not succeed. But the attempt at character assassination of a leader of the women's group crippled the whole anti-alcohol movement in Santosh Nagar. Even the literacy programme in the community came to a halt after that.

Women demolished liquor dens. They fought their husbands on the issue, wrote a collectively signed letter to the police authorities, compelled the police to take action against the den owners, submitted a written appeal to the Prohibition Minister of State and established alternative leadership in the community. The 'dumb dolls' of yesterday became fire-brand personalities. A group of twenty-five to thirty women were taking rounds in the community twice a day to see that no illicit liquor was sold. They were literally afraid of nothing. Sonabai emerged as one of the two leaders of this movement. Her level of response to stimulus was high. She narrated,

> I was not a learner in the literacy class. I used to take my grandsons every day to the main road for a walk when I would see these women sitting in the class, writing, reading. But I never thought of going and learning there. One day these boys [literacy activists] invited me for a women's *melawa* (get-together). Since the transport arrangement to attend the get-together was available free of cost and even tea and snacks were to be served [with a laugh], I went along with other women. There we heard how women from Pune, who looked similar to us [appearance, non-literate] resisted the alcoholic habits of their husbands. That started some thinking in our mind.

Sonabai took the initiative to mobilise women and speak without any inhibition. In her own assessment, she became leader of the activity because she was very tall, had a loud voice, and spoke too much and too fast. She was not a literacy learner earlier but started attending literacy classes regularly after the anti-alcohol action. The attendance in the literacy classes improved after the anti-alcohol activity. One of the learners aptly described their success, saying, 'Enhancement in women's courage was the success.'

Sonabai excitedly recalled how the women defied the den owners' demand for payment of the liquor purchased by the men on credit. Sonabai stated, 'We asked them, "Did you give them sweets? You ruined our lives. We refuse to pay you any money."' The collective force was so powerful that the den owners could not retaliate against this mass disobedience to pay. Sonabai narrated, 'Get-together was the first instance when we went out for such a reason (for listening to somebody, for some social programme).'

Vijubai made a very interesting disclosure. She referred to her husband as a *malak* (owner), which is a general custom in rural areas, especially among Dalits. She said:

> My malak used to drink [alcohol] a lot. I started threatening him that if he drinks, I will call all the 'literacy' women and beat him. He was really scared. In spite of being a 'man' he was afraid of us. He bought a white sari and a blouse for me to wear when I go out for the meetings.

The vision, perspective and actions of CORO were helpful to this movement. CORO activists were instrumental in accelerating the process. Whenever and wherever women felt themselves inadequate to handle any situation, CORO stepped in as a partner to the movement and devised new training programmes for the women to overcome their inadequacies. The male activists of CORO stood by the women all throughout the movement and that was very helpful. The feeling of solidarity that was developed among women in the process of the acquisition of literacy was crucial to the women's anti-alcohol movement. Women had been helplessly suffering from alcoholism among men for a long time. Individually they were mutely accepting all the excesses associated with alcoholic habits among men but collectively they gained the courage to fight this devastating habit (Sakhubai).

Agitating women got a lot of attention and recognition from the press and public figures. This further enhanced their motivation. Representatives of All India Radio, and some prominent local magazines, interviewed some of the participants in this activity. The Minister of Prohibition, State Government, who was also the chief of the Republican Party of India, a party with a large Dalit following, publicly felicitated the leaders of the activity. The women immediately formed a *mahila mandal* (women's group) which was regarded as active by women from other communities. This recognition was altogether a new and unexpected happening for the community women. Sonabai articulated this very well in rightly saying, 'We were nowhere. We were not [present] on any maps. Literacy brought us to the forefront.' Emergence of leadership from among women in the community was something that 'never happened before'.

The processes of literacy learning and of the emergence of women's activism in Santosh Nagar were neither linear nor were they only about successes. Dominant patriarchal structures that initially had welcomed literacy activities as 'good' and 'noble' later sharply contested women's anti-alcohol movement. These forces aligned together to suppress the women's initiative that challenged unequal gendered relations in the private and public domains. When all efforts to break women's solidarity failed, the attempt at character assassination of a woman leader proved to be an effective tool to stall women's initiative.

Alcoholic men in the community were very upset with women because women's assertion itself was a blow to the power relations that existed within the community and within the family. Men thought that women were crossing their boundaries and going beyond limits. Husbands vehemently started harassing wives for going out of the house. Sons restrained their mothers from going out, saying, 'People talk about you, it's embarrassing.' Women were criticised for not being good wives and/or good mothers. As a group men were cursing the women's group for its insanity.

Men's opposition to their wives/family women attending literacy classes was further fuelled with this collective action. Men used their preferred gendered position in the family to ensure and reinforce women's subordination.

It should be noted here that women who could challenge men's alcoholic habits collectively did/could not directly challenge gendered relations within their family very powerfully. Through interaction with them I realised that many of them perceived the anti-alcohol movement predominantly as an issue of family well-being, rather than as an issue of increased violence against them due to alcoholism. But their actions challenged gender equations both in the public and in the private domain. The women's movement posed a real threat to established male leaders in the community. They made every effort to break solidarity among women. Women resisted these onslaughts very well. However the intense confrontation at every moment inside and outside the house was really draining their energies.

A vulgar anonymous postcard was written to Latabai (fifty-five), another leader of anti-alcohol activism. Photocopies of this postcard were sent to many houses in the community and the letter was discussed in the local political party office even before it reached Latabai. Attention was shifted from the anti-alcohol movement to this letter. Generally women felt very bad about the letter. Latabai felt humiliated. The discussions about her moral character started in the community. This divided women into two groups. Strong and wrong notions about the woman's character among women, and jealousy, were some of the reasons for this division. Latabai's family members pressed her to withdraw from the movement because they felt that the letter and the subsequent discussions were a blow to their family respect.

Ratan, a CORO literacy activist, said, 'Such an attack was possible because the leader was a woman. Such a letter would have never been written to a male leader.' This letter proved to be an effective tool to stall the women's movement. When all efforts to break women's solidarity were in vain, the femininity of their leader was exploited to stall the movement. The stalling of all anti-alcohol efforts and also of literacy classes in this community after the anonymous letter episode vividly explains how women's assertions and initiatives in the public domain were controlled by using their gendered identity.

Conclusion

It is seen that the events and processes in Santosh Nagar unfolded against the background of alphabetical literacy learning. It is also observed that it was not literacy *per se* that enthused women for the 'anti-alcohol movement' but literacy learning as a collective process which culminated in confidence building of the women, challenging gendered power relations. Literacy classes provided the women with the most needed mental and social space (also see Millican in this volume) and a platform for sharing and ventilation of grievances. An opportunity to communicate with women of similar status, within a homogeneous group, helped the literacy learners to break the 'culture of silence'.

Literacy *per se* was never a perceived need of the community women. Literacy learning (*per se*) could make sense only when it became emotionally appealing or functionally 'relevant'. Later, this learning became instrumental in enhancing the self-esteem of the learners. Writing letters to the police authorities and to the State Minister enhanced this self-esteem further, though CORO literacy activists had drafted it (in consultation with the learners) and individually women had only signed it. This indicates that social networks and supports are important in literacy communicative practices. In urban contexts like Mumbai, where all administrative, legal procedures follow only the dominant literacy mode of communication, acquisition of this skill becomes necessary even as part of one's survival struggle, struggle against denial of basic human rights.

CORO's literacy efforts can be seen as a combination of Emancipatory Literacy (Freire 1972, 1993) and the Social Literacies approach (Street 1984, 1995) with the focus on gender. While all CORO's efforts were aimed at social change, it built on local perceptions, needs, practices and aspirations. Though CORO's literacy programme was initially inspired by government's autonomous model of literacy (Street 1984), soon it became delinked from the target-oriented, linear approach to literacy and was developed with flexibility and reflexivity in response to the stimulus provided by the community women.

As Rogers *et al.* point out in this volume there cannot be a 'one size fits all' literacy programme. However the challenge remains to integrate ethnographic perspectives into large-scale literacy implementation programmes. This is more true in countries like India with a massive number of non-literates, a wide range of cultural diversity (gender, castes/subcastes, religions, regions, languages) and inadequate resources. Again the inevitable lack of highly skilled facilitators (see also Fiedrich and Millican in this volume) in the implementation of reflexive literacy programmes makes it more difficult to scale up such approaches.

Participatory approaches to implementation are discussed extensively in this volume. Whether an 'ideal' participatory approach is possible and preferable (see Millican's chapter) is an issue of debate. Ideally, the mere fact that one chooses to work/research with a particular section of society (geographical/social) itself could bring into question the participatory approach. For intervention what is important is that the programme continuously creates larger spaces for reflexivity, for participants to be 'actors' in every capacity and to 'own' it.

It should also be noted that the women's anti-alcohol movement in Santosh Nagar unfolded the changing alignment and realignment of social and political forces in the community as reactions to the movement. When the established political leadership and men in the family together opposed the women's initiative, women aligned themselves with CORO and also with the male activists of literacy to build on their strength. Women's gendered identities were used as weapons against them to stall their initiatives. While strategising, implementing organisations like CORO should take such anticipated backlash into account and make an effort to create necessary support structures.

References

CORO (1992) 'A Brief Note on CORO Activities', a note prepared for wider circulation by CORO Executive Council, Mumbai: CORO

Freire, P. (1972) *Pedagogy of the Oppressed*, London: Penguin

—— (1993) 'The adult literacy process as cultural action for freedom' in J. Maybin (ed.) *Language and Literacy in Social Practice*, Adelaide: Multilingual Matters, pp. 252–63

Kumar, R. (1995) 'From Chipko to Sati: the contemporary Indian women's movement' in A. Basu (ed.) *The Challenge of Local Feminism: Women's Movements in Global Perspective*, Boulder CO: Westview Press, pp. 58–86

Longwe, S. (1997) 'Education for women's empowerment or schooling for women's subordination?' in C. Medel-Anonuevo (ed.) *Negotiating and Creating Spaces of Power: Women's Educational Practices Amidst Crisis*, Hamburg: UNESCO Institute of Education, pp. 17–24

Rangari, A. (1984) *Indian Caste System and Education*, New Delhi: Deep & Deep

Street, B.V. (1984) *Literacy in Theory and Practice*, Cambridge: Cambridge University Press

—— (1995) 'Introduction' in B.V. Street (ed.) *Literacy in Theory and Practice*, Cambridge Studies in Oral and Literate Culture, Cambridge: Cambridge University Press, pp. 1–16

13 Functional participation?

Questioning participatory attempts at reshaping African gender identities: the case of REFLECT in Uganda

Marc Fiedrich

Ruth abruptly stops picking beans, jumps to her feet, swiftly brushes the dirt from her dress and marches across the small courtyard to proudly pose in front of a little reed table: 'Without REFLECT I would never have known about drying racks.' I try hard to conceal my disappointment while Ruth continues to enthuse: 'This is where everything must go, the pots, the plates, the knives, everything. You wash it and then you put it there on top until it's dry. If it's not dry and you eat from it, that's it, you fall ill. That is what I learned in REFLECT.' Any reader familiar with the smart housewives who routinely appear on Western television screens to marvel at the life-transforming effects of a new dishwashing liquid will have a fairly accurate image of the way Ruth strutted around the shaky construction upholding her meagre collection of as yet unwashed cups and plates.

Ruth's courtyard was a regular port of call on my walks through the central Ugandan village, Kilemba, where I had set up camp the year before to find out about the place adult education classes occupy in the lives of women learners. When I was not sitting in a class observing how learners and facilitators grappled with the learning tools offered by the REFLECT method, I was walking the far-flung paths to make visits and gain a sense of how learning in the classes may or may not contribute to the 'empowerment' of women in rural Kilemba. A reflection on my disappointment with Ruth's parading around the drying rack is perhaps a good starting point to my discussion of adult education, gender relations and the varying expectations of change that learners and development agents bring to the process.

The first sting of disappointment was, of course, that Ruth put on a performance for me. She was acting as if we were meeting for the first time, as if I was a gullible consultant sweeping through the villages to be fed neat little success stories. It was an insult to any ethnographer's honour. I had spent hours, days and months trying to weave myself into the cultural fabric of Kilemba, and Ruth's courtyard was a favourite because I felt she treated me as she would any other of her neighbours, even those who were not white men employed by a large international NGO with a brief to do research on adult education programmes. On other occasions Ruth had been refreshingly blunt. Once, when we were also discussing the merits of the REFLECT programme, she cut our elaborations short, stating that adult learning was well and good but unless she was given some 'seed money' soon she would consider the whole affair a waste of time. A bit like her husband. At the time I had admired her sharp wit, and the circumstances of her statement were such that I felt I had been taken into her confidence. By contrast, now Ruth's posturing around the drying rack appeared sycophantic, exactly the scene one would lay on for a project evaluator on a fleeting visit.

Apart from my sense of being relegated to outsider status, I was also disappointed at the object Ruth had now chosen to illustrate the merits of her participation in the REFLECT circle. Drying racks, I suspected, were a mildly disturbing relic from a previous generation of adult education programmes whose main objective had been to imbue African women with European standards of housewifery. To speak in the idiom of Paulo Freire, drying racks would have to be classified as a tool for 'domestication', not 'liberation', let alone 'empowerment'. Nothing for Ruth to be proud of. And to make matters worse, drying racks did not even deliver on their limited promise of improved domestic hygiene.[1]

The dilemma I faced with Ruth's story was replicated many times. Perspectives on the 'impact' REFLECT participation was having on a woman learner's life were often contradictory and appeared highly contingent on the circumstances of the moment, how a woman felt on the day of our meeting, what she wanted to present to me and what not. At the same time, it was also clear that my assessments of situations were coloured by the way I felt included or alienated, or, most likely, constantly tittered between the two sentiments. To add further complication, my growing appreciation of the messy realities women learners inhabited further hampered any attempt to recount their trajectories in terms of the empowerment narratives familiar to those working in development contexts. It is rare to hear of empowered women who use their newly gained personal freedoms to act selfishly, immorally or even just indifferently. Instead, to become empowered is often taken to be synonymous with becoming community-minded, health-conscious, economically prudent and, on the whole, morally upright. In this sense, to become 'empowered' through participation in an adult education programme is not worlds away from earlier paradigms of becoming 'modern' through a functional literacy programme. And yet, while literacy's potential to harness modernity has rightly been challenged, the notion that participation is empowering remains a much-coveted truism. In other words, there is a real danger that adult education programmes, having (barely) come to terms with the idea that literacy will not transform people in preconceived ways, substitute participation for literacy and continue to promote themselves as trusted manufacturers of progress.

In fact, this study started at a point in time when many REFLECT practitioners questioned whether the 'three Rs' still had any place in adult education, whether visual tools such as PRA graphics were not a more valid, less imposing form of literacy in participants' contexts. Those REFLECT programmes that focused exclusively on participatory debate were widely considered more progressive than those which still dedicated much time to the teaching of reading and writing. While this tendency was not strictly upheld, it did affect the programmes under discussion here, limiting the amount of time participants spent on learning how to read and write. This chapter is then not overly concerned with literacy as a tool, nor does it say much about literacy practices. Instead, I explore how concepts such as 'literacy' or 'participation' often act as a convenient proxy to make the complex self-transformations that adult education programmes seek to encourage appear linear, logical and straightforward.[2]

To most adult educators Ruth's building of a drying rack would represent a story of learning success, where participatory analysis led to the identification of a problem and provided a solution that was duly implemented by her. While this would confirm widely held expectations of what participation achieves, it would leave half the story untold. Ruth's motivations, to which I shall return later, would become negligible since 'participation' is seen to be the active agent acting on her.

My first aim in this chapter is to unsettle understandings of participation, to make some of the assumptions behind the concept explicit and thus vulnerable. To be sure, I am not setting out to 'attack' participatory approaches, instead I seek to counter a perhaps understandable trend to stylise participation as 'the' answer to all kinds of development-related problems, a trend that mirrors earlier belief in the power of literacy and, in my view, invites unwarranted dogmatism and unnecessary rigidity. To this end, I analyse a participatory tool, the gender workload calendar which is widely used in many REFLECT programmes to facilitate debates on gender relations. In a second step, I discuss ways in which women in Kilemba attempted to use adult education classes to negotiate gender relations, sometimes drawing on the participatory ideology promoted through the classes, and sometimes not.

Gender and REFLECT: tools and subtexts

Attempts to use participatory approaches to foster 'open debate' in adult education are often contradictory. Discussions on gender relations in

REFLECT programmes are a good example of this. On the one hand, the importance of respecting privacy and cultural difference is usually recognised by programme initiators, while on the other hand, the need for intervention is justified through normative assertions about relationships being unequal and unjust, perpetuating the subordination of women. The innovators of REFLECT evince this ambiguity in their proposed approach to gender, which:

> recognises that both men and women have practical and strategic gender needs; and that although in most societies (both North and South!) women tend to be subordinate to men, and to have a heavier work load; both women and men would benefit from a more equitable balance in gender relations. . . . Literacy participants, both male and female, have the chance to discuss a range of issues (from nutrition to income and expenditure) in open-ended but well structured discussions – rooted in their own experiences. There is no pressure to reach a pre-decided conclusion.
>
> (Archer and Cottingham 1996: 17)

Here the rejection of 'pre-decided conclusions' contrasts with certainty about the 'benefit from a more equitable balance in gender relations'. But how could one be certain that 'open-ended but well structured debate' will necessarily result in learners endorsing greater gender equality? Taking the gender workload calendar as an example, I argue that the desired effect can be reached only if learners, somewhat paradoxically, go into the debate already sharing concerns for gender equality similar to those the exercise is designed to instil in them.

Among the objectives the REFLECT manual sets out for discussions on the gender workload calendar are: 'To analyse work done by men and women, and to consider whether the division of work is fair' (Archer and Cottingham 1996: 126). It is proposed that facilitators start out by asking participants to define what they mean by work before men and women split into two groups to graphically construct calendars detailing their respective work loads over the year. Once completed, it is suggested that the two calendars are brought together for comparison and debate which, if the facilitator deems fit, can be structured by asking some or all of the following questions:

- Do women work harder than men or more than men – or not?
- Is the work that women do recognised as work? Should it be?
- Is collecting fuel-wood work? Is cleaning work? etc.
- Why is work divided up as it is between men and women?
- Has it always been like this?

- Has it changed in the last ten or twenty years? Is there any need to change it now?

(Archer and Cottingham 1996: 127)

Assuming for the moment that circles roughly follow these guidelines, there are three major conceptual issues to be raised. The first concerns the way individual learners are asked to position themselves within this debate. The answer to this question is simple: individuals are there either as men or as women, no more and no less. But what happens when, as is the case here, individual men are conflated as 'men', or a woman is taken as representative of 'women'? Articulation of their 'own' experience in this calendar is subject to individual men and women filtering out aspects of their lives which they deem untypical of 'a man' or 'a woman'. To achieve this abstraction, participants must agree, at least tacitly, on what constitutes a 'typical' woman or man, a category that effectively removes all other axes of difference, other than sex, from the analysis. Any suggestion that such a calendar is an authentic representation of participants' realities as perceived by them then precariously reinforces the erroneous assumption that 'all (wo)men are the same'.[3] Ironically, it is near impossible for participants to complete the calendar without first conjuring up those same stereotypes about gender that this tool is designed to criticise. Barred from considering work loads as a factor of anything other than being a woman or a man, participants' options are limited to fictionalising 'women's work' or 'men's work'.

A second important cultural assumption implicit to the gender workload calendar is that work exists prior to its division between men and women. It suggests that work is not *per se* gendered but becomes so only in the process of its division. In fact the gender neutrality of work itself is the prerequisite for debating its subsequent division in terms of equality and fairness. In short, the division of work is considered a reversible, contractual arrangement between men and women. Participants who answer the guiding questions and construct the calendar may easily appear complicit with this view, seemingly sharing the same concern for equality and fairness between the sexes as many Western observers. And yet, even if the debate ends in women accusing men of being lazy, this should *not* automatically be taken as further evidence of the argument that women the world over are fighting the same battles. In Kilemba and other villages women learners often complained about their husbands' laziness but usually did so with reference to specifically male and female obligations. They rarely couched their criticisms in terms of equality or fairness. This may be so because they do not regard the division of work but work itself as gendered and therefore are not primarily struggling to enter male-defined work domains or to get men to partake in female-defined responsibilities. Instead, they may be keen to remind their partners of their obligations *as men*. This may be a well justified demand in the case of some men, but it does not help the case of those who, irrespective of their own efforts, have no realistic prospect of satisfactorily assuming the role of male provider that modern Bugandan society ascribes to them.

The third issue to be raised concerns a contradiction that feminist writers have previously recognised with respect to broader debates on Gender and Development (GAD). Kandiyoti (1998: 136), commenting on her earlier work (1988), self-critically remarks on the difficulty of characterising women as simultaneously immersed within dominant gender ideologies while also considering them rational and autonomous actors. The gender workload calendar replicates this tension in a simplistic, time-bound fashion where the existence of hegemonic constraints on women first necessitates but then does not hinder women learners formulating and expressing their own, rational interests when discussing the implications of the graphic. While increased autonomy is often one of the desired outcomes of women's empowerment, it is, at least in this case, also one of its prerequisites. This is a circle that is not easily squared, as Attwood *et al.*'s (this volume) description of REFLECT circles in Lesotho demonstrates vividly. For example, participants and facilitators in Lesotho were, perhaps unsurprisingly, not familiar with the distinction between gender and sex. Attwood *et al.* then describe a process of gentle coaxing which allowed 'more skilled facilitators' to stir participants towards speaking about relationships between men and women from what you and I would recognise and probably value as a 'gendered perspective'. What participants thought they were expressing, or their motives for putting matters forward in the way they did, does however remain elusive.

I am not suggesting that the tensions, contradictions and assumptions highlighted here necessarily inhibit circle debates. Neither does my criticism aim to encourage the redesign of participatory tools with a view to ensuring truly undistorted, authentic and representative debates in the circles. On the contrary, I suggest that participatory adult education practitioners should accept that circle debates are inevitably contrived. Once we stop to routinely claim that participatory debate offers a linear path to an authentic representation of learner perspectives there should be much greater freedom to recognise cultural difference and to explore how learners, in practice, engage with approaches such as REFLECT. The second half of this chapter aims to provide some ideas on how such a shift in perspective may change our perception of how women learners use adult education in the negotiation of gender relations.

Returning briefly to Ruth and the pride she expressed in her new drying rack, while I was still wondering how best to react to her display of enthusiasm, Ruth changed tone. Smiling meaningfully, she intimated that another advantage of the drying rack is that it makes a public exposition of the cups, plates and cooking utensils one owns. I couldn't grasp why that would be beneficial, particularly since Ruth's possessions were comparatively modest, nothing that could be shown off to passing neighbours to any great effect. But that, Ruth retorted, was precisely the point: by virtue of exposing her lacklustre collection of cooking utensils to the passing public she had managed to embarrass her husband into buying a few new pieces that she had long wanted to have.

There are two aspects in this story that appear to me to be symptomatic of the way in which women learners use adult education to wiggle and wrangle gender relations – as opposed to negotiating them. The first is to do with the way Ruth, at least initially, fashions herself as a dutiful disciple of education, claiming that education did exactly what education had set out to do, i.e. convince her of the health-and-hygiene benefits of a drying rack. I will argue that in a society such as that of Buganda, where education is an important signifier of status, becoming proficient with the lingo of educational messages, being able to replicate them convincingly, can be a major boost to one's respectability. In this context, building a drying rack or a latrine may well have been a more meaningful signifier than the ability to read or write. The ability to sign one's name or to write a few words mattered to most participants but only a few pursued the ambition to become more proficient than that. The second aspect of Ruth's story that connects with a common theme in this research is the way in which she uses education to exert pressure on her husband, to appeal to his honour as a married man.

Before going into more detail on these two topics, it is necessary to briefly justify why I am not spending more space exploring how learners, in practice, approached learning units that addressed gender issues explicitly. After all, the gender workload calendar was only one of several units where my Ugandan NGO colleagues had inserted suggestions on how to explore the gender dimensions of a given issue. Yet whenever we discussed the gender-sensitive credentials of the programme, curriculum content was mentioned last, and often only after probing. Made aware of this, my colleagues confirmed that they believed measures such as the recruitment of female facilitators (which was possible in a limited number of cases), or the initial emphasis on encouraging women to register for the classes, were more effective than attempts to get learners to discuss gender relations as part of the curriculum. From my own observations of circle sessions it soon became clear that my colleagues had a point. In the context of discussing the reasons for sending children to school, for example, the facilitator might ask whether boys benefit more from education than girls or the other way around. Answers to this question varied but tended to be brief and factual in intent. In anticipation of this, staff had designed the next guiding question to probe further as to why participants chose either girls or boys, or both. Among the answers overheard commonly and in different classes were 'Girls are stupid,' 'Everyone should learn,' 'It is good to learn,' 'When they get older, girls don't have a mind to learn,' etc. Far from provoking debate, guiding questions were often interpreted as points of information and participants seemed mainly concerned to come up with a 'right' answer. This aspect was not limited to discussions on gender and it should also be noted that very lively discussions on controversial issues did often take place before the sessions officially started or when they had ended. Needless to say, these more animated debates were not nearly as systematic, structured and egalitarian as participatory ethics would prescribe.

Rather than further document how and why circle debates deviated from the participatory framework that the REFLECT approach anticipates it is now perhaps more constructive to look at some ways in which participants sought to draw benefit from them.[4]

Flaunting the 'practical' in search of the respectable?

As earlier pointed out, I initially found it difficult to cope with instances where learners presented me with educational messages that I knew to be impractical and suspected they did too. While observing class debates I was often struck by the ease with which participants made solemn resolutions to take actions that seemed way beyond their scope. Thus the learners in Kilemba collectively decided that as of that day they would all boil their drinking water. No matter how well advised this action would have been, nobody present had the means to procure the pots, the fuel wood and the time to put it into practice. And nobody really liked the taste of boiled water either. Similarly optimistic actions were decided upon to reduce the incidence of malaria. All standing waters were to be covered forthwith. Again, in this tropical region this was a task that went well beyond the capacity of the women either as individuals or as a collective.

To be sure, not every action learners discussed in the circles was unrealistic, but it was rare to come across a circle that would stop short of deciding on an action simply because it was clearly impossible to achieve. The usual pattern seemed to be for unrealistic actions to be adopted and then ignored. This sounds more obtuse than it actually is. Obviously, when discussing a problem in the circle it is comforting to believe that an action can be taken to address it. And given that learning units were generally structured to culminate in a decision about actions to be taken, it is not surprising that learners felt they had to come up with something before moving on to the next topic. It is also true that learners enjoyed making resolutions, not least because it offered an opportunity to prove to oneself and others just how serious a learner one was.

While I could explain dynamics in the circle with such reasoning, I was still puzzled about the situations I encountered when I spoke to learners in their own homes. A few weeks after the resolution to boil drinking water, for example, it was clear the action was unviable and I expected those learners I knew better to tell me as much. To my surprise several of them first spent a good chunk of time explaining to me in onerous detail why it was so vital that drinking water was to be boiled and how REFLECT had opened their eyes to this novel fact. Later in the same conversation, learners were usually frank and unapologetic in stating that they had known well before the literacy classes about the arguments in favour of boiling water and no, of course they did not boil theirs. Still, it seemed as if I was the only one who noticed a disjuncture, a contradiction. If learners had wanted to convince me of their diligence in reproducing educational content, why would they be so relaxed about flaunting it the next moment? Why were they not more disappointed or even bitter at the fact that at least some of the educational content produced in the circles was so clearly of no use to them? Attempts to discuss this disjuncture with learners were not fruitful, since, as pointed out, it seemed that I saw one where they saw none.

Before I could grow too impatient with this pattern, I realised that I was not the only one at the receiving end of learners' lectures about the necessity to wash one's hands before eating, the need to eat a varied diet, or to plant one's crops in orderly lines. On a couple of occasions I overheard how learners also patronised others with wisdoms derived from the circles and then I noticed how often it occurred that learners proudly reported to me occasions when they, to the surprise of their audience, had shown mastery of 'proper school knowledge'. It now dawned on me that I was too fixated on the notion that the educational *content* of REFLECT sessions had to be the key element from which learners would draw benefit. Instead, it seemed that to many women it was at least equally important to be able to 'parade' prestigious forms of knowledge. In other words, whether one actually boils one's drinking water or not is secondary to one's ability to convince others that one is the kind of educated person who effortlessly deals in Western (read 'modern') health and hygiene practices. A university graduate, or even a secondary school leaver, does not have to prove such fluency, it goes with the degree, but adult literacy classes tend to be of more doubtful repute and learners cannot expect to gain status simply by attending, they need to demonstrate to the outside world that they have indeed become legitimate bearers of sophisticated school knowledge.

Judging by the satisfaction visible on the face of an elderly lady who told me of the surprise she caused when, on a visit to a relative, she suddenly insisted on being given water to wash her hands before eating, there can be little doubt that learners experience such moments of status enhancement as gratifying and empowering. Perhaps the sole difficulty is how to recognise this type of progress in a tradition of adult education that is, at times, exceedingly puritan. Since colonial times, the main criticism adult educators have levelled against each other is that adult education is not practical enough, does not translate smoothly enough into learners engaging in concerted self-reform. When we find, for example, that learners have learned to read a little but make virtually no use of it, we are certain to have found a failing literacy programme, since the usefulness of a skill must surely be in its application. I do not suggest that we do away with such performance measures but I do suggest that we also recognise that to many learners it can be of equal importance to be seen to be 'learned', regardless of whether reading and writing skills find application or not.

One impediment to adult educators recognising status gain as a genuine benefit is that it is so often achieved by means that are incompatible with the way adult educators perceive their learners. Learners who gain respect by showing off their newly gained knowledge often do so at the expense of others. The intent in lecturing a neighbour about the nutritional value of vegetables is often not to 'share knowledge' but to demonstrate one's superiority. Self(ish)-interest and vanity undoubtedly form part of the approach in such circumstances. This is difficult to square with the widespread perception that adult education, by definition, encourages virtuous self-reform. One often hears of women who become numerate and thus protect themselves from being cheated by rogue traders but one never hears of the adult learner who uses her newly acquired abilities to do a bit of cheating herself. In a similar vein it is common to learn that participants start up small businesses and these would always be community-oriented and irreprehensible in nature (i.e. sowing, baking, agricultural sales, etc.). It is exceedingly rare to hear of adult learners who take up drug dealing, moneylending or, for that matter, any highly profitable activity. The gains adult learners make from their honest work are predictably invested sensibly in schooling, health, food or housing. We do not hear of the adult learner who uses her meagre earnings to buy, say, make-up or to pay for a consultation with the witch doctor. I argue that the expectation that women who join adult education quasi-automatically embark on a virtuous spiral of progress prevents us from recognising how women use adult education strategically, expressing their own vision of progress as they go along.

One area where women learners seek to capitalise on their status of 'being educated' is in relations with their sexual partners. Ruth embarrassed her husband into buying new cups and plates, while a few other women started to construct latrines or kitchen buildings themselves, thus pressuring their husbands into action, since construction work is considered a male responsibility. On a few occasions, women also reported successfully arguing that their newly educated status obliged them to wear better clothes or to visit the health clinic (as opposed to using herbal medicine) and that their husbands had obliged.

However, these are exceptional cases whose significance should not be exaggerated. Most women did have some access to income that was independent of their husband and the wrangle was predominantly about the division of expenditures between husband and wife. Despite first impressions to the contrary, it is, in my view, a misconception to depict gender relations in Buganda as embedded in self-assured patriarchal structures. Many men in the field sites emphasised the strength of male rule so often and so loudly that one could not help wondering why it was necessary if male dominance was indeed as firmly embedded as they claimed. A more accurate description of gender relations in Uganda would recognise that the male desire to be effortless patriarchs is strong, yet rarely fulfilled. This results in women often having a substantially higher radius of action than is publicly acknowledged or condoned. To many women the fact that they have more effective control over crops and household expenditure than their husbands would care to admit may widen the scope for discreet manoeuvring but it is not necessarily a source of comfort. One day a husband may turn a blind eye to a woman selling off some coffee but the next he might accuse her of mismanaging his affairs and the day after she stands accused of stealing. Tensions around resources were permanent in most households and therefore few women were keen to raise the confrontational stakes beyond where they had already reached.[5]

It is in this context that one has to read women learners' often-made assertion that adult education has made them 'better wives'. During a survey exercise in 1999, nine out of ten women participants claimed that respect from their husbands had increased in the past year. Those who elaborated on the reasons stated that they were now working harder, that they were cleaning the home well, and that they were speaking well to their husbands. To many readers this seeming embrace of female docility may confirm a deepening rather than a transformation of gender roles. But it must be remembered that the context in which women took this position is one where they are already in permanent confrontation with their husbands. It is also interesting to note how husbands chose to interpret their wives' participation in adult education. Many asserted that their wife's domestic management had indeed improved, some noting that there was now less need to command their wife, since she had become 'more reasonable'. Men often had a tendency to portray education as an ally in the project of controlling their wives. For men to depict women's education as aiding their own position as master is not only to diminish its threatening potential but also helps to explain the liberties women do take not as a lapse in male control but as a new form of it. In other words, if a woman participant in REFLECT decides to go to the market without seeking her husband's permission he is no longer forced to see this as insubordination, he can also choose to accept it as suitable behaviour for an educated woman.

Even with the important addition that most women who claimed to engage their husbands through redoubled efforts at being housewifely appeared to do so with clear aims in mind it is self-evident that this is not a strategy that would normally be recognised as empowering to women. Some women made a more convincing case for this strategy than others but the reason for describing it here is by no means to advocate it as a new avenue to women's empowerment. The purpose is merely to suggest that it is highly likely that learners – women or men – appropriate education in ways that appear awkward, perhaps even objectionable, to outsiders. Particularly when it comes to gender relations, it seems far more promising for women learners to wriggle and wrangle, exploiting opportunities wherever possible, than to engage in the kind of 'open' negotiation suggested in tools such as the gender workload calendar. The changes occurring as a result of such struggle are, by definition, difficult to attribute to any single factor, are incremental and are likely to be far more modest than the resolutions adult learners adopt in their learning environments.

Conclusion

At the end of this chapter the question why women come to literacy classes, and some come back time and time again, should be much less clear than at the beginning. At least in the case described here, literacy achievement could not have been the driving force. It would also be difficult to insist on participatory practices having rendered the programme irresistible and empowering to women. And yet they were there. One motivation, I have argued, was women's ambition to become recognised as educated. Coming to 'school' (the term preferred by many participants) was in itself sometimes more important than what actually transpired during sessions. This is not to say that process does not matter but it is to say that it often pans out quite differently than the well worn empowerment narratives would have us believe. Recognition of women learners' ambitions, whether selfish or altruistic, becomes much easier if we manage to occasionally put the blueprints that are much needed for action to the side.

Acknowledgements

Field research was carried out from June 1997 to June 2000 under the auspices of the British international NGO, ActionAid, supported by a grant from the Department for International Development, London. For further details about this research see Fiedrich and Jellema (2003). Names of places and persons have been changed.

Notes

1 Other activities advocated in the REFLECT circles, for example the building of latrines, could equally be labelled domesticating but could still be justified on grounds of the tangible hygiene improvement they encouraged. And yet drying racks in Kilemba seemed a failed attempt at education being 'practical'. The daily rhythm of activities was such that few women did the dishes straight after a meal and, even if they had done, they could not have left them out to dry, since they themselves were either inside the house, to sleep for the night, or away, working in the fields. Therefore the used pots and pans (some still containing leftovers) had to be locked away in the huts and were only brought out and washed once the next meal was due to be prepared.

2 The link between this and other chapters of this book is closer than may appear on first sight. Contributions such as that by Rogers (*et al.*) explore officially accepted definitions of literacy and how the ambitions for change expressed within them (mis-)represent those whom they are to serve. My starting point is not literacy as a concept but literacy programmes as an institution and yet the focus is on the same dynamic: the knee-jerk reaction that still automatically links 'literacy' with all too clearly defined visions of social progress, making it so difficult to leave the proverbial 'illiterate woman' behind (see also Robinson-Pant, this volume).

3 I am here touching on controversial debates among feminists about the usefulness of categories such as 'women' and 'men'. In short, postmodernists such as Mouffe (1993), Fraser (1998) or Butler (1990, 1998) question whether individuals can be subsumed under such a singular identity, insisting on the multifaceted, creative and fluid nature of identities. Authors such as Stromquist (1988) or Kandiyoti (1988, 1998) recognise the value of such enquiry but insist that singular identity categories are not only commonly accepted as a given by women's organisations in the South but are also, at least for Stromquist, a prerequisite for unity in feminist political struggles. My comments here relate to the way in which developmental tools can reinforce specific notions of singular identity rather than merely representing what is commonly accepted. This does not resolve the tension but it further underlines the dangers of assuming unity (rather than constructing it) where individuals are deemed to belong to the same category.

4 It is not possible here to explore the range of motivations which animated circle debates; for more details see Fiedrich (2003) and Fiedrich and Jellema (2003).

5 On the issue of why women may downplay their levels of skills, see also Betts's discussion (this volume) on El Salvador.

References

Archer, D. and Cottingham, S. (1996) 'Action Research Report on REFLECT. Regenerated Freirean Literacy through Empowering Community Techniques. The Experiences of Three REFLECT Pilot Projects in Uganda, Bangladesh, El Salvador', Education Research 17, London: Overseas Development Administration

Butler, J. (1990) *Gender Trouble: Feminism and the Subversion of Identity*, London and New York: Routledge

—— (1998) 'Subjects of sex/gender/desire' in A. Phillips (ed.) *Feminism and Politics*, Oxford: Oxford University Press, pp. 273–91

Fiedrich, M. (2003) 'Domesticating Modernity: Understanding Women's Aspirations in Participatory Literacy Programmes in Uganda', DPhil thesis, Brighton: University of Sussex

Fiedrich, M. and Jellema, A. (2003) *Literacy, Gender and Social Agency: Adventures in Empowerment*, Educational Papers 53, London: Department for International Development/ActionAid UK, or http://www.dfid.gov.uk-Pubs-files-litgenemp_edpaper53.pdf

Fraser, N. (1998) 'A future for Marxism', *New Politics*, 6: 95–8

Kandiyoti, D. (1988) 'Bargaining with patriarchy', *Gender and Society*, 2 (3): 274–90

—— (1998) 'Gender, power and contestation: rethinking bargaining with patriarchy' in C. Jackson and R. Pearson (eds) *Feminist Visions of Development*, London: Routledge, pp. 135–51

Mouffe, C. (1993) *The Return of the Political*, London: Verso

Stromquist, N.P. (1988) 'Women's education in development: from welfare to empowerment', *Convergence*, 21 (4): 5–14

14 'Out of school, now in the group'

Family politics and women's il/literacy in the outskirts of Mexico City

Claudia Flores-Moreno

In Mexico, the 2000 census showed that 6 million people out of the 63 million aged fifteen or over were regarded as illiterate. The gender illiteracy gap proved then that seven of every 100 men and eleven of every 100 women in the population of fifteen years of age or over were considered illiterate (INEGI 2003a). Moreover, the biggest disparities were in relation to age: whereas 1.5 million people out of those 6 million of illiterate Mexicans were in the sixty-five-year-old and over group, the fifteen-to-nineteen-year-old group included only 300,000 people (ibid.). Gender and age differences mean that it is not rare to find that more women than men of a mature age attend literacy groups run by the National Institute for Adult Education (INEA), since its foundation in 1981.

It is then arguable whether the majority of attendance at INEA by women can be considered as women's successful access to adult literacy programmes or whether there is still need to look at their schooling as girls. Arguments about women's access to literacy have concentrated on barriers to their attendance (Stromquist 1992; Ballara 1991), while girls' access to schooling has classically been looked at as unrelated to illiteracy rates (King and Hill 1993). Throughout cultures, families are important for girls and boys during schooling years, and have a key role in the gender literacy gap. As in other countries and cultures, Mexican families have a range of constitutions and dynamics. An important link for the understanding of women's literacy that has been under-explored so far is the role of family politics for girls' access to education and its relationship to enrolment in literacy groups. Family politics can be considered as an intricate set of nettings formed by covert and overt commands, negotiations, oppositions and support within kinship relations, according to which some members of the family take decisions and get involved in practices regarding themselves and others. Family politics is then worth exploring to look at women's literacy in relation to their education as girls.

This chapter thus explores the role of family politics for women in determining whether they had access to school when they were girls, and also in their motives for attending literacy sessions in adulthood. I will first look at how factors for women to prevail illiterate and their motives to attend literacy sessions are regarded in relevant research literature in the area, with particular reference to Latin America. I will second present the case of the group of La Paloma in Mexico City, to consider the motives of participants for not having been enrolled at school and why they were attending literacy sessions. Finally, the role of family politics is discussed in relation to the literature on women's literacy, based on the experience of the group in La Paloma.

Il/literate women with a past: families and girls' access to schooling

It has been acknowledged that particular interactions that take place in the family constitute a certain politics for girls' enrolment. Tackling the concern about why women remain under-educated as compared with men, mainstream education and development research approaches have proposed that gender differentials in education endure because those persons who bear the private cost of investing in schooling for girls and women fail to receive the full benefit of their investment. Thus it is regarded that parents' views have an influence on gender differences in education:

> although the returns to schooling go primarily to the student, the decision and the resources usually come from the parents, especially in the early school years. Thus the perception of parents may be the key factor. And parents may have different perceptions regarding their sons' and daughters' education.
>
> (King and Hill 1993: 23)

However, as Kabeer (Kabeer and Humphrey 1993: 81) has identified, a notion of the family as an 'unproblematic unity', dedicated to the collective interests of members, underpins many neo-liberal analyses. This model of the household is based on a Eurocentric commonsense view of the nuclear family, in which both parents are seen to have symmetrical power in decision making. Such a model is thus patently inadequate to deal with the flexible structures, the plurality of family and household composition, domestic relations, and residential arrangements which characterise domestic groupings around the world (Kabeer and Humphrey 1993: 82). What is more, it is now accepted that the extended family does not necessarily disappear with 'modernisation' or 'urbanisation' (Moser 1998: 17). In countries experiencing stringent adjustment conditions, the extended family remains vital for low-income survival strategies, with widely different and complex structures. Schultz (1993: 237) also shows that most policy makers operate with an oversimplified view of the family and its dynamics.

Regarding cultural patterns and customs, Ballara (1991) states that many parents in Latin America believe that it is not worthwhile to invest in girls' education, as daughters are seen as additional resources of household labour who will provide support for them when adult, and once married, will become part of the (re)productive labour force of another household.

> Husbands, fathers and men in general have such attitudes towards women's education, especially when it results in the possibility of learning new skills which give women a new role in the family. Better earning prospects tend to give women more independence and change their economic status in the family, and this may give rise to family tensions, particularly if women's earnings are controlled by the husband.
>
> (Ballara 1991: 11)

Ballara (1996: 41–2) explains the hegemonic familial pattern in Latin America. Since their early childhood, girls particularly from low-income families are socialised to do housework and take care of their younger siblings, as women are socialised towards the satisfaction of family needs regarding childcare, nurturing and household maintenance. In the region, the reproduction of such ideology begins at home, where, as responsible for basic food provision and childcare, mothers do productive work and get involved in tasks of community management. They transmit this role to their daughters, who grow up perceiving such work and sometimes the tasks as women's responsibilities. But this role is as well reaffirmed by other family members and society in general, relegating women to an inferior condition assigning 'natural' roles of family care and education, as well as the sexual division of labour and the control over their sexuality. Girls are thus kept close to their homes to ensure their future as wives, often with restricted freedom, to avoid risk of teenage pregnancy.

However, the most important non-nuclear family household structure still 'invisible' in many contexts relevant to women's literacy programmes is the female-headed household. These are in either *de jure* female-headed households, in which the male partner is permanently absent owing to separation or death, and women are legally single, divorced or widowed, or in *de facto* women-headed households, with male partners 'temporarily' absent. In the latter case, women are often perceived as dependent although for most of their adult lives they have primary if not total responsibility for financial and organisational aspects of the household. It is estimated that in urban areas in Latin America women head one-third of the households, and the phenomenon seems to be increasing (Moser 1998: 17).

To understand the complexity of decisions for the schooling of girls in a wide range of contexts in non-wealthy countries, it becomes necessary to reconsider neoclassical formulations of the family as a unit engaged in satisfying a single set of goals, following the stereotypical view of the family as a 'normally' male-headed institution (Moser 1988: 16). For many contexts, this urge is particularly relevant for policy makers to perceive that the background of decisions for girls' access to schooling needs to be seen in the light of parental decisions, and to look at the wider family politics.

Families and adult women's access to literacy

Braslavsky (1984) found that the gender gap in literacy in Latin America has tended to be reduced since 1980. However, the main familial obstacles identified for women's attendance of literacy courses include lack of time, fatigue, frequent pregnancies, caring for children and the wider family (Ballara 1991; Bown 1990: 24). In relation to women's motivation to participate in literacy programmes, Ballara (1991: 13) highlighted familial roles in terms of child and health care, such as the desire to help children to study.

A key phenomenon for Latin American women to be involved in literacy programmes is the emigration of men to towns to take up employment. Internal migration in the region in the 1980s created vast 'new settlements' in which a substantial number of squatter families are (as Moser says, ibid.) female-headed *de facto*. In these new settlements on the outskirts of huge urban agglomerations such as São Paulo, or Mexico City, the skills needed for survival are economic, political and health-related (Conway 1993: 250–1). Literacy practices of women in the new settlements take place in the context of dealing with Latin *machismo*, managing family hygiene and diet in the urban setting, and learning how to avoid repeated pregnancies. As Lind and Johnston (1986: 47) acknowledged, women often attend literacy sessions because of their perception that it will help them to cope with their responsibilities, read their husband's letters and to write back without the help of other people.

In contrast with the notion of families embedded in the literature of girls' access to schooling, the diversity of familiar constitutions and roles of women within them are recognised in relation to the barriers that women face enrolling in literacy classes. Van der Westen (1994: 258) suggests that high rates of female illiteracy emanate from lack of educational opportunities in childhood. She reports that in the literature, the determinants mentioned with regard to the low educational level of girls and women are often distinguished in factors related to the family and to the provision of schools and the school system. In her study of under-schooled women and the meaning of literacy in Mexico City, Kalman (1998: 28) shows that attending classes and learning to read and write are 'a response to the women's direct and collective challenge of asymmetric power relationships with their husbands or fathers'.

In this way, some authors have acknowledged the key role that families play in determining whether women enrol in literacy sessions (Ballara 1996; van der Westen 1994). However, in contrast to neoliberal concep-tions of the family (King and Hill 1993), the interrelationships that keep women out of school, and also motivate them to enrol in sessions have not been explored comprehensively so far. Some elements found in the case of the literacy group in La Paloma may provide insights in this regard, as presented in the following section.

'Out of school, now in the group': women attending literacy sessions in La Paloma, Mexico City

In early 1998, I carried out participant observation for almost six months in the local literacy INEA group at the community of La Paloma, located in the geographic-political area of Tlahuac, on the south-east outskirts of the federal district (DF), often equated with Mexico City. Despite the fact that the population of the district has the highest education provision in the country, around 133,000 women out of a total about 181,000 of fifteen years and over were counted as illiterate in the most recent national census (INEGI 2003b). At the time of my visits, communities were organ-ised in semi-rural areas, where services such as water, electricity and public transport were still poorly provided. This INEA group was selected as part of a wider multi-institutional programme to target literacy with a gender perspective. One of the basic criteria to have been chosen was that it hap-pened that most of the participants were women. Women in La Paloma attending the literacy group had already some literacy skills from their scarce early years' school attendance, although they had not achieved a primary education certificate.

The group used to gather in a small room with a wire door, lent to the regional INEA by the local general practitioner, and they had been gath-ering for four months before I first met the participants. Carmela, the instructor, used to hold two-hour sessions twice a week, with eight regular participants, five of whom attended most frequently: Adela, Tita, Luz, Martha and Juanita. The language of instruction was Spanish, native to all of them, as they had lived most of their adult lives in urban areas within Mexico City. Although they did not regard themselves as part of any ethnic group in the country, these participants had migrated as girls together with their families from towns, having a rural/migrant culture and integrating themselves into a rather urban context. Whilst they were included by the language of instruction, the complex interplay of racial, class, gender and family politics also represented a challenge for their involvement. Trust between the instructor, the participants and myself evolved throughout the time of my visits as we began to feel more comfortable with each other.

Adela was Carmela's eldest sister-in-law, in her early fifties. She had nine daughters and sons over the age of eighteen at the time and most of them were married. This implied that at least Adela had relatively more time for herself at that time, as they were not economic dependants any more. Her husband had abandoned her when the kids were little, and Adela recalled that he used to drink too much. She used to work as a janitor in a factory one hour away from La Paloma by public transport, and she would take care of her granddaughters in the afternoons, sharing with them some literacy practice while doing their homework. Despite the fact she frequently said, 'I did not know how to do them,' she had some basic skills in reading and writing, and was able to do basic calculations. She used to attend the classes with Juanita, her daughter, who was twenty-eight years old. Juanita was married and had three children; she had attended until second or third grade of primary school and had no permanent job at the time. In the group, she was the most advanced in reading, writing and basic calculation.

Martha was the youngest sister-in-law of Carmela. Unlike Adela, she lived in the same household as Carmela, with their mother-in-law. Martha was also twenty-eight years old and had six children. She used to bring her youngest two, a four-year-old girl and her one-year-old boy, to the sessions. In those days, her husband was a migrant worker in New York, but had suffered an accident and had no insurance. This had left them with very little money, so she used to work in a shoe shop and her ability to read was better than her writing skill. Martha, together with Adela, was one of the most active participants: it seemed as if becoming heads of their households, working for income and at home, had given them more assertiveness to deal with their learning. Tita was approximately twenty-five years old, married, and had a four-year-old girl. She used to help the doctor of La Paloma with the cleaning and in first aid. Despite losing some fingers in an accident when she was a child, she never regarded herself as disabled. She had attended school only for a couple of months. Luz was about twenty years old, married, and was pregnant at the time of my visits. She was Tita's sister-in-law, and used to live in the same household with Tita's family. Luz's knowledge of written language was very basic (knowing a few syllables), and she had attended only one year of primary school.

Tita and Luz had a forty-five minute walk to get to the sessions because they lived on a nearby hill.

For Carmela, teaching as a literacy instructor came from her learning through INEA's open primary and secondary school. She had three sons and a husband still living in the same household. Carmela had also developed literacy, numeracy and health care knowledge since her youngest child had a kidney transplant and she learned how to treat his condition. Sometimes she could draw on that 'real world knowledge' to teach numeracy issues, such as learning how to use the thermometer. Although she had to interrupt her secondary school to take care of her youngest child, she remained committed to finishing it. Becoming a literacy instructor also represented some autonomy for her as, although the payment is extremely little, since it is regarded as just a recognition of voluntary work, she could have some control over her budget and her time, and could socialise outside the household with a specific purpose.

As Marchand observes (1995: 71), testimonies are probably the only means for (marginalised) Latin American women to conduct their struggle(s) at the level of the production of knowledge, and they can situate their life experiences as a form of resistance to the dominant discourse. Indeed, life stories of women in relation to literacy have in common both the reasons why they dropped out from school and why they are participating now in literacy classes. The following dialogue between the researcher and women in La Paloma took place on the first visit to their literacy group, where they told about their initial motives for attending the sessions.

> RESEARCHER: So you were saying that for some of you it is the first time that you go to school. Did you ever attend it before?
> MARTHA: No, I didn't.
> RESEARCHER: Why is that?
> MARTHA: Well, because we are too many in my family, and besides, as I was the youngest one. My dad died when I was ten years old, and we are eleven in the family, we started going to ... but we were not given schooling. And then, some of us had to work, to help the others. And it is hard as well, because children nowadays ... one cannot help them with their homework. And for everything, because when we go out, we have to be asking over and over – we don't know where we are. And that is my problem. And for everything I have to do, I have to be asking.
> RESEARCHER: And is it the same for the others?
> TITA: Well, I only [went for two months], because my stepfather said that school was useless. He used to say that school was only for lazy people, and then he put me to work.

RESEARCHER: Luz?

LUZ: I used to go to school, but I was not sent any more after the first year. And as we moved to here, I didn't keep on going.

RESEARCHER: And why do you want to keep on studying?

LUZ: Because I want to learn. If my child asks me 'What is written in here?' or 'How can I write it?' I want to know (more or less).

JUANITA: I attended only till third grade. My father left us when we were children. My mother used to go to work, and I had to, as I am the youngest, the only woman. I have [two brothers]. I had to stay at home and I had to help her, to serve the food.

RESEARCHER: Adela?

ADELA: I didn't go because when I was young my father used to drink a lot. He never sent us to school, because, well, he didn't give my mother any money, not even for her necessities. He drank a lot, he didn't work ... We were young when I helped my mum, yeah, to look after my brothers too. And when we grew up, I got married, and I didn't study. And now, it's like I've got this opportunity, I want to learn something not to be ... to be someone in life.

In a rather schematic way, the relationships between family politics and the motives of women in La Paloma for looking for access to literacy sessions could be presented as in Table 14.1. It is noticeable that in all cases of the five women doing literacy classes in La Paloma, their fathers, and not their parents, are referred to as those who took the decision over their heads for them not to carry on studying. However, exploring their family politics beyond describing constraints or barriers, it is possible to notice that while in some cases participants referred only to the family politics which kept them out of school, in a couple of cases it is also expressly linked with the motives for attending literacy sessions. While their motives for attending – such as helping their children, or becoming able to interact with urban life – confirm what most of the literature on women's literacy provides, their narratives show that their motives and reasons for attending literacy sessions are not solely to repair personal histories, to express determination or the usefulness of literacy in the social world and the market place. Their narratives are also used for them to develop another sense of the self, which is related to their family politics. Besides the usefulness of being able to sort out practical needs while using literacy, they also position themselves in a different family politics, as if being a literate mother would confer the authority of being the head of household. Participants then reposition themselves in their family politics through their narratives.

Despite the fact that most participants took account of their family poli-

Table 14.1 Family politics and motives of women in La Paloma

Family member	Family politics	Motives to join the literacy group
Martha	Having ten siblings (coming from a large family) Being the youngest one Her **dad** passed away The need to work and sustain the family	To help her children with their homework To be self-sufficient To handle travel through the city
Tita	Her **step-father** said that school was useless **He** put her to work	
Luz	Her family moved	To help her child (as she was pregnant)
Juanita	Her **dad** abandoned her family Her **mother** therefore had to work Being the **youngest** and **only woman** Stay at home for nurturing	
Adela	Her **dad** used to drink a lot Her **dad** never sent them to school **He** did not work (no provision of money) Therefore, she helped her **mum** to **sustain** her siblings She got married	'To be someone'

tics in what was sometimes a covert way, kinship relations in La Paloma instruction can be looked at as in Figure 14.1. Nevertheless, women joining literacy sessions in La Paloma took account of family politics in an overt way as well. Though most of them came from male-headed households, they took responsibility for the females in their households. Whilst Carmela was extending her role to include women's access for her female relatives, they also attended the sessions, knowing that Carmela could have some earning capacity from doing her teaching. It was not altruism among women or only motivation that kept the group coming together for at least ten months: rather, it was an interplay of negotiations within the extended family to keep the learning space as part of their family politics. Adela and Juanita never treated each other as mother and daughter in the classroom, but still they could help each other with homework. Adela and Martha were distant relatives, but they had in common being head of the household, in the case of Adela on a long-term basis, whilst Martha was still expecting to rejoin her husband, as he was a migrant

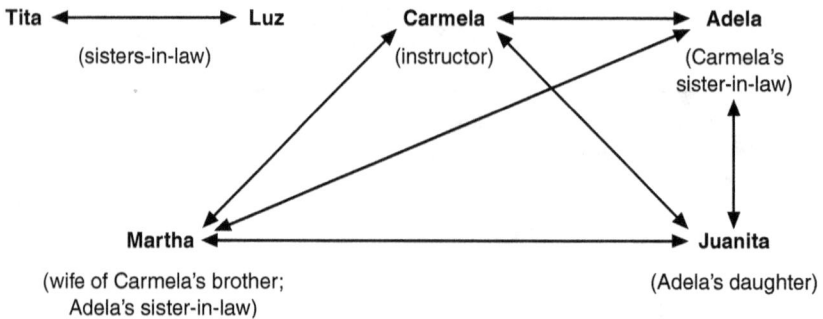

Figure 14.1 Women and literacy in La Paloma: kinship relationships.

worker. As they were sisters-in-law, Tita enrolled Luz into literacy sessions, and while she helped Luz with her learning disability in reading and writing exercises in the sessions, Luz would also help Tita with the tasks that were often physically difficult. Rather than only mutual support, it is possible to find that the enrolment and attendance of the two were intertwined by negotiation and support to get involved in literacy practices.

Family politics and women's il/literacy

Based upon the case of women in La Paloma, it seems clear that families may not take decisions about investment in children in a rational way, as King and Hill (1993) maintain. Family politics is a complex interplay of covert and overt commands, negotiation, opposition and support within kinship relations that has a great influence on women's literacy. For women attending literacy classes in La Paloma, the decision of not having been sent to school and therefore remaining illiterate is taken by their *fathers*, and not by the generic *parents*. While the decisions of fathers are regarded as the main reason to keep girls out of school, mothers of the La Paloma women seem to have had little power to decide over girls' schooling. However, the implicit agreement of the mother was necessary to back the father's command, so that girls could help with housework. In the adulthood of women participants, when they become head of their own household while their husband is absent, they enrol each other in literacy sessions in various ways. The case of La Paloma shows that joining the literacy group in order to be someone means that enrolling for literacy sessions occurs along with a process of collective support among women, intertwined with kinship relations.

As has been acknowledged (Stromquist 1990), women's illiteracy is a phenomenon not only of gender, but of class dynamics as well, in which families are highly implicated. In agreement with Schultz (1993), it is crucial to reconsider the family politics in households in a non-static form, as it adopts different dynamics. What Stromquist (1995: 14) calls the reliance of women on 'networks of reciprocal exchange' can be reconsidered as a starting point for understanding the wider family politics of women's motivation and enrolment in literacy sessions. While family politics in which female relatives encourage each other to become literate may not necessarily be a cross-cultural phenomenon, the network support among kinship relations needs to be reconsidered within literacy projects. While women in La Paloma were kept out of school by the decision of their fathers and the implicit agreement of their mothers to take care of household responsibilities and younger brothers and sisters, they give each other as adults the opportunity to enrol in literacy classes.

In the case of the group in La Paloma women excluded by their fathers and included in literacy programmes by their female relatives expand a net of mutual support. Family politics in this case backs up challenges that poor women face while becoming heads of households. Although their fathers made commands over them as girls so that they remained illiterate into adulthood, as women they oppose them and support each other to gain access to literate practices, entangled with their kinship relations as mothers and daughters or sisters-in-law. While negotiating in various ways the dynamics that keep them at home or work outside the household to make a living, literacy sessions can form part of the network for the contestation of power relations in family politics.

Acknowledgements

I would like to thank Dr Judy Kalman, a researcher at the Departamento de Investigaciones Educativas in the Centro de Investigación y Estudios Avanzados in Mexico City for permission to use a classroom record that I collected as her assistant on the postdoctoral study 'Literacy in the struggle to survive: a study of literacy learning and use in a community education project for underschooled (and unschooled) women in Mexico City', sponsored by the National Academy of Education of the United States and the Spencer Foundation.

References

Ballara, M. (1991) *Women and literacy*, London: Zed Books
—— (1996) 'Educacion de personas adultas desde una perspectiva de genero: responsabilidades publicas y sociales', *La Piragua: Revista del Consejo de Educacion de Adultos para America Latina*, 12–13

Bown, L. (1990) *Preparing the Future: Women, Literacy and Development*, London: ActionAid

Braslavsky, C. (1984) *Mujer y Educacion. Desigualdades educativas en America Latina y el Caribe*, Santiago de Chile: UNESCO/OREALC

Conway, J.K. (1993) 'Rethinking the impact of women's education', in J.K. Conway and S.C. Bourque (eds) *The Politics of Women's Education: Perspectives from Asia, Africa and Latin America*, Ann Arbor MI: University of Michigan Press

INEGI (2003a) http://www.inegi.gob.mx/inegi/contenidos/espanol/prensa/con-tenidos/estadisticas/2002/alfabeti02.pdf

—— (2003b) http://www.inegi.gob.mx/est/contenidos/espanol/proyectos/censos/cpv2000/definitivos/Nal/tabulados/00ed02.pdf

Kabeer, N. and Humphrey, J. (1993) 'NeoLiberalism, gender and the limits of the market' in C. Colclough and J. Manor (eds) *States or Markets? Neo-liberalism and the Development Policy Debate*, Oxford: Oxford University Press, pp. 78–100

Kalman, J. (1998) '"*Dile que haga la comida el!*" On the Meaning of Literacy and Schooling in the Lives of Poor Undereducated Women in Mexico City', draft to the 1998 fall postdoctoral forum, National Academy of Education/Spencer Foundation, Stanford University, 15–17 October

King, E.M. and Hill, M.A. (eds) (1993) *Women's Education in Developing Countries: Barriers, Benefits and Policies*, Washington DC: World Bank

Lind, A. and Johnston, A. (1986) *Adult Literacy in the Third World: a Review of Object-ives and Strategies*, Stockholm: SIDA

Marchand, M.H. (1995) 'Latin American women speak on development: are we listening yet?' in J.L. Parpart and M.H. Marchand (eds) *Feminism, Postmodernism, Development*, London: Routledge, pp. 56–72

Moser, C. (1998) *Gender Planning and Development: Theory, Practice and Training*, London: Routledge

Schultz, T.P. (1993) 'The economics of women's schooling' in J.K. Conway and S.C. Bourque (eds) *The Politics of Women's Education: Perspectives from Asia, Africa and Latin America*, Ann Arbor MI: University of Michigan Press, pp. 237–44

Stromquist, N. (1990) 'Women and illiteracy: the interplay of gender subordination and poverty', *Comparative Education Review*, 34 (1): 95–111

—— (1992) 'Women and literacy in Latin America' in N. Stromquist (ed.) *Women and Education in Latin America: Knowledge, Power and Change*, Boulder CO and London: Lynne Rienner, pp. 19–32

—— (1995) 'The theoretical and practical bases for empowerment' in C. Medel Anonuevo (ed.) *Women, Education and Empowerment: Pathways Towards Autonomy*, Hamburg: UNESCO Institute of Education, pp. 13–22

UNESCO (1997) *Adult Education in a World in the Process of Polarization: Education for All. Situation and Trends*, Hamburg: UNESCO Institute of Education

Westen, M. van der (1994) 'Literacy education and gender' in L. Verhoeven (ed.) *Functional Literacy: Theoretical Issues and Educational Implications*, Amsterdam: Ben-jamins, pp. 257–77

Afterword

Reading ethnographic research in a policy context

Lalage Bown

A new tapestry

It isn't the purpose of an afterword to write a review, but I must start by saying why this book has been worth reading, because it is only honest to declare my sympathy with the whole project.

The theme is important, moving on from past discussion of literacies without a gender dimension and parallel discussions about women in social and economic change, to melding them together, with literacy as the linking topic. The book's well organised structure (research; policy and programming; learning from experience) has created a unity which might have seemed unlikely, given a group of nineteen contributors from different national backgrounds and different professions. Perhaps because a shared gender perspective and a general acceptance of the validity of an ethnographic approach have provided a broadly common understanding, they have produced a tapestry and not just a patchwork (as usually happens with multi-authored works).

There is an underlying warp of common assumptions and also of common conclusions about women's literacy. While remaining faithful to the view that women cannot be seen as a single social category, the authors have generalised several findings about women as literacy learners. Julia Betts in Chapter 4 gives expression to the agreed finding that women creatively and cleverly take hold of dominant discourses and of literacy for their own purposes and also notes that in her research area 'Language and literacy practices ... do not merely reflect social relations, but rather are major forces in their construction'.

Also in the warp threads of the tapestry is acceptance among most authors of the responsible nature of ethnographic research. As Chizu Sato says (Chapter 6), researchers are multiply accountable, while Shirin Zubair (Chapter 5) reminds colleagues that this kind of research is 'for' and 'with' its subjects, not just 'about' them. Interestingly, the one researcher who seems to prefer a more distant style of observation is one of the only two male contributors.

In the weft, the overall pattern is enriched by some threads not usually to be found, such as the direct testimony of a literacy NGO activist (Sujata Khandekar, Chapter 12) and the viewpoints of facilitators in large-scale programmes (Juliet McCaffery, Chapter 9). The result of all this is a fresh *new* tapestry.

Perhaps this is particularly exciting to me, as I first attempted in 1990 to produce qualitative research on these issues, with the intention of affecting policy makers, in a study quoted by several authors here. Interest in women's literacy among researchers, theorists and policy makers has increased dramatically since then; much more qualitative evidence has been gathered and there is a context of new thinking.

In that context, first are the New Literacy Studies, so vigorously advanced by Brian Street (see Chapter 3 here), which mean that any writer on literacy can take it for granted that literacies are multiple and their uses multiple. Second, notions of development have moved into accepting that poverty is about poverty of justice and in academia at least there is no longer any need to knock down economistic straw figures. Third, gender studies have matured, so that concepts of sexual politics can be taken for granted, as can understandings of women's multiple roles, statistical invisibility and so on. This book shows that there are now other questions to be asked – some of long standing, and some emerging from the new research.

Questions outstanding

I have referred to the consensus of approach here. Perhaps this has led to the position that while we tackle issues around literacies in relation to personal and social change and while we question the assumption of literacy as instrumental to development, but observe that it can be used for oppressive or incorporative purposes, we don't really address our own standpoints on literacy. We should challenge ourselves along the lines suggested by a number of Indian theorists, going back to Ananda Coomaraswamy's *The Bugbear of Literacy* (1947). There are some fascinating questions raised by D.P. Pattanayak in Olson and Torrance (1991):

There is little evidence that literacy has civilized mankind [*sic*].

Both non-literates and illiterates are placed in the literate milieu, and therefore literate and illiterate modes of discourse complement rather than contrast one another. It is to be understood that literacy is not a solution to all problems, but a problem to be looked into in its own right.

Adult education *sans* literacy links directly personal experience to objective environment. In adult literacy, writing mediates between personal experience and objective environment. Under conditions of orality, people identify and solve problems by working together. Literacy brings about a break in togetherness ...

He is asking us who live in the literate postmodern world not to take any literacy for granted, to examine our relations with non-literate people and to enquire whether literacy, rather than empowering, actually isolates people. This provides a plausible explanation for the failure of much literacy endeavour to result in concrete change, although I want later to refer to literacy within a social movement context.

The topic of relations with the non-literate brings us to the continuing question of the researcher's role. Part I of this book has, I have suggested, made a useful contribution, but there are still contradictions between the stand, dear to ethnographers, of *understanding and not promoting* and at the same time recognising that researchers cannot locate themselves in a world of 'ivory tower distancing' (see Street 2001). We cannot expect to influence policy makers unless we address some of their concerns; if we don't wish to answer their questions, we have to convince them that our questions are important to them.

There is one further point about ethnography as a research tool, whether linked with policy or not. Case studies such as those reported here provide real insights into complexity and an accumulation of evidence which makes it possible to draw useful conclusions. For instance, the chapters on the REFLECT method (Gillian Attwood, Jane Castle and Suzanne Smythe, Chapter 8, and Marc Fiedrich, Chapter 13) together point substantively to the flaws in controlled or enforced participation. But it could be suggested that focusing on individuals may sometimes limit an understanding of the social context and an awareness of emergent social action. Unlike Pattanayak, I believe there is evidence of an interplay between women's involvement in literacy and their involvement in social action. The current discourse of 'civil society' and the co-option of some social activism into the agenda of international NGOs has perhaps obscured the existence of women's campaigns and movements, dependent on some solidarity through literacy ... Sujata Khandekar (Chapter 12) provides a suggestive example. Other possible examples could be movements in Somalia against female genital mutilation and environmental movements (see e.g. Vandana Shiva, 1988).

New problems

One of the new issues brought out here relates to social action. Because of our understanding that politics are much broader than activities in the formal public arena, we have perhaps come to downplay women's efforts in that arena and how far literacy and language are factors in those efforts. Three authors (Anna Robinson-Pant, Chapter 1, Brian Street, Chapter 3, and Donna Bulman, Chapter 10) mention rights-based education. This is a pointer to a new interest in legal literacy and in women's struggle as a struggle for justice. In some countries it is about equality with men, in others it is about men and women allied against a dominant or alien group, as in Palestine or southern Sudan. Research is needed across the whole spectrum of women's political action and its interplay with literacy.

Among other new problems, one has been indicated by Donna Bulman (Chapter 10) and, very cogently, by Juliet Millican (Chapter 11): how women confront the HIV/AIDS pandemic. Is it pushing older women into acquiring literacy for family survival? On the other hand, are policy and programme makers distorting literacy needs to fit the urge to educate on this one health issue?

Another, more technical, new research question (rather than a problem in the colloquial sense) emerges from the very interesting work of Claudia Flores-Moreno (Chapter 14). She reminds us of two increasingly common situations for women, which are likely to affect their literacy interests. One is large-scale displacement into new settlements and the other is the increase in female-headed households (also mentioned by Julia Betts, Chapter 4).

Engaging with policy makers

The various issues and questions which I have derived from this book could all be bases for dialogue with policy and programme makers. The work has been about 'reading ethnographic research in a policy context', which should then make direct engagement possible. What should we try to communicate? Obviously we must share our questions with them; and we must also constantly attempt to shift mind-sets which still want to hold on to jejune concepts of 'functional literacy' (which Alan Rogers, Archana Patkar and L.S. Saraswathi take apart in Chapter 7) and of women's literacy programmes as purely instrumental.

Our main predicament is that we are concerned about *diversity* in literacies, in women's interests, in locales and methods of literacy learning, while policy makers, with costs in mind, are concerned about *uniformity*. Is there any hope of convergence? I suggest that we modify our discourse and perhaps engage their interest by talking about 'customisation'. This is an acceptable concept in the world of mass markets. We need to put forward ways in which we think it could be realisable in large-scale literacy programmes. Alan Rogers has one proposal for use in urban areas – small centres or 'one-step shops' where women (and men?) could come for what they wanted in literacy. We need to develop more such practical ideas; but the most potent means of enabling diversity is the existence of well trained facilitators in local communities.

The vision

One very positive point we can put to policy makers, the outcome of all experience and research reiterated here, is that literacy acquisition evokes new confidence in women. Formally educated people may be looking for other outcomes, but the fundamental reward for women participants in any form of literacy programme is that confidence – perhaps because of the symbolic value of literacy referred to by several of this book's authors, perhaps because of a greater sense of identity, perhaps because of a release from fear. It has been expressed to me many times: by a Pakistani woman who knew (unlike the class facilitator) that her newly acquired skill would not get her a job and said, 'I have learnt to read so that I can respect myself'; by a Ugandan war widow squatting on the ground to write her name in the mud with a stick and who when I could read it back to her laughed with delight and said, 'Now you know who I am'; by a South African maidservant who had been sent to class by her employer so that she could write down phone messages, but who said, 'I sent my son a Christmas card and I wrote in it *I love you.*'

These encounters are what make worthwhile research and attempts to develop better women's literacy programmes. They also make it worth strenuously engaging with policy makers. They underlie any vision – and as Juliet McCaffery says in Chapter 11, 'Without a vision, little changes.'

References

Bown, L. (1990) *Preparing the Future: Women, Literacy and Development,* London: ActionAid

Pattanayak, D.P. (1991) 'Literacy: an instrument of oppression' in D.R. Olson and N. Torrance (eds) *Literacy and Orality,* Cambridge: Cambridge University Press

Shiva, V. (1988) *Staying Alive: Women, Ecology and Development,* London: Zed Books

Street, B.V. (2001) *Literacy and Development: Ethnographic Perspectives,* London: Routledge

Index

For Product Safety Concerns and Information please contact our EU
representative GPSR@taylorandfrancis.com
Taylor & Francis Verlag GmbH, Kaufingerstraße 24, 80331 München, Germany

www.ingramcontent.com/pod-product-compliance
Lightning Source LLC
Chambersburg PA
CBHW070355270326
41926CB00014B/2552